THE MAKING
OF MODE
POMPEY
& THE MEN WHO MADE IT

THE MAKING OF MODERN POMPEY
& THE MEN WHO MADE IT

MICK COMBEN

Editor
Colin Farmery

First published 2024

PHS Publishing
c/o Fratton Park
Frogmore Road
PORTSMOUTH
PO4 8RA

www.pompeyhistory.org

Copyright © 2024 Mick Comben.

The right of Mick Comben to be identified as the author of this work has been asserted in accordance with the Copyright, Designs & Patents Act, 1988

All rights reserved. No part of this book may be reprinted or reproduced or utilised in any form or by any electronic, mechanical or other means, now known or hereafter invented, including photocopying and recording, or in any information storage or retrieval system without permission in writing from the publishers.

British Library Cataloguing in Publication Data
A catalogue record of this book is available from the British Library

ISBN 978-1-7391813-1-4

Design and typesetting by Colin Farmery for PHS Publishing

Printed in Great Britain by Bishops Printers, Walton Road, Portsmouth PO6 1TR

Other books by PHS Publishing

POMPEY Champions of England (2022)
Comben M, Middleton S, James R & Spraggs G, Editor Farmery C
ISBN 978-1-7391813-0-7
The Official History of POMPEY Cards & Stickers (2023)
Emptage E
ISBN 978-1-7391813-2-1

CONTENTS

		Page
	PREFACE	7
	AUTHOR'S NOTE	8
	FOREWORD by Richard Oliver & Jane Byrne	9
	INTRODUCTION	10
	Section One: **THE MAKING OF MODERN POMPEY**	
Chapter One	**RISE OF PROFESSIONALISM**	20
Chapter Two	**FOUNDATIONS**	33
Chapter Three	**RAISING CAPITAL**	45
Chapter Four	**BUILDING FRATTON PARK** with Michael Saunders	59
Chapter Five	**CREATING A CLUB**	71
Chapter Six	**PREPARING THE PLAYERS**	84
Chapter Seven	**LET PLAY COMMENCE**	97
	Section Two: **THE MEN WHO MADE IT**	
I	**THE MOVERS**	114
II	**THE SHAKERS**	121
III	**THE ADMINISTRATORS**	131
IV	**THE FOOTBALL MEN**	135
V	**LEGACY MATTERS**	140
	APPENDICES	150
	BIBLIOGRAPHY	154
	ACKNOWLEDGEMENTS	156

ABOUT THE AUTHOR

Mick Comben

A Pompey fan for almost 60 years, he is the knowledge specialist within the Pompey History Society on the early years of the club between 1890 and 1920. He co-authored *POMPEY: Champions of England* (2022) and *The Official History of Portsmouth FC* (2023) and is presently chair of the society. Now retired, he was a specialist in HR and organisational design and governance for a financial services group. He lives in Southsea.

ABOUT THE EDITOR

Colin Farmery

A teacher, journalist, photographer and fan for more than 50 years, he has been involved at Pompey, on and off, since 1979, from painting the goalposts that summer, through to being the club's head of inclusion and safeguarding until he retired in 2019. In 2012/13 he managed the PR & communications campaign for the successful community bid to buy the club and was executive producer of *Our Club* (2019) the full-length documentary film about the bid. He has written several books about Pompey and edited *POMPEY: Champions of England* (2022) and *The Official History of Portsmouth FC* (2023).

ABOUT THE POMPEY HISTORY SOCIETY

Registered Charity No: 1201687

Founded in 2016, the Pompey History Society converted to a charity in January 2023. The society has two key remits: to preserve and conserve the archive of the club and to share it with the public. It does this through its website www.pompeyhistory.org, social media channels, as well as conducting tours of Fratton Park for the club, to help raise funds. In 2019-22 the society managed a £81,000 Heritage Fund oral history project called *POMPEY: Champions of England* and it has also spent £25,000 after commissioning replicas of the division one and division three trophies which are in the club's trophy cabinet.

Cover: Portsmouth FC team in 1899 and John Brickwood. / PHS Archive   *Colourised by Ed Emptage*

PREFACE

COLIN FARMERY

This book is long overdue in more ways than one. Its roots can be traced to the 2008 second edition of my book *17 Miles From Paradise* which told the story of the Pompey-Saints rivalry. The first edition, four years previously, had attracted the attention of the team at Hagiology Publishing which, by coincidence, had produced at the same time, its own **Saints v Pompey A History of Unrelenting Rivalry**. Presumably, we'd both got a bit excited at the same time about the resumption of derby-day hostilities as Pompey cruised to promotion to the Premier League in 2003. Anyway, to cut a long story short, a handful of factual errors in my first edition were, somewhat brutally, exposed in a Saints' match-day programme in November 2004. Fair enough, I was bang to rights. For my second edition, I reached out to Dave Juson, one of the authors of the Hagiology book, to get some help to put them right and he generously agreed. Thinking about it, I might still owe him a bottle of Merlot for it but I digress again.

As I traded Southampton facts back-and-forth, Dave one day said to me: "Do you know what Colin, no one has done the story of how Pompey were founded justice. It's always seemed very 'top level' to me. You ought to do it..." Whether I ought to have or not, the fact is I didn't, which is where Mick Comben comes in. I've known Mick for more the 20 years and he and I also share a quite complicated, but real, extended family relationship. A Pompey fan all his life, in 2020 he was newly retired and had just moved back to Portsmouth. With my encouragement, he decided to get involved in the Pompey History Society, which I was chairing at that time. His lockdown/retirement project had been to research the origins of football in Portsmouth, which he was very excited about. In fact, he still is. However, I told him not to worry about that and instead help me with, first **POMPEY Champions of England** and then the 125th anniversary official history of the club, which he expertly did.

When I finally sat down to read his 300,000-odd words in October 2023, I realised Dave's complaint - that the story of Pompey's founding has always been, including by me, largely glossed over - could now be addressed. Much of Mick's research into the mid-19th century roots of football in Portsmouth has had to be culled, although there are plans afoot for it to see the light of day, as this book does what it says on the tin. It tells the story of how the modern club we know today was formed, which turns out to be a tale far more nuanced than previously thought and introduces us to the 13 men who made it, some barely heard of in the traditional account of the club's founding. It is, quite simply, the most significant book on Pompey's history I have had the privilege to be involved with.

AUTHOR'S NOTE

As with the River Nile, pinning down the precise source from which the modern Portsmouth FC club sprang is not straightforward, but four key dates certainly contribute to the flow. December 15, 1875, when the first recorded Portsmouth Football & Athletic Club was founded at the Castle Hotel can make a case for being when the club we now know was set in train. Similarly, October 8, 1884, when the Portsmouth (Association) Football Club or "the borough club" was formed in the Albany Hotel has a claim. More obviously, the famous meeting on April 5, 1898 at 12 High Street, held to propose a new club, has a strong case but the company didn't actually come into formation until May 13. And that's not to mention the role of the Royal Artillery (Portsmouth) club which, by an historical quirk, became one of the foremost amateur teams in England during its bright, but brief, brush with glory between 1894 and 1899.

This book draws largely on contemporaneous newspaper reports. In the late 1890s one could have purchased several papers. The daily **Evening News**, **Portsmouth Times** and **Southern Daily Mail** often had a number of editions on the streets, from Late Morning to Final, each carrying different or extra information. In addition there was the weekly **Hampshire Telegraph**. There are good financial records in the club's first cash book, which shows all income and expenditure, but there seem to be no minutes remaining of any meetings, apart from what was set out in the press. In consequence, we can't fully understand why things might have happened, but some tentative conclusions on the available evidence will be drawn. There are various documents at the National Archives in Kew, such as the original Memorandum & Articles of Association, but some of the newspapers of the time, for example the Football Mails from 1898, have disappeared from both the Portsmouth Central and British Libraries.

The events which took place in the run up to the formation of the club have never been researched in depth and this book seeks to answer a number of key questions. What was the state of football around Portsea Island by 1898? Why have a professional club at all, especially when the Royal Artillery team was so strong? What brought the founders together at 12 High Street in 1898 and what were their backgrounds? How was the money required raised and who else invested in the club? Who built the ground and how did they get a team together so quickly? For me it has always felt strange that of Pompey's 'six' founding fathers, all one ever read was the fact that they came together in the High Street followed by their names and occupations. In reality, there is so much more to tell and those six have a more-than-supporting cast of another half dozen at least.

FOREWORD

RICHARD OLIVER & JANE BYRNE
Great-Grandson and Great-Granddaughter respectively of George Lewin Oliver

Our father was invited to join the board of directors of Portsmouth Football Club in 1958. On my first visit to the boardroom not long afterwards, I, Richard, admired the splendid painting of HMS Victory at Gibraltar after the Battle of Trafalgar and noticed that the brass plaque below was engraved "Presented to Portsmouth Football Club by Arthur Lewin Oliver in memory of George Lewin Oliver." On the way home my father explained that his grandfather George had helped found the club. That was it. The two of us knew nothing much more than that until we met with Mick Comben last year. What a revelation being involved in the production of this book has been.

When was Portsmouth FC founded? Who were the founding fathers? What's the history of Fratton Park? These questions, as my and Jane's superficial understanding indicated, were questions which have bigger answers than we ever imagined. It is a tribute to the painstaking research undertaken by Mick, the author of this informative and authoritative story of the making of modern Pompey, that we now know so much more about this period.

You need to be a truly dedicated Pompey fan to embark on a project such as this. We doubted Mick knew what he was letting himself in for when he first sat down to explore the plethora of local newspaper articles of this period. These articles relate the joys as well as the trials and tribulations of those formative years. They also provide insights into the people who founded the club and nurtured it through those early years. There were the inevitable disagreements, resignations and threats of bankruptcy, as well as the good times, such as when people stood up to save the club, our great-grandfather notably it would seem. They have all been cleverly woven together in this book. It shows that in football, as in many other areas, history repeats itself.

For true Pompey fans, especially those with an interest in the club's history, this book is a must for the bookshelves. The same applies to historians studying the city of Portsmouth. On a lighter note it offers new material for all quiz setters in the city. On behalf of the relatives of all those stalwarts of the past who helped in the creation and development of Pompey, the two of us would like to say a big thank you to Mick and all the others who have helped in the production of this book. It has been a true revelation to us all.

INTRODUCTION

No one knows for sure when football was first played although *The Football Encyclopedia,* published in 1937, suggests that it began in ancient China and was used as a form of military training. The introduction of the game to the British Isles is equally uncertain, but the same book claims that in AD 217 the men of Derby drove a body of Roman soldiers out of the town and then celebrated the event with a "football carnival". Whatever the truth, there is no doubt that various versions of football have been played in the UK for more than a thousand years. Portsmouth would have been no different, although it was a relatively small population centre until the 19th century. The game was a little more violent then too, with players sometimes recorded as dying from injuries sustained during matches. One of the earliest documented uses of the English word "football" in 1409, was when Henry IV issued a proclamation forbidding the levying of money for "foteball". Another type of football was recorded in Scotland and prohibited by James I by his Football Act of 1424 due to the mayhem caused. The act was not formally repealed until 1906. Meanwhile Henry VIII, no less, might have conceivably played in Portsmouth before watching the Mary Rose founder. He had been known for his sporting prowess in his younger years and owned one of the first recorded pairs of football boots. The royal footwear collection from 1526 was itemised by Dr Maria Hayward on the *BBC News Channel* in 2004 as including boots: "...45 velvet pairs and one leather pair for football". However, perhaps due to his increased waistline and thus inability to compete at the highest level, Henry had banned the game in 1540, claiming that it incited riots, so it's fair to say the chances of him turning out in Pompey are slim. Indeed, by 1667 football had been banned at least 30 times, either by monarchs or local authorities particularly in London and Manchester.

The reputation of football as a violent game is documented across the British Isles throughout the 16th and 17th centuries. According to the Hampshire FA Golden Jubilee Handbook published in 1937: "[The game] as played for centuries before the Football Association was formed ... in Hampshire [it] consisted of crowds of young men chasing a blown-up pig's bladder, roughly cased in leather, over fields and through ditches, or the streets of towns, in a tumultuous riot." However, once the Victorians got hold of it, the game quickly developed into a game of skill, with clear rules, reflecting an increasingly civilised society. In the mid-19th century, public schools picked up the game using it to help instil a sense of order for pupils. Winchester, for example, had a complicated dribbling game with the pitch marked off with rope. Eton had two versions, the 'wall game' and the 'field game', with rules first recorded in 1847 which didn't allow handling. According to Paul Brown (2013) in *The Victorian Football Miscellany* the latter game was "a clear predecessor of association football." Cambridge University's rules, drawn up in 1848 by Eton Old Boys, were closely related to the field game and an updated version of those rules, written in 1863, were used as the template for the FA's first edition of the 'Laws of the Game'. One of the first clubs in Portsmouth was also formed by pupils from Eton - the 'Sunflowers' - and the development of football in the town owes much to them. Newspaper reporting, which found a growing audience for accounts of matches, also helped its spread. By the 1880s reports were quite detailed. For instance, in November 1886 the **Evening News** covered a game involving the Portsmouth Grammar School and Portsmouth AFC - including Arthur Conan Doyle, of Sherlock Holmes' fame - playing under the name of 'AC Smith'. The report of the match, played at Hilsea, gives a good insight into how football was played then:

> The school, though playing a skilful and plucky game, were defeated by five goals to two in front of a loud crowd. They started with the wind in their favour, but the combined play of the Portsmouth forwards led to a series of attacks being made on their citadel; and after the School had retaliated, Godfrey, who had made several good shots, succeeded in registering a goal for the borough team. A second was kicked by G.L. Pares, and then some neat passing between the school's Smith, Owen, and Edmonds resulted in the latter scoring for the School in pretty style. The next point for Portsmouth was registered by Boyle, so that on changing ends the PAFC were to the lead. Rain came on, but the School worked well against the wind, and Smith obtained for them a lucky goal, PAFC's A.C. Smith putting the leather between the posts in trying to head it back out. The Borough eleven then put on a spurt, and Godfrey kicked a fourth goal, while Boyle secured a fifth by a fine screw shot.
>
> For Portsmouth all the forwards did well, the passing being rapid and correct and the shooting pretty true, while Kindersley and the other half-backs, supported them efficiently, the heavy kicking of A.C. Smith also proving serviceable. For the School, Smith was a useful centre, and Edmonds and Owen dangerous on the right wing, Seddon also showing promising form on the other wing, while the Rev. Norman Pares worked with characteristic energy at half-back and Henry also saved his side several times when hard pressed. It should be stated that the School would have had a third goal but for the leather being handled by one of the Portsmouth half-backs, and that on a free kick being given near the Portsmouth uprights Smith put in a shot that the borough club found difficult to save.
> Portsmouth Team:- Goal, W.G. Adames; backs, A.C .Smith and R. Hemingsley; half-backs, A.E. Kindersley (captain), J. Fin-

lay and Stimpson; forwards, W. Boyle, centre; G.L. Pares and F.J. Seddon, right wing; A.H. Godfrey and Simpson, left wing.

Note the 2-3-5 formation, with two forwards out wide on each side with a centre forward in the middle. This was an early use of this tactic as most games saw teams line up 1-2-7, basically a gang of forwards trying to force the ball into the opponent's goal. Match officials were supplied by each team and Montague Sherman (1887), in *Athletics & Football* summed up their complicated lot: "Each side has its own umpire, who is armed with a stick or flag; the referee carries a whistle. When a claim for infringement of rules is made, if both umpires are agreed, each holds up his stick, and the referee calls the game to a halt by sounding his whistle. If one umpire allows the claim, and the referee agrees with him, he calls a halt as before; if the other umpire and referee agree that the claim be disallowed, the whistle is not sounded. Two of the three officials must therefore agree in allowing the claim or the whistle is silent, and players continue the game until the whistle calls them off. Both umpires and referee, therefore, must lose no time in arriving at a decision, or so much play is wasted."

In 1895 a team called Royal Artillery (Portsmouth), based at Cambridge Barracks, started winning cups and quickly had a significant local following, after winning the Army Cup in 1895 and getting to the final of the FA Amateur Cup in the following year, so interest in the game was taking off. Newspapers in those days often published five or six editions daily. In 1890s Portsmouth, the biggest newspaper was the **Southern Daily Mail** and in September 1896, to meet demand for sports news, it started a 'football edition' of the regular paper. However, many readers continued to complain that the growth of sport was encroaching on the other content so in September 1898 the Mail started trailing its new standalone paper, the **Football Mail**, with the editor confident "that complaint will be got rid of". *Volume 1 Edition 1* was issued on September 17, 1898 as, according to the editor, "the success of the Football Edition of the Southern Daily Mail in the past years has encouraged the proprietors to make an extraordinary departure in local journalism". It proudly declared that on a Saturday evening in Portsmouth "there will not be a match played within the Borough the result of which will not appear in the Football Mail". By October 9 they went further: "the Football Mail is acknowledged to be the only representative football journal in the South of England." A dedicated football paper for the district followed the success of **Pearson's Athletic Record**, a national periodical which gave football in the south much prominence. Started by C Arthur Pearson it ran until blindness stopped him editing. The **Southern Daily Mail** subsequently amalgamated in 1905 with the **Evening News**, which by then had its own separate **Football News & Southern Sport**, started on September 5, 1903. Printed on green paper and costing one halfpenny - or 2s 6d to 'any part of the world' - it was a carbon copy of the **Football Mail**. On September 19, 1903 the Mail took a swipe at its new rival, saying that clearly their editor had a copy of the original in front of him when he put it together. They reminded readers that they had all the original and the best content which would continue. The new paper was to cover in full all the football in Portsmouth, Southampton and Plymouth with a correspondent recruited especially for the latter. Relationships between Portsmouth and Plymouth were really friendly in those early days, as shall be discovered in due course. After the amalgamation, the combined **Football Mail & News** was printed pretty much every Saturday from January 2, 1905. It did suspend publication for the first and second world wars and seemed to have shut for good in October 2012, but was revived when Pompey became community owned a few months later. It published its last copy definitively in July 2022.

There was also a political angle to newspapers in the late 19th century, which would resonate in due course with some of the club's founding fathers. The **Westminster Gazette** in January 1905 discussed the merger of the Mail and News which had "occasioned much excitement among Liberals in Portsmouth." The Conservative-leaning **Southern Daily Mail** - started in 1884 - was owned by Sir Alfred Harmsworth. The **Evening News**, established in 1877 by James Niven as editor, reporter and distributor, was older and eventually owned by Samuel Storey, a Sunderland-based businessman, with Niven as his managing director. Storey had first purchased the **Hampshire Telegraph**, in August 1883. Storey was a radical Liberal, we'd call him left-of-centre these days, and a prominent businessman, representing Sunderland for some years as MP. He had started the **Sunderland Daily Echo** in 1873 when he realised how powerful a newspaper could be to spread his world view. With Andrew Carnegie, a wealthy Scottish American industrialist, he built up a publishing empire, establishing or buying out several, mostly evening, papers across Britain including in Portsmouth.

Carnegie's charm, aided by his money, afforded him many establishment friends, including then Prime Minister William Ewart Gladstone. Carnegie and Storey's aim was to circulate newspapers in support of Radical principles. In fact, the **Evening News** already had a reputation as "the radical organ", in other words, to the left of centre, although in the late Victorian era it was said to have had more right wing "tariff reform" leanings which meant supporting the movement against unfair foreign imports to protect British industry from competition. When Storey purchased the **Hampshire Telegraph** some were uneasy as it meant another paper under Liberal sway. He also started the **Southern Standard**, but he and Niven soon realised there was no room for two evening papers in Portsmouth. Niven sold most of the business to Storey, retaining a quarter share and his job title. He died suddenly at the age of 55 in 1899. The Standard had only survived for eight issues.

The **Hampshire Telegraph** and **Evening News** had merged in October 1883 and when Storey and Carnegie eventually split their business, Storey retained the News and the Telegraph as well as the **Sunderland Daily Echo** and **Northern Daily Mail**; hence the company became Portsmouth & Sunderland Newspapers Ltd which published the titles until the late 1990s, when it was acquired by Johnston Press. Incidentally, Samuel's obituary in the **Evening News** in 1925 explained it was also down to him that Sunderland AFC acquired the land for Roker Park when they moved there in 1898. He subsequently arranged for their earth banks to be terraced, so it's no wonder his papers were always big on local sport, given his evident personal interest. The main sports writers didn't go under their real names but used the noms de plume *Sentinel* and *Linesman*. In those early years, the reporters were involved with the club's setting up and let slip their real names, FJH Young and TL Dines, in articles in 1922.

As newspapers grew, the organisation of football developed through men like William Pickford, the secretary of the Hampshire FA, who later became president of the Football Association, driving more professional administration. Football on Portsea Island, the Isle of Wight, and the surrounding district began to thrive only well after the FA was formed in 1863, taking until 1875 for the creation of the first club to bear the town's name, the Portsmouth Football & Athletic Club, which only lasted a year. Incidentally, note that Portsmouth was still municipally-speaking, a town for the core period this book covers, as it wasn't accorded city status until 1926. The Hants & Dorset FA formed in 1884, and was joined almost at once by the newly-formed second club to bear the town's name, Portsmouth (Association) FC. 'Association' was added to distinguish it from the rugby club which confusingly called itself Portsmouth Football Club. It soon became clear though, the game needed more local focus so there was a move to create two separate FAs. In 1887 the Hampshire FA was founded. A number of men stand out in this period, for their role in developing football in the area, notably the journalist Robert Hemingsley, who was also one of the backs for P(A)FC. He helped found the Hants FA after becoming P(A)FC secretary. In addition, there was Will Grant, the headmaster who played both football and cricket for Hampshire. He founded the Portsmouth FA with Alfred Wood who was Conan Doyle's great friend and private secretary. Another headmaster, Charles Crisp, 11 times Mayor of Lewes, founded the Portsmouth & District Referees Association around the same time. Clubs sprang up all over the district, including the Portsmouth Grammar School men's team previously mentioned and Southsea Rovers. Further afield teams set up in Havant, Petersfield, Ryde, Cowes, Fareham, Emsworth and Gosport, but it took until both the county and the Portsmouth FA were in place from the mid-1880s for there to be a formal competition structure.

Until then newspapers were full of requests from clubs asking for games to fill their diaries. Another issue was having enough good grounds to play on. This didn't change much even when the new Stamshaw Recreation Ground was opened in 1891 (see page 51). When P(A)FC was formed, it involved Conan Doyle, the Southsea-dwelling medical doctor. Its committee, led by Hemingsley, inspired the creation of organised competitions. The Portsmouth Senior Cup started in 1886 after P(A)FC brought together representatives from several clubs to organise it. This, in turn, spawned the Portsmouth FA. P(A)FC soon became the 'borough club', and were widely regarded as representing the whole town. However, they folded in 1896, primarily due to the lack of an enclosed ground to enable it to generate income. The club had initially played on land which is now Stubbington Avenue, then utilised Stamshaw Rec, but it never found a place to truly call home. For a while, the club even had the use of a field opposite the present day Shepherd's Crook pub, a stone's throw from what would become Fratton Park.

The demise of P(A)FC left a gap which was filled by the RA (Portsmouth) team in the mid 1890s. For the first time army players started to be chosen, not just to represent the army, but also to represent the Portsmouth FA. Six of the RA team played for a Portsmouth FA XI who beat the Brighton FA 5-0 in 1895. In 1896 they were the first Portsmouth team to win the Hampshire Senior Cup and on their return to the town station they were met by the artillery band and congratulated by senior army officers as it played. By 1898 they had reached the top league available to clubs in the south of England: the Southern League. Its success attracted large crowds to its Burnaby Road ground until the Gunners – as they were known - fell foul of the rules concerning amateurism ahead of an FA Amateur Cup quarter-final tie at Harwich & Parkeston in February 1899. Cigars and brandy claimed on expenses by the players during a pre-match training camp meant the defeated Harwich protested to the FA, who upheld the complaint. They deemed the RA's players professional and expelled the club from the competition. Relegation from the Southern League swiftly followed and, despite an ultimately successful appeal, the team retreated to anonymity. How and why a civilian professional club came to be formed in Portsmouth just as the amateur army team were enjoying such success, will be covered in due course. However, The Gunners bequeathed the emerging professional club three significant things: the colours used from 1909 until 1912 – white shirts and navy knickers - quite possibly the nickname 'Pompey' and without doubt the 'Chimes' - the song created around the melody of the town hall bells. The town hall was in High Street, Old Portsmouth until a new one was built in 1890 on the site of the current Guildhall. It was opened by the future Edward VII on August 9 that year. Bells would chime every quarter hour to the now familiar refrain, which is named the Westminster Quarters, after the Palace of Westminster's bells, although the full four lines of the chimes is only used on the hour. As the RA primarily played their home games at the United Services' ground in Burnaby Road, the bells could be heard from there. Referees would use the clock to let them know when the match should finish. In winter that was around 4pm. A fan named *Fair Play* told the Football Mail in September 1899 about his first game in 1897 and mentioned that just before 4pm the crowd would "lilt in unison" with the chimes of the hour to encourage the referee to blow the final whistle. He added that fans soon created some words to fit the chimes which they used often and "with aplomb". The lyric went: *Play up Pompey; Just one more goal; Make tracks, what ho; Hallo, hallo.*

It certainly fits the rhythm when sung to the tune of the chimes. Fans quickly started to use the song to signify a goal or a potential goal or to chivvy the team along to do better. Fans were also said to ring bells throughout their games. The description "Town Hall Chimes" soon became simply the "Pompey Chimes" a fact backed up by Kevin Smith (1999) in *Glory Gunners*. In December 1898 the **Evening News** reported that a fan, John Tonks, was charged with using obscene language at one in the morning in Commercial Road. In court, witnesses said that the defendant was only singing "the Pompey Chimes". Amidst much laughter, they demonstrated the chant to the judge, who wasn't amused. He found Tonks guilty, and fined him 4s 6d with 10s 6d costs. Another fan, calling himself *Play Up Pompey*, wrote to the **Football Mail** in September 1899 and said that his recollection of the chimes was that it was used to take the "mickey" out of RA fans. In 1898 a group of about a dozen Southsea Rovers fans – then a major amateur club – were at the RA match versus Tottenham and when Spurs scored the first goal the "chiming" started. "Every time the Spurs passed the Portsmouth RA players, the cries were repeated as a shout of derision," he said. Another letter in the same year from a *Mr TL*, claimed that the "Pompey Chimes" war cry "is not entirely new to the south" as "for a few years the chimes have been the war cry of the supporters of the Worthing Football Club, the Champions of the West Sussex Senior League", adding it is "just possible that they may have been imported from Worthing". He asked if other fans would change the words to: *Hallo, hallo; Play up Pompey; Hallo, hallo; Pompey one goal.* A week later other fans replied, telling him not to be so ridiculous. However, soon letters started arriving with various suggestions. One of the paper's own attempts, published on September 30, 1899, coincidentally the day of Pompey's record win, 10-0 in the English Cup against Ryde, was: *Play up Pompey; With heart and soul; Add two more points; And one more goal.* There have been variations to the song over the years - for example in November 1914 the **Evening News** reported the crowd singing a version aimed at the German Kaiser. The tune is uncertain - 'My Old Man's a Dustman' certainly works - but the chorus matches the chimes:

> *God bless the lads of Pompey, the boys in red and blue,*
> *Who one and all, rose to the call, to see old England through,*
> *We're proud of every Briton, from near or far away,*
> *But we're extra proud, of the little crowd, of Pompey boys today,*
>
> *Hallo Hallo,*
> *Play up Pompey,*
> *Kaiser must go,*
> *Offside is he.*
>
> *They're mighty fond of football, they bubble over with fun,*
> *But when their country calls them, they quickly shoulder gun,*
> *You wouldn't think it in them, when cup tie crowds go by,*
> *Who said they'd fear the Prussians? And wink the other eye,*
>
> *Chorus*
>
> *They've heard their brothers calling, from trenches on the Aisne,*
> *They've heard the call appalling, of Belgium in its pain,*
> *They see the goal of duty, they mean to fight and win,*
> *Give back to louvain Beauty, and crush the men of sin.*
>
> *Chorus*
>
> *God bless the Bonnie Laddies, increase their numbers too,*
> *Be with them as they rally to see old England through,*
> *Go with them to the conflict, and bring them back once more,*
> *Triumphant over the vandals, to sing on England's shore.*

The present version of the Chimes plays on part of a continuous loop in the National Football Museum in Manchester and the name 'Pompey' spread widely, in part at least, due to the success of the Royal Artillery team, but its origins remain subject to claim and counter claim. Richard Coates (2009) in an article entitled 'Pompey as the Nickname for Portsmouth' in the *Journal of the Society For Name Studies In Britain and Ireland* investigates many theories as to why Portsmouth might be called Pompey. The most likely origin remains the simplest. In the 19th century the town of Portsmouth was concentrated on the south western corner of Portsea Island. For many centuries the main point of the harbour entrance to aim for, if you were a ship coming into port, was Portsmouth Point, or Spice Island, known as such as it was the "spice of life" with a seedy reputation. By the 18th century, the 'island' had become a popular destination for sailors on leave from the hundreds of ships often moored at Spithead. 'Portsmouth Point' was commonly shortened to 'Po'm.P' when handwritten in a ship's logbook. After all, writing at sea was often shortened to save time, ink and, besides, was simply difficult on a rolling ship. Nautical maps and records back this terminology up. It seems eminently possible 'PomP' entered the vernacular as sailors looked for a short form to describe the location of the impending night ashore.

However, it is not the only claim. In March 1898 the **Woolwich Gazette**, reported on the impending professional team and state in the article that Portsmouth is called "by our sailor friends as 'Happy Pompey', where the band plays". The evidence certainly points to a military or nautical connection. However, using the name Pompey didn't catch on widely until the town had a large number of fans of a decent football team, the Royal Artillery. Prior to the establishment of the RA there are few references anywhere to 'Pompey' in connection with Portsmouth. To add weight to the military argument for the origins of the nickname, there is a story in the **Hants & Sussex News** about the Volunteer Battalion of the Hants Regiment competing against a company from Havant in a training exercise in Winchester in April 1896. When Portsmouth lads approached the saluting platform after winning the contest the others shouted "good old Pompey". Clearly the nickname for the town was in existence at that time in military circles but, for the most part, references only start truly proliferating once the 1898 club had established itself. The connection with the RA was also referenced in the **Harwich & Dovercourt Free Press** on February 25, 1899, ahead of that fateful FA Amateur Cup tie: "Portsmouth RA are known in their own neighbourhood as 'Pompey'." The **Evening News** of December 8, 1912, confirms the origins lay in the Royal Artillery club, but suggests the prosaic Po'm P explanation may have to give way to a more exotic explanation: "Pompey is a nickname for Portsmouth generally now. Originally it applied only to the RA Portsmouth, association football club. At infantry inspections on Southsea Common, the parade ground used to be kept by garrison artillery. An officer, never intending to create a nickname, remarked that the ground at big reviews in Paris was kept by *les pompiers*, in other words by the fire brigade." RA (Portsmouth) FC were christened Les Pompiers and it soon morphed into "Pompey" goes the story. Given some of their fans were said to ring bells throughout their games, that adds credence to this theory. In 1911, the **Pall Mall Gazette** reported: "There is a recent fashion springing up amongst

Introduction

certain classes of calling the town 'Pompey' and as old campaigners there have no recollection of such a nickname down to 1890, the presumption is that it was given to the football club about 1896." Unfortunately, it doesn't specify the club, but it was most likely the RA, as Portsmouth AFC was pretty much defunct by then. The article added: "It dates from Nelson's time and was used by sailors."

Other theories have been shared over the years, including a possible Roman connection – *Magnus Portus* - the great port - was Portsmouth's Roman name – reminding folk of Pompeii perhaps, or the Roman General Pompey. Another claim is that sailors from Portsmouth climbed Pompey's 100-foot pillar near Alexandria in Egypt thus becoming known as the 'Pompey boys'. **The Chronicle** recorded in 1837 how the colours of England were flying from the top of the pillar and a "discharge of musketry" was heard "as sailors from Portsmouth-based HMS Hermes had by means of a huge kite managed to get a rope to the top and create a rope ladder for a party of ten to climb up and toast 'Her Majesty Victoria' although the sway of the column in the wind [was] sufficient to shake the wine out of their glasses." This challenge had been going on since 1781 or 1782 according to the newspaper. In 1798 Nelson is reported to have said to Emma Hamilton in Naples, prior to the battle of the Nile on August 1, "see you back in Pompey" which would fit the time frame of that theory. It was definitely 'Pompey' recorded and not the nearby Pompeii. Other possible origins include a ship called HMS Pompey based in Portsmouth in 1762 referenced in the **Evening News** in 1935. In addition, there had been a prison ship *La Pompée* moored in the harbour for many years before being broken up in 1817 and also a connection with slavery, where the name Pompey was often given to slaves in the USA and then possibly brought back by the sailors to Portsmouth.

In conclusion, whatever the derivation, it was the success of the Royal Artillery football team which is most likely how the name became synonymous with the town. Newspapers, both local and national, used it from the earliest games to describe the club and it stuck. In the club's first handbook, the opening page starts with the title: "Play Up Pompey" and new Secretary/Manager Frank Brettell, writing the introduction to the second handbook in 1900, starts with the full words of the song. He then goes on to make reference to "the sporting public of Pompey", emphasising that Pompey also refers to the name for the town and not just the club. But we digress. Whatever the origins of the nickname, what is unquestionably true is that the RA's successes had whetted the appetites of local followers for first-class football. It was also increasingly obvious that the town was big enough to support a professional club along the lines of those already established in Southampton, Brighton and Reading. The sporting public of Portsmouth were soon to get their wish. What follows is the story of how it came to pass and an introduction to the men who made it happen. And within just three seasons, Pompey would become regarded as one of the best teams in England with a fine ground to match.

SECTION ONE

THE MAKING OF MODERN POMPEY

Chapter One
RISE OF PROFESSIONALISM

By the late-1890s association football was polarising into two distinct worlds: amateur and professional. Every major, and not-so-major, town or city wanted its own professional club with the best players, who of course wanted to be paid for their efforts. Portsmouth was no different. To play at a high standard, clubs needed to have players who could concentrate on their sport and were fit and healthy. Victorian diet and working life did not, in general, help much, so football needed professionals if it were to properly succeed. Professionalism had been sanctioned at a special meeting of the Football Association in July 1885. This vote had followed several years of allegations of enticements being made to amateur players to turn out for particular clubs. One obvious way was to give jobs to players in exchange for turning out for the work's side. Blackburn Olympic didn't fall into that category, but they would win the 1883 English Cup beating one of the southern bastions of amateurism Old Etonians in the final. What provoked bad feeling was Olympic's decision to hold a pre-final training camp at Blackpool. To do such a thing meant players had to take time off work, so therefore someone, somewhere must have been paying them, went the amateurs' argument. Olympic's superior fitness told in extra-time. With football increasingly being seen in the north of England as a business, footballers became a commodity. Clubs were widely starting to unofficially make payments to players, making a rule change inevitable.

The dominance of northern football was further illustrated by Blackburn Rovers, picking up where Olympic left off, who won the English Cup three years in a row from 1884-1886. The differences between the amateur idealists from southern England and the increasingly unofficial professional teams from the north came to a head in 1884. The **Glasgow Evening Times** at the time talked of the "strong feelings about the present chaos" that existed. After Preston North End won a fourth round English Cup match against a devoutly amateur team from the capital, Upton Park, the Londoners protested that Preston's players had been paid, which was against the competition rules. Preston were kicked out of the competition, but it brought matters to a head and the FA almost split over the issue. In the end, professionalism prevailed although the south held out for quite a while longer. However, just because the FA said it could happen, did not mean that it did. In the mid-1880s no payments were made across areas controlled by the Hampshire or Dorset FAs, due to their predilection for the amateur game. The Hampshire FA sanctioned just one professional player, William Winkworth from Winchester Rovers, and that not until 1887. Its 1937 handbook records that he holds the distinction of being the first professional player in the south of England. The county did not even pay expenses for their own representative matches. Players chosen to represent the county had to pay their own fares to travel as far as Brighton or Reading, as well as purchase their own county shirts. On one occasion the whole team had to cough up sixpence each to get entry to the ground at which they were playing and when a Portsmouth AFC player, Pinfold, broke his leg playing for Hampshire against Sussex he had to pay all his own medical bills for a lengthy hospital stay.

So, all professional clubs were based in Birmingham or the north west with many from the urban industrial powerhouses of Victorian England such as Blackburn and Accrington in the north or West Bromwich and Stoke in the Midlands. Charles Sutcliffe *et al* (1938) in *The Football League's Golden Jubilee History*, said that the league could have covered the whole country when it was formed but "there were then no professional clubs south of Birmingham." Even by the Southern League's first season, 1894/95, it still had four out of the nine clubs stating they were amateurs. In South Wales, the association there held out longer, outlawing player payment until 1900. The Football League had been founded in 1888, comprising 12 professional clubs and quickly proved popular. In response, a general meeting of the London-based Football Association had been held to consider the best means to "secure and promote" amateur football in the south of the country, but it was not going to stop the march of professionalism. There were rumours that the Royal Arsenal Football Club were to turn professional, but many still hoped that legislation would be introduced to preserve the amateur game. One vocal critic of professionalism, reported in the **Woolwich Gazette**, said that since 1884 "it had been tolerated" and felt it was not right that professionals should now run the game as they had "not had the benefit of the earlier education that had made the amateurs gentlemen" . Some in the meeting did not feel that the introduction of professionalism in the north had done anything to improve the game. However, various other speakers disagreed and felt that professionalism was coming and here to stay. William Pickford (1939), wrote in his autobiography *A Few Recollections of Sport*, that there were also doubts in county football about the merits of a league structure. Of the national set-up he said: "In its inception the League was almost entirely a north and midland affair. We, in the south, did not for a time take much interest in it. Twelve clubs struggling under the handicap of having to pay players wages, as a consequence of their success in securing the recognition of professionalism, bound themselves by simple rules, to meet home and away, to keep their fixtures as arranged, and to play their best available teams. That was about all."

Increasingly though, amateur teams were struggling to compete as paying players meant clubs could attract the best talent. In many ways, this explains the 'why?' of there being a move towards creating a professional club in Portsmouth during late 1897 and early 1898. On the face of it, RA (Portsmouth) had filled the gap for 'top class' football in the town. It was successful in the FA Amateur Cup, which was almost as prestigious as the English Cup in those days and, in early 1898, the club was on course to win promotion to the top division of the Southern League, which was as high a level of football as it got for teams south of Birmingham. However, RA (Portsmouth) were an amateur team, made up of professional soldiers, subject to the whim of Her Majesty's Government and the army top brass, who could and would deploy battalions overseas at the drop of a hat to protect any real or perceived interest of the British Empire. More prosaically, even sentry duty could intervene on player availability from time to time. Tensions also arose from a cavalier attitude to registering players. A letter to the **Southern Daily Mail** in January 1898 summed up the issue:

What do you think?

> I didn't know what the general feeling on the matter is, but I must offer a protest against the playing of men from other regiments under the title of "Portsmouth R.A." I allude, of course, to the appearance of Ward and Lewis, of the 1st Battalion East Lancashire, at Warmley on Saturday. In these days when competition is so keen one can understand the legitimacy of strengthening a regimental team by recruiting in the ordinary way or transfers from other battalions of the same regiment, but to take the pick of another club in order to bring the eleven up to the required standard, and to label the combination thus produced "Portsmouth R.A." is a practice certainly to be condemned. Civilian clubs would describe such conduct as poaching.

In November 1897, the same newspaper had also noted: "That there is growing interest in football in Portsmouth is undoubtedly true and a really strong civilian club with a private ground, in any accessible part of the town, would soon have a large following and sound finances." Despite the success of the RA, and the enthusiasm it undoubtedly engendered, the Army FA regulating the club set it apart. To many in the town's football community it wasn't strictly a 'Portsmouth' team or professional either, and that was the combination which was wanted. A letter from *TAF* to the **Evening News** in January 1898 made the point:

> What is wanted is some gentleman connected with the football world to come forward and start the ball rolling by calling a meeting in this town for the purpose of testing the public feeling, and it would be very favourable. A committee could be elected from the gentleman at the meeting to draw a pay scheme to place before the public for approval, and, if approved, shares could be offered for sale, and I express the opinion of hundreds when I say they would be snapped up.
>
> Why is it that this town is so backward where sport is concerned? Little towns in comparison, such as Luton, Sheerness, Chatham, and Cowes, have splendid civilian teams and it is reasonable to assume that Portsmouth could run a better one. In regard to attaining a suitable ground, it seems to me that the ground along the old canal near Fratton station would be very well adapted, being near the station for the teams coming into the town.

And, of course, fans could see what was happening 17 miles up the road. Southampton, which had been formed as a church team in 1885, but had been paying some players since 1892, were considered fully professional by 1894, when they joined the Southern League. On Boxing Day 1897, the **Southern Daily Mail** reported that 14,000 went to watch Saints play, with many from Portsmouth: "A goodly crowd who travelled to Southampton by special trains and steamers". Pickford added in his memoirs that "professional clubs were now too strong for any amateur sides to compete with any hope of getting near to the closing stages [of the English Cup], unless it might have been the Corinthians, but their rules forbade entering any competition, and it is only by real professional competition that a team can attain to its highest level".

In consequence, it was widely felt in Portsmouth, based on the experiences of the Royal Artillery team, playing in front of up to 8,000-strong crowds, that with a good ground a professional team would attract the public and money could be made. The large number of service personnel based around the town, many of whom were familiar with the professional game in the north, also helped fuel optimism. The press started comparing football in the south and north. The **Southern Daily Echo** in March 1898 praised the results of the Southampton team after a draw against Nottingham Forest in the English Cup and quoted a Blackburn paper: "Since the Rovers [Blackburn] rose on the horizon, followed by North End [Preston] and professionalism, the south of England has cut a pitiable figure in the game. But last season there was a movement in the dry bones and now the corpse of the game in the south seems infused with a life and vigour that we have been accustomed to regard as the monopoly of the north."

The **Southern Daily Mail** talked of the increasing popularity of the game, saying that at one time "700 to 800 was quite a decent crowd, and even for the visit of Preston no more than 3,000 were expected [but now] one thinks of the 15,000 that witnessed Southampton defeat Bolton Wanderers." It noted "the energetic efforts of the local branches of the Football Association and the gradual decay of the rugby game, admirers of that code having slowly but surely dwindled away and deserted to the other camp, with the promotion of the leagues and the gift of cups to 'friendlies' has all given an impetus to the game". For good measure it added: "It will be a long time, probably, before the gates will be of such huge dimensions of those frequently taken at Sheffield, Birmingham, Liverpool, and other famous centres, but for consistent and enthusiastic support, the large crowds that gather at Southampton, Tottenham, Bristol, et cetera, would be hard to beat." On January 22, 1898, the **Hampshire Telegraph** gave impetus to a professional club following a visit to Portsmouth by Nat Whittaker, the secretary of the Southern League. He said in its columns: "A really good team could be supported here considering the population is a quarter of a million and that the soldiers are very keen on the association game." The paper duly approved:

> This is not the first time that opinions have been expressed in favour of the formation of a professional team in Portsmouth, but the difficulty which has always risen on the first consideration of a scheme has been the provision of a suitable ground

sufficiently near the town, though, of course, this is an obstacle which might be overcome. Whether Portsmouth will ever possess a 'really good' professional team it is hard to say, but local enthusiasts are to be found who say that it is only a matter of time. They point to two or three facts which cannot be denied, viz, the growing interest in football among the youth of the town, among the Servicemen, and among the Dockyard men, many of whom come from the North, and the steady increase of the 'gates' at the R.A. matches, cup ties, and other important contests. Any number between 2,000 and 4,000 people now usually attend an R.A. match, and an experiment recently tried at Stamshaw showed that there were close on 200 boys willing to pay for admission to a Portsmouth cup-tie. These are 'signs of the times' which encourage those who look forward to seeing the formation of a Portsmouth professional team.

It is believed that there are several good players in the town who would gladly join a local 'pro' eleven. They now go to teams outside Portsmouth to play, because there are openings for them as paid players in neighbouring towns, and no scope for them in Portsmouth as amateurs. These, with some professionals from the North, who would have to be men who would not demand too high a salary at first, might no doubt form a nucleus of a team which would in time develop quite up to the standard of many clubs run in towns [of] similar in size.

A reader *SJN* wrote to the **Evening News** "in support of the formation of a professional team for Portsmouth" thinking "it quite possible with the great advance which the 'soccer' game has made in the town, that something can be done to raise a team." He suggested: "A company might be formed, with £1 shares", believing that "the working men of the town would take the matter up." Momentum was building. An unidentified reader of the **Southern Daily Mail** on January 25, 1898 added:

Advice Of A Well Wisher

Will you kindly ventilate through the medium of your valuable paper the opinion held by a large section of the football loving public in Portsmouth with respect to a professional football team for the town? If it is to be in any sense a success there must be no half-hearted measures. Portsmouth will have to work on similar lines as those of the people of Bristol and get together from class teams throughout the country the best possible men and talent available, so that we might reasonably hope to see the team admitted late into the Southern League and Western League in the first season.

In the event of this we should have attractive fixtures from the beginning, but to do this no cheese-paring policy must be pursued, or the venture can safely be predicted to become a failure. On the other hand, if the constitution of the team as suggested be a good one, the sport-loving people of Portsmouth will undoubtedly rally to the help of those who are organising the team, and endeavour to make it one of the most successful teams (financially and otherwise) in the South of England.

A day later, on January 26, it seemed like a wish had been granted. Under the headline "PROFESSIONAL TEAM FOR PORTSMOUTH", the Mail reported that "it is not at all unlikely that before next winter comes round Portsmouth will be able to boast of a professional team." JF Wells, secretary at Southsea Rovers and a confidant of William Wigginton, told the paper that "a public announcement as to shares etc, will be made in your columns on Saturday next." This did not go to plan and the announcements were delayed some months, but he was fundamentally right. He added: "The football loving public may be assured of one important point, ie that those at the head of the movement are experienced in the management of a football club." Presumably, that referred to Freddy Windrum and Richard Bonney from the Royal Artillery, but more of them in due course. Later that week Wells acknowledged he might have jumped the gun: "I am sorry that I cannot fulfil my promise of Tuesday week but the promoters of this proposed professional team are most anxious to get all the preliminaries thoroughly settled before they place the prospectus before the footer public of this town, and you will, I am sure, agree that this is the better course. We are getting all the information possible, and, after our next meeting on Monday (31st inst.) hope to publish the prospectus. Our capital will be rather large, and we shall try for election to the Southern League, but you will understand that I am not at liberty to detail our proposals. The ground difficulty has been overcome, and the footer public may rest assured that if they will give the undertaking practical support, success is almost assured."

Pearson's Athletic Record was convinced that Portsmouth "would prove to be as great a hot bed of association football as has Bristol with the dockyard town having an advantage in that it isn't handicapped by the presence of another professional team." On January 29 the same paper picked up the story that moves were afoot to create a professional team in the town: "We are informed that a movement has been started by several well-known sporting gentlemen to establish a professional football team that shall be the equal of any other in the South of England and that a public announcement as to shares etc will be made." The **Bournemouth Guardian** of the same day stirred the pot: "Some gentlemen that are interested in the game have already been taking advice from some of the experts. The [Evening] News does not despair of a suitable ground being found and suggests one close to Fratton Station. With a strong club in the Naval town the Saints would have to look to their laurels." The **Southern Daily Mail** also waded into the debate and amplified rumours an announcement was imminent, while after a game between the Royal Artillery (Portsmouth) and Warmley from Bristol in January 1898, watched by between 7,000 and 8,000 fans, an article in the **Hampshire Telegraph** on 29 January 1898 stated that the paper had been informed that "a movement had now been started by several well-known gentlemen and the secretary pro tem was to be Mr JF Wells of 38 Manners Road Southsea, the secretary to William Wigginton at Southsea Rovers."

On February 5, 1898, the **Southern Daily Mail** opined: "If 500 people will travel to Southampton from Portsmouth to see a good match, how many would go to Fratton if a professional football team were suddenly to spring up in that salubrious neighbourhood." The well-connected paper clearly knew a professional club was coming and that it would be close to Fratton station. With the western side of Portsea Island already urbanised, it was a logical location. On March 25 the **Woolwich Gazette**, even went as far as to suggest that players had been approached already, praising the efforts of a proposed new club to rival those clubs of the north: "At least four players have been secured from Blackburn Rovers for a new organisation being formed 'Hampshire way', about 70 miles SW of London, like New Brighton Tower with no league connection..." In other words, a team in Portsmouth. New Brighton Tower and its football club, also set up as a limited company to generate income for the resort's observation tower, built to rival Blackpool, illuminated – pun intended - the model Portsmouth would follow. Tower had spent big to sign good players, entered the Lancashire League, won it, and were then accepted by The Football League for 1899.

In March 1898, an **Evening News** reader unfavourably compared Portsmouth attitudes to sport with Southampton: "The public men of Southampton understand a thing or two. We find that in yet another respect they are ahead of their nominal peers at Portsmouth. Members of the Southampton Corporation are sportsman first and public men afterwards. They have worked up no small amount of excitement over the replayed cup tie match between Southampton and the Bolton Wanderers, which takes place at their own doors today. Of course they were bound to see the game, and so those of them who are members of the health committee, and who had been summoned to meet today, signed a 'round robin' to the chairman asking him to postpone the meeting. When may we expect to see the humdrum Portsmouth Council take a lesson from Southampton, and adjourn, say, in the middle of a debate on waterworks purchase, so as not to miss a Royal Artillery match on the Officers' Ground?" They were referring to an English Cup game involving Bolton, who were a Division One club managed at the time by Frank Brettell, more of him later, and Saints, who won the game 4-0. Spectators not only came by train from Portsmouth, but from all over the south including London. It was a sensation, particularly as Saints had already eliminated two Football League second division sides, Leicester Fosse and Newcastle United in rounds one and two respectively. Portsmouth football fans were happy for Saints, with many letters to the **Evening News** singing their praises. Leicester had the dubious distinction of being the first Football League club to be eliminated from the English Cup by a Southern League club and likewise Wanderers now became the first Division One club. Saints were knocked out eventually by Nottingham Forest in a semi-final replay, but only by two late goals scored while they defended against a blizzard.

However, there were rumblings from elsewhere in England that profits were starting to fall due to rising wages and other costs. Aston Villa's accounts, published in June 1897, showed a very small profit on "the best year so far of their existence" and **Pearson's Athletic Record** asked a pertinent question: "What on earth is the margin on the wrong side going to be in a bad season?" But press locally remained overwhelmingly positive and on May 14, 1898, a little over a month after the announcement that Portsmouth FC were to be formed, the **Southern Daily Mail** remained a staunch advocate for professionalism:

> It is impossible to do great things in the football world nowadays unless the team is run on professional lines, and from a thoroughly business point of view. Portsmouth is, therefore, to be congratulated on the fact that hence forward it is to take its place among other large towns and being represented by a first-class team of its own.
>
> For we make no doubt that this team of the Portsmouth Football & Athletic Company Ltd., will soon come to the front in the football world. It is not our place here to deal with the concern as a financial investment, but we only hope that we are only re-echoing the feelings of the sporting public in Portsmouth in hoping that the new club which is about to be inaugurated may soon enter upon a career so prosperous as it may be credible to the town which it will represent.

Initially there had been confusion as to whether there might even be two professional teams in Portsmouth. The **Southern Daily Mail** reflected that on Friday April 29 when it reported: "We [the town of Portsmouth] will have a great club, but it won't be Southsea Rovers." It had been rumoured Rovers, were also turning professional and several papers had carried reports that the club had told the Hampshire FA that this was to be the case. It turned out that they were referring to the new club and not themselves. It is interesting to see what the paper had to say about professionalism though:

> Our report of the Hants. F.A. meeting on Monday contained a reference to the Southsea Rovers which, it now appears, was the result of a misunderstanding. Mr Wells, the Rovers honorary secretary, wrote to Mr. Pickford applying for permission to the Hants. League and simply mentioned the fact that the movement was on foot in Portsmouth to form a professional club - quite distinct from the Rovers, who had no intention of adopting professionalism – which would probably seek to gain admission into the Southern League (first division) not next season, but in 1899 to 1900. Portsmouth, therefore, is to start a new century in splendid fashion as regards Football.
>
> The new club is, of course, to be a limited liability company, and the ground is already secured, while the prospectus will in all probability be placed before the public shortly. The board of directors will be found to contain the names of several well-

known local gentleman who take an interest in the propagation of healthy sport. Let us hope that the early years of the coming century will see the new Portsmouth team fighting for the English cup at the Crystal Palace!

Indeed, Wells constantly wrote to the **Southern Daily Mail** to keep them abreast of the new club. It will be seen in subsequent chapters that Pompey founder Wigginton was almost certainly encouraging him on behalf of the syndicate intending to form the club. If Wells was involved, then "all must be well" appeared to be the consensus as he was clearly highly regarded. The **Hampshire Telegraph** went on: "At last active steps are being taken re the question of a professional team for Portsmouth, and the fact that Mr. Wells is associated with the scheme would seem to point to the fact that the Southsea Rovers are involved in the matter. But if the promoters wish to make the organisation a success it must be a town club and a first class one, that can put in the field an 11 capable of meeting on equal terms Southampton or any other club in the south. If this be the idea, I am confident as to its success, and there is no doubt that shares would be easily taken up, while the gate at the R.A.'s match on Saturday conclusively prove that a really good team would be splendidly supported by the public." Wells never took up a position in the new club and his name completely drops out of the picture from formation onwards. One more than plausible reason is that John Brickwood wanted his own man as secretary...

MAKING THE CASE
Enthusiasm can be infectious and Dave Juson *et al* (2004), raise a valid point in ***Saints v Pompey: A History of Unrelenting Rivalry***. In the rush to have a team to rival Saints and others, it was asked whether Portsmouth really could support a professional team in the prevailing climate. Whilst Juson *et al* noted that should a Portsmouth club get to the top of the Southern League they "would be well placed if a national league was formed" they added "that it was becoming self-evident that, although lot of money could be generated through the gates of the successful big city clubs, healthy profits - as the critics of professional football were constantly pointing out - were elusive." One, unsurprisingly, did not hear this line of argument too much around Portsea Island at the time.

In the late 19th century newspapers were the main source of news, with the inhabitants of Portsmouth avidly buying the various papers on offer. An emerging theme was reports of football clubs losing money. Juson *et al*'s healthy scepticism is backed up by Southampton's experience. Saints' 1898 AGM, just after the first new Portsmouth club share offer had opened, was widely reported. Saints' chairman, Dr EH Stancomb, reported that they had had a "really good year." The club had won the Southern League for the second season in a row but that came at a cost as **Hampshire Independent** of July 2 acknowledged: "Owing to the large sums that had been expended in bringing about these results, a loss was shown on the seasons workings of £234." In the intangible credit column, the directors felt that the "greatly increased prestige and popularity of the team justified the expenditure" but Stancomb was "disappointed with the loss" and felt they had "been too generous [and] perhaps paid too much out in bonuses." The directors advised the investors that no dividend was to be paid for that year. The previous year Southampton had also reported a loss, after having formed a limited company, as the flow of income and expenditure was getting too large for any other business model. The club's overdraft would be growing to "between £600 and £700 before the 1898/99 season commenced, and they did not want to ask the friends of the club to guarantee such a large amount." Income for 1897 had been £3,322 and expenditure £3,490 leaving "an adverse balance at the end of the season of just over £200."

As well as the success and, albeit quick, demise of Royal Artillery (Portsmouth) FC many felt that Southampton's exploits, on the field if not on the bottom line, were another catalyst which led to Portsmouth gaining its own professional team. **The News**, the successor paper to the Evening News, wrote in an article commemorating Pompey's centenary in 1998: "Organised football had begun [in Southampton] in the mid-1880s and by 1891 Southampton St Mary's were to be found in the English Cup for the first time. By 1892 they had signed their first professional and two years later they became founder members of the Southern League. In Southampton, the change from amateur to professional promised success. Revenue in Saints' last amateur season was £800. By 1897 it was £3,300." And after all Portsmouth was a more affluent community, better known, thanks to its military significance, and had a bigger population to support a club. In the 1901 census it had 189,907 inhabitants to Southampton's 105,500.

Along the coast, Brighton United, which had pipped Pompey by a few months to become the first club to be set up from scratch as a limited liability company, were also suffering. Tim Carder and Roger Harris (1993) in ***Seagulls! The Story of Brighton & Hove Albion*** show that the forerunner club had been struggling financially in the Southern League first division during 1899/1900, despite having managed to get elected straight into the top division only the year before. The book noted: "[Attendances] dropped on occasion below four figures when a gate of 3,000 was required to ensure a successful company. The club was living from week to week, relying on home games for money to pay the players wages: clubs were obliged to meet only their visitors' expenses and these were often slow in arriving". Indeed, it got so bad that by their last home game of the season, which was due to be against Southampton, but followed by six away games, meant "the directors were hoping for a bumper gate to see the club through the remainder of the season." When Southampton reached the English Cup semi-final and then drew their game they had no choice but to postpone. Carder and Harris concluded: "This was the death-knell for United, and a meeting of shareholders on the Monday evening decided that a motion to dissolve the company must be put to an extraordinary general meeting ten days later." An FA-appointed commission to inquire into the affairs of United concluded in the August "there was no reckless trading and [the club] had been managed with due care up to the date of liquidation".

What was clear was that clubs needed capital and a model that worked for the town and the people involved. Across the country clubs had been set up in different ways. Some, like West Bromwich Strollers, latterly Albion, had been set up by companies – Salters Spring Works in this instance – to give workers something to do in their leisure time. Thames Ironworks, which became West Ham United, had a similar story as did Newton Heath, eventually Manchester United, which was formed by the Lancashire & Yorkshire Railway Company. A number of teams formed a limited liability company to allow them to grow, such as Small Heath, latterly Birmingham City, the first club to do so. Subsequently, ambitious clubs started using that business model, seeking to attract that capital investment from the wider public, including clubs such as Bolton Wanderers or Tottenham Hotspur, which had sprung from churches or cricket clubs.

In the **Bristol Times & Mirror** another article appeared in 1898 going a little further. From the editor, it talked about the dangers of professional football spreading from the north to the south and how "the southern clubs had held out for a long time but have succumbed generally during the last two years." They felt that the system was "bad for the players, worse for the spectators as the former learn improvident habits, become vastly conceited, whilst failing to see that they are treated like chattels, and cannot help but be brutalised." The latter were thought to get injured physically and morally. Moreover, it continued: "Instead of playing themselves or taking other exercise on their only half holiday, they stand still during cold, wet afternoons, on cold, wet ground. The number of lives indirectly sacrificed to football must be enormous. Out of 20,000 people who stand to watch each winter Saturday, many must catch severe colds, a certain proportion is bound to fare worse. The physique of the manufacturing population is bad enough already. It is rapidly growing worse under the pleasures of football. And the money that some said would be made hasn't yet come to fruition, perhaps this was a conceit as well." A bit strong perhaps, but this article and others like it were appearing just as potential investors in professional football in Portsmouth would have been thinking of risking their savings. There were evident problems too in The Football League. Sunderland's shares didn't sell as expected for instance. **Pearson's Athletic Record** reported in July 1897 that of the 5,000 they put up for sale, only 1,746 were taken up. Apparently, this was the fault of fans who "hadn't ever supported the club as they should have." The **Sporting Life**, weighed in on July 19 in the same year: "If one looked at the finances of all Football League clubs one would find many were in difficulties."

There seems little doubt these kind of stories resonated with potential investors in the new club in Portsmouth, especially those looking for a return. A story on August 17, 1898 in the Evening News tried to balance things, pointing that two clubs had made a profit: Derby £1,066 and Sheffield Wednesday £1,063. However, even this article went on to show that both Villa and Everton had spent well over half their costs on wages. All in all, it didn't paint a very positive picture. And then on September 3, 1898 the same paper reported further concerns: "The South had seen a tremendous growth of professionalism and there was a sudden demand for professionals from Midland and Northern clubs to Southern teams, and a great emigration has taken place. Southampton for instance have signed on at least ten men from the North to play on their magnificent new ground. This competition has resulted in a rise in wages, which have reached a ridiculous pitch. A prominent Liverpool player, for example, is now receiving £7 per week and seeing that more than half the League clubs finished up last season in debt, the prospect financially does not look rosy for them, and it puzzles one to know how some of the best clubs are going to get through the season. Higher wages, 40 players to pay, bonuses, summer wages, and travelling expenses. It is no wonder that most of the big teams are very nearly bankrupt."

The evidence clearly shows that in the late 1890s the whole financial landscape for the game was changing fast. The FA had limited the payment of dividends to a maximum of 5% and the new company's Articles of Association expressly covered this point. There were several newspaper reports around this time warning investors not expect to profit from the fortunes of a football club. Besides, whilst the average return from the UK stock market had been around 5% from 1829 until 1929, there were some bigger dividends to be obtained elsewhere. Water company stock was paying double what football could pay and banking stocks were a great investment as they went through a period of expansion and rationalisation. By way of example, the Capital & Counties Bank paid 16% per annum on its shares in 1898. In November 1899 the **Sporting Life** discussed how the description "limited liability company" suggested that football was all about finance adding: "In a mad moment one might dream of the possibility of exploiting the game and discovering therein a gold mine". In other words, that wasn't going to happen. The Life felt likewise that 5% was never going to be achieved from a football club investment as any bad playing year would simply drag the finances down: "Happy is the football shareholder that ever comes within a reasonable distance of this," it concluded. It went on to set out all the restrictions the FA placed on anything to do with a limited company. Shareholders couldn't sell season tickets separately from the shares given to them free of charge and because of having those shares. There was also a restriction on the number of free tickets, restrictions on the number and the type of shares that a company could issue and a rule that even when a company was wound up, the owners, that is to say the shareholders, couldn't profit from any excess value after all the debts had been paid off.

This meant in practice that if a club had to close down, the money left from the sale of the ground, after they had received their initial investment back, was to be given to another club or similar institution, as agreed by the FA Council. In an earlier **Sporting Life** article in January 1898, the paper warned its readers about the dangers of converting existing clubs to limited liability companies, although this wasn't what the entirely new club in Portsmouth was proposing to do. However, the FA had clearly introduced rules to protect supporters of clubs, including the maximum dividend rule "in order that financial consideration might be excluded from the management of the sport", concluded the paper. It added rules from 1897/98 meant that any new club had to have ratified all manner of things including "the terms of purchase, the offer of shares, and the articles and memorandum of association." In other words, all the legal documents setting out the governance of the club. It said that "the rotten financial condition of a large proportion of professional clubs is the subject of general comment just now" and "every one of the less important clubs is anxious to run on lines similar to the magnificence of Aston Villa, Glasgow Rangers and other great models and they are apt to overlook the fact that high wages and a long list of players are only permanently possible in the great centres of population where an assured gate of many thousands can be relied upon." Experience had shown that it was only possible to run a professional club in the bigger cities, the paper continued, citing the example of Woolwich Arsenal, in those days situated in an area well away from central London, which had gone professional, spent a lot of money and were no better off than before. The fact that teams based on smaller population centres, such as Cowes, Chatham and Bedminster, on the outskirts of Bristol, would ultimately struggle to compete in the Southern League underlined the issue. The **Sporting Life** also published details of the average crowd of clubs in the Football League, from 21,000 at Aston Villa to 5,000 at Bury and with an overall average of around 10,000.

Royal Artillery (Portsmouth) had proven that this was a support level to which a professional club in the town should, at the very least, be able to aspire, especially as the limitations of the amateur club were, by now, apparent. According to Smith (1999), it had been a bit of a surprise when they got into the Southern League in the first place. After two rejected applications, they were only accepted due to Southampton-based club Freemantle's shock resignation at the end of 1896/97. However, they justified their presence by winning promotion at the first attempt in April 1898. The **Evening News** was delighted: "They have done so much for local football that they deserve their congratulations on their promotion." However, by the August, as the RA prepared for its first season in the top flight of the Southern League, the same paper damned its prospects with faint praise: "It is a great undertaking for an amateur team like the RA to take its place among the professional teams, as its the only one that doesn't rely on paid players, so it might just, at best, keep its head above bottom place." No matter it seemed, as by now there was a new fish frying in the Portsmouth football pan…

THE MAKING OF MODERN POMPEY: KEY DATES

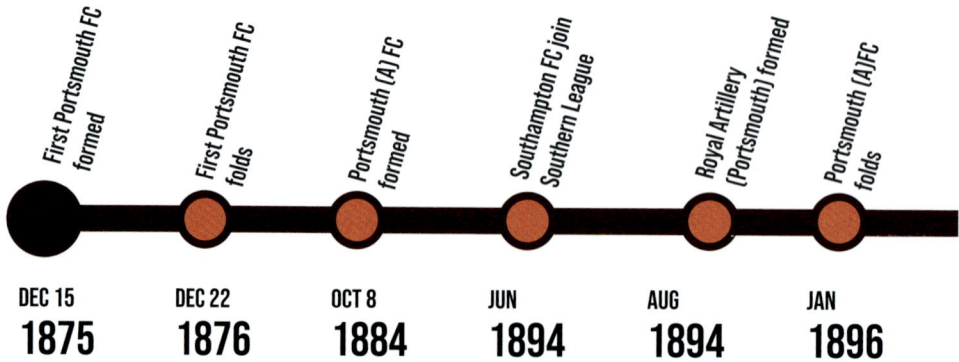

THE MAKING OF MODERN POMPEY

Chapter Two
FOUNDATIONS

While the story of how Portsmouth Football Club was founded is superficially well-known, in reality very little has been published previously about the events leading up to the formation, notably how and why the men involved came together. Clearly they were linked through business, and most, if not all, would have had money from business or family or both. Most importantly, they possessed the right mix of skills to run a large football business and there were links between them through both the military and freemasonry. Dave Russell (1997) in *Football and the English, a Social History of Association Football in England* describes the profile of a football club director. Most were from wealthier backgrounds. They needed to be, as the maximum 5% dividend allowed by the FA limited the opportunities for money making. Many were, of course, football enthusiasts and the opportunities for indirect benefit were substantial. At Portsmouth, opportunities to supply drinks and catering were there for John Wyatt Peters, Bernard Murtough and John Brickwood, who were all in that trade one way or another. For the likes of William Wigginton, the prospect of contracts clearly existed too. Russell also suggests that there was also evidence of opportunities to exert political pressure. At Portsmouth a number of the new club's leaders were involved in politics. For instance, John Pink would become town mayor and Irishman Murtough was active in Liberal politics in Portsmouth. Brickwood was an avowed Conservative. Whatever their reasons, the club's 1948 jubilee handbook, written by FJH Young, talks of the founding directors fondly as "men of vision and discernment." As *Sentinel*, the **Evening News** reporter, he would have known them well. After all, it would be Young who stood up at the club's 1913 AGM and toasted their good health. He followed it up with a eulogy in the club's 1948 Golden Jubilee handbook:

> Their prognostications concerning the popularity and future prosperity of first-class football in Portsmouth have been abundantly justified. Many years of stern struggle, financial sacrifice, personal risk and responsibility, and endless worry to make ends meet, had to be endured, however, before the present happy days of success were reached. It is almost impossible to adequately assess how much present day enthusiasts owe to the enterprise, sporting proclivities and sound business acumen of those five gentlemen who so successfully laid the foundations and built up a successful and flourishing Pompey Club. They have, alas, now passed to the Great Beyond, - but let us never forget to revere

and honour their memories. They were, indeed, great sportsmen. And who were they, apart from their connection with football?

The first Chairman, John Brickwood, who afterwards became Sir John, was head of Brickwood's Breweries, one of the biggest private businesses in the City. A keen, clever businessman, he was an ideal leader. Mr. Alfred H. Bone was a well-known architect and surveyor, whose professional experience and knowledge were invaluable ; Mr John Wyatt Peters, head of the local-firm of wine importers, was a man of resource and enterprise, whose many and varied interests and love of all manly sport fitted him for the prominent part he played in the formation of the Club ; Mr. William Wigginton, a successful Government contractor, from his youngest days a keen follower of sport; and, last but not least, of Mr. George Lewin Oliver, founder and proprietor one of Portsmouth's most successful private schools, who from the start was always to the fore with practical advice and a ready purse to promote the welfare of the Club and its' players. He later became Chairman of the Board of Directors and was always affectionately referred to as 'Father of the Club'. Right well he deserved the title, for no man did more for Portsmouth in its early days or sacrificed more in its interests.

That a professional club was wanted in Portsmouth by the late 19th century is indisputable, even if the finances didn't necessarily stack up. The prevailing mood among the proponents seemed to be that the marginal benefits of being involved in football would soften any financial blows. A potted history of the club in the **Sports Mail** during the 75th anniversary season in 1973/74 concluded: "The six businessmen knew they were not taking a reckless plunge, for professional soccer was spreading like a brushfire towards the turn of the century. League wages had spiralled to an unprecedented £7 a week, clubs were prepared to splash out £300 in transfer fees, and the fans were flocking to the grounds. Portsmouth felt distinctly out in the cold when Southampton opened a spanking new ground capable of accommodating 25,000 spectators at The Dell and recruited 10 Northerners to strengthen their squad."

It was easy to understand why Brickwood was involved in the project. The **Football Mail** in 1899 stated that he "liked the idea of mixing sport and business" and he would have seen this as a good way to increase his profile even further in the district. Never one to pass up on an opportunity, he quickly built the Pompey public house next to the ground in 1901, paying for it but keeping the profits and also charging for the food and drink that he supplied on match days and for club meetings during the week. Brickwood was involved in some of the biggest business deals of the time, and his involvement was seen as inevitable. The **Evening News** recorded in 1895 that "he could even afford £100", a lot of money in those days, to move a twenty-ton cedar tree across Portsea Island to put up in his new house in Southsea, so his credentials as a leader were self-evident.

It also made sense that Pink was involved. The club would need a solicitor as forming a limited company required legal expertise. He was also solicitor to Brickwood's Brewery, so a man starting to do well with good links to the political movers and shakers in the town. Not so much was known about Wigginton, although the assumption must be that his involvement was to do with building Fratton Park as he was described as a "government contractor". As it turned out he was neither the contractor or builder, but as a director he could offer advice and contacts for materials and labour. Wigginton was also a sportsman and then the president of Southsea Rovers, one of the better clubs in the area before 1898. He would have known Gorge Lewin Oliver through the latter's school at Mile End and it is pretty clear that they both, as men who liked sport, came to the conclusion that a professional team was needed in the town. They went and made it happen, organising the initial meetings along with Murtough, who like Brickwood and Wyatt Peters was in the drinks trade, namely the supply of mineral water and soft drinks to the armed forces.

Wyatt Peters was described in the 1891 census as a "wine importer" albeit part of the family firm of George Peters & Co, which also had a significant brewing and public house element to it. However, there was a "Peters" who played for the forerunner club, Portsmouth AFC, playing as a full back alongside Conan Doyle, which was almost certainly him. He was also a good friend of business rival Brickwood, so good that he was his best man at his second wedding in 1893. Knowing that, it is easier to understand why he was asked to come on board. He knew the people involved and could help with his knowledge of the game and business acumen. Alfred Bone was a surveyor and one of the two architects, the other was Arthur Cogswell, that Brickwood's retained for its public houses. The new board would have needed an architect to build what would quickly come to be regarded as one of the best grounds in the country. In those days the person usually performed a dual role of architect and project manager, so who better to get on to the board than Bone who was extremely well known around the city and already working with Brickwood. Portsmouth City Council planning records show that he had also just undertaken some work for Pink on his offices so perhaps he was already in mind when invitations were considered.

Traditionally, the founders of Portsmouth Football Club are regarded as the six known to be at that first meeting in April 1898. However, there is more than enough evidence to suggest it really should be eight men, if Pink's legal clerk George Preston and Percy Whitney are included. Preston was definitely present at the formation meeting and is recorded on the minute. Whitney isn't, but he was Brickwood's clerk and reports of other meetings suggest he was usually present wherever the boss was. He would also become the club's first secretary so it seems inconceivable that he wouldn't have been there, or at least been kept fully abreast of the outcome. In 1907 the **Hampshire Telegraph**, reporting on his untimely death, seems to confirm indeed he was at the formation. The total of those present might even have been nine if Alfred Jelks, Peters' 'managing clerk' is included. He certainly signs some of the first legal documents but there is no proof one way or another of his attendance. In addition, there is more than a strong possibility that another, Murtough, was part of the founding group but simply couldn't be at that first meeting due to other commitments.

What has undeniably been established here are two key groupings, which comprise men who for differing reasons can clearly be considered to be among the men who made Pompey. At the core are the prime movers in Lewin Oliver, Wigginton and Murtough, along with shakers such as Brickwood, Wyatt Peters and Bone. Between them they brought foresight, enthusiasm and, above all, credibility. They were inter-connected, whether professionally, militarily, via sport or through freemasonry, and sometimes by all four. They were also well-connected giving the enterprise the gravitas it needed to succeed. They were aided and abetted, though, by the men who had the essential skills to make their vision a reality. Generally younger and, no doubt, wanting to prove themselves, Pink brought legal expertise and Preston, Whitmey and Jelks the financial and administrative backbone of what was, and remains, the highly-regulated and rules-based industry that is professional football.

It was clear that in the first few months of 1898 the case for a professional team was growing apace, but how did the wheels get set in motion to form the club? The first step seems to have been taken by Lewin Oliver, along with Wigginton, and Murtough. Wigginton's son played for the football first XI of Lewin Oliver's school and Lewin Oliver and Murtough would have known each other as they were both in the education 'trade', Lewin Oliver through running his Mile End School and Murtough through his service to the Portsmouth School Board. They were also all freemasons. Although Murtough has never previously been listed as a 'founder', he clearly helped get the project off the ground, took shares early on and was on the first board of directors. Between them they organised two public meetings to specifically promote the idea of a professional club. The first was run by Lewin Oliver with Wigginton. The club's 1927 souvenir handbook explained: "Messrs G.L. Oliver and W. Wigginton got to work and called a meeting at the old Albany Hotel to take into consideration the desirability of starting professional football in Portsmouth. More than 70 supporters attended. After lengthy discussion, a most successful start was apparently made with many promises of substantial support; and the matter was finally adjourned for a week. At the second meeting only the two promoters were in attendance. They got in touch with Mr J.E .Pink their solicitor through Mr G. F. Preston and a strong committee was formed and brought about the great change in the winter sport of the city."

The subsequent meeting is also referred to in the 1948 handbook. It adds that there were several meetings, at least one more organised by Lewin Oliver, this time with Murtough, described as "a friend of John Brickwood". At this meeting, town councillor Alfred Amatt also spoke powerfully in favour of the scheme. The 1948 handbook concludes that the events leading up to the formation meeting included "much negotiation and several public meetings." It went on:

> At the latter, speakers emphasised the 'glorious opportunity that presented itself for introducing professional football to Portsmouth'. These, by the way, were the words of Councillor Alfred Amatt, a great sport and an enthusiastic football fan, at a preliminary public meeting held at the Albany Hotel, Commercial Road. That particular meeting was called by Mr. G. Lewin Oliver and Mr. B. Murtough following a good deal of correspondence in the local Evening News, some advocat-

ing and others deprecating the formation of a professional Club. Southampton, by the way, had already taken the plunge, and not under such favourable circumstances as existed in Portsmouth for the town was, of course, smaller and there were not the same opportunities of securing a freehold ground as there ~ were here. There is no doubt that the warm advocacy of Councillor Alfred Amatt who, incidentally, had long been a keen supporter of the old Portsmouth Wanderers - for which club Dave Halliday, Dick Pook and George Preston were among the players - went a long way towards persuading the meeting to vote for the formation of the proposed Club and to give it every support. Anyhow, be that as it may, the meeting paved the way for rapid developments. Within a few days the proposal was formally ratified and the first Directors met, discussed preliminaries, and unanimously brought the Company into being.

Many years later an undated **Hampshire Life** magazine article added some vivid, if possibly apocryphal, colour to the proceedings: "To the seventy men assembled in the dimly-lit, smoke-laden room of the Albany Hotel, back in 1898, [Amatt's] bold words were perhaps tinged with more than a degree of optimism." Our three promoters then went to see Pink, Brickwood's solicitor, and he was charged with setting up a further meeting to "move the idea forward." That meeting was the momentous one of April 5 at 12 High Street. As an aside, Amatt was probably the council's 'go to' man for most sporting activities. His name crops up in many reports, all connected in one way or another with sport. He is recorded on numerous occasions as participating in events and dinners, donating a five guineas' billiards cup and other trophies to good causes. He was also recorded as an official of various sporting clubs including the vice chair of Portsmouth Wanderers FC in 1895 and their president by March 1898. In 1897 Preston was recorded as Wanderers' secretary, so would have known Amatt well.

As well as the education connection, Wigginton and Lewin Oliver also played cricket against one another. The Mile End school staff team and Wigginton's Southsea Rovers played each other and the two would have surely met and discussed their mutual love of both football and cricket. It can be surmised that Wigginton was one of the people described by the press when it was reported that the syndicate being formed to set up Portsmouth FC "included those who were used to running high level sport", although the use of the plural hinted at the involvement of Frederick Windrum and Richard Bonney from the Royal Artillery club too, but more of that later. This all points to the proposed club having more football experience than in many other start-ups at the time. William Pickford, the well-regarded administrator, secretary and general driving force of the Hampshire Football Association said in his memoirs that "some of us had the advantage of having taken part in football control previously but to most of the newly drawn enthusiasts in football everything was fresh."

Both Wigginton and Lewin Oliver clearly felt there was an opportunity for players on Portsea Island to have their own professional club to aim at, something which would have been a shared aspiration. Indeed, one of the first players in the new club's first squad, the aforementioned Halliday, was one that they might have had in mind. He captained the Mile End House first XI for Lewin Oliver, after Wigginton's son left, and then played for Southsea Rovers. After the two meetings had taken place in early 1898 confirming sufficient interest on the island, the promoters initially met with Preston, Pink's confidential clerk. Preston - who incidentally himself played for Portsmouth Wanderers - reported back to Pink and a committee was formed. It is doubtful if it will ever be known for certain if Brickwood and Wyatt Peters were already involved, or if Pink subsequently whetted their appetite for the project, but the enterprise had been widely reported for some time as involving a group of local businessmen, suggesting their prior involvement. As seen already, Brickwood was an obvious person to lead and having his own company architect, in Bone, helped further. However, they also needed good administrative support to make it happen and that was what Preston and Whitmey, Pink's confidential clerk, added to the mix.

There is a strong link between most of the founding fathers too through freemasonry. Most prominent people were freemasons in those days, as it was considered a necessary step on the path to success in many professions and, of course, they undertook many good works to help others in the district. Brickwood, Murtough, Bone, Pink, Wyatt Peters, Wigginton and Lewin Oliver were all members of one lodge or another in 1898. They would have met at their respective lodge meetings or at the masonic social club in Commercial Road, which could be used by all lodge members. Richard Oliver, Lewin Oliver's great grandson, has researched their family tree and the received wisdom is that the core group which founded the club used their lodge connections to meet and discuss the matter. Some, like Brickwood, had masonic leadership positions, in his case in the Phoenix Lodge, the oldest in Portsmouth. He undertook several senior roles and initiated new members, including Arthur Conan Doyle. There are also a number of people heavily connected to the founders, names that will surface more in the chapters that follow, who were also masons including Arthur Cogswell, the designer of the Pompey public house, Samuel Salter, a retained builder at Fratton Park and John McCarthy, the original builder of Fratton Park.

The formation meeting of what would become 'Limited Company Number 57335' took place on Tuesday April 5, 1898 at solicitor John Pink's offices in Old Portsmouth. It wasn't called 'Old' in those days though, as the location was the hub of the town, albeit one getting over a smallpox epidemic according to the **Evening News** published on that day. Companies House records confirm 12 High Street would be the club's registered office until it was changed to Fratton Park on May 2, 1903. Although April 5 is the club's official birthday, like the King or Queen, it has two. Its true birthday comes six weeks later on Friday May 13, when The Portsmouth Football & Athletic Company was legally incorporated. To be precise, the meeting on April 5 was merely to note the founders' resolve to form a limited liability company to run the club. We know who was there for sure. The club's 1927 handbook said: "It will be noticed that the original minute was proposed by Mr. George Lewin Oliver and seconded by Mr. John Brickwood. Also present were Messrs J.W. Peters, A.H. Bone and W. Wigginton, together with Mr. J.E. Pink who was appointed solicitor to the company and later [in 1905] became a director, and Mr. George F. Preston, Mr. Pink's confidential clerk". Unfortunately, there are no records of any of the board meetings from this period, so much of the history of that first year can only be deduced from irregular newspaper reports. However, in the club archive is its first cashbook and share register, enabling us to see the day-to-day detail of the first year's expenditure and receipts, which was meticulously recorded.

The formation document was preserved by Preston and a copy of it is framed and on a wall in the South Stand to this day. Whitmey was nominated as company secretary with Pink as company solicitor. The formation resolution is only agreed to by five of the founders – Brickwood, Bone, Lewin Oliver, Wyatt Peters and Wigginton – with Pink adding his offset signature at the end, presumably in his capacity as legal advisor. Those "desirous of being formed into a company" in the Memorandum of Association were actually seven in number. The Companies Act (1856) had established a principle that, to quote verbatim: "The number of subscribers must not be less than seven and every subscriber must take one share at least." In this case to the five cited above two clerks, Whitmey and Jelks could be added. Pink witnessed the signatures, as was required by the law. The signed page from the memorandum also shows a distinct gap between the businessmen's signatures and those of the two clerks. The pecking order of Victorian society writ large.

The legally binding Memorandum & Articles of Association would have been approved by the FA under their rules. Directors were barred by the articles from receiving "any remuneration in respect of the office" - that was FA Rule 34 - which remained the case until 1981. Also, under the rules they signed up to, each director had to own at least £50 in shares, all fully paid. This was clearly ignored from the outset, as according to the share register only one of the five directors is recorded as having purchased £50 worth of shares until well into 1899. This was Wyatt Peters, recorded as buying 200 shares on June 13, 1898, and then only just before he entered into the agreement on behalf of the company to buy the land for the ground from the Goldsmiths. It seems likely – although it is impossible to be definitive as the articles could, in theory, have been amended – most of the directors seem to have acted beyond their legal authority for more than 12 months. This is backed up by the first Form E - which is the legal return of shareholders to Companies House sent in September 1898 - where the directors names are not recorded as shareholders, although some of their family members are. However, the page for 'P' is missing, so it must be assumed Wyatt Peters' name at least was recorded.

It was also common in those days for the company solicitor to attend all board meetings and shareholders meetings so Pink didn't need to be a director and didn't become one until 1905, but on the evidence he still more than qualifies to be considered as one of the founders. In his role as company secretary, Whitmey initially based himself at Brickwood's head office in Admiralty Road, at the Portsmouth Brewery and ran the football club from there. The new club's first entry in the Hampshire FA Handbook for 1899 gives the club's first formal address as the Brickwood's Brewery although adverts for games and tickets in early 1900 also said they could be obtained from "the office of the company" at

12 High Street, namely Pink's offices. There is also a note, on headed paper in the football club's name, but with the address at the brewery, in the National Archives in Kew. It is from Whitmey to Companies House asking a question concerning the paperwork required to run a limited company. In many respects it is strange that he must ask the question, as he should have known the answer from running the brewery. As we shall see, there was an issue of not obtaining planning permission for the building of one the new stands, with the council taking umbrage when it came to light, so perhaps Whitmey was simply a little bit cavalier over certain matters, including the share issue mentioned above.

Twelve High Street was the obvious place for the founders' meeting and Simon Parker, writing in **The News** on the centenary of the club in 1998, evoked the occasion: "The first meeting is believed to have taken place in the first-floor drawing room of the elegant town house which dates back to 1750. A century on, the house, which stands 200 yards from Portsmouth Grammar School, has hardly changed from that day." He went on to say that no one knew for sure in which room the meeting took place, although from the layout of the house it was likely that it was upstairs. Having a reception downstairs would be logical for the business and having been inside the building myself in 2022, it is clear that the original door to the reception office downstairs is still there, with what would have been Pink's office on the first floor. The owner, John Reynolds, recalled that the first thing he saw when he bought the place was the walls. The owner before him had lived there since just after the second world war and had hardly changed a thing. When Reynolds moved in she told him she thought that the orangey-pink paint had been there since well before then. Coincidence perhaps, but the colour of Pompey's first shirts was salmon pink...

The original formation minutes certainly existed in the 1940s, as at the Golden Jubilee dinner in November 1948 a copy was presented to all the guests, but the original is now missing. Young wrote in the Golden Jubilee handbook that: "The original Minute [was] passed by a syndicate of sportsmen who afterwards became the first Directors of the Portsmouth Football & Athletic Company Limited at a meeting held at the offices of the late Alderman J. E. Pink, 12 High Street, Portsmouth, April 5th, 1898, is an appropriate prelude to the history of the Club which is this year celebrating its Jubilee. The meeting held 50 years ago definitely decided whether there should or should not be a professional Football Club in the town. Fortunately, the 'ayes' had it. The Minute was carefully preserved by Mr G.F. Preston and presented to the Club on his election as a Director and, needless to say, the memento is highly prized."

The **Southern Daily Mail** reported in May 1898: "It is impossible to do great things in the football world nowadays unless a team is run on professional lines, and from a business point of view. Portsmouth are to be congratulated on the fact that henceforward it is to take its place amongst other large towns, in being represented by a first class team of its own - for we make no doubt that the team of the Portsmouth Football & Athletic Company, Limited, will soon come to the front in the football world. It is not our place here to deal with the concern as a financial investment, but we fancy that we are only re-echoing the feelings of the sporting public of Portsmouth in hoping that the new club which is about to be inaugurated may soon embark upon a career as prosperous as it may be creditable to the town which it will represent." The prospectus for the new club was soon drawn up, with Pink and Preston the likely authors. The directors chose to set up a limited liability company, just like many other clubs at the time, with ownership through shares anticipated to be spread widely around the community to generate the cash they needed to build the ground, find players and pay wages until the gate receipts started rolling in.

MAKING A PITCH
A limited liability company with shares that can be bought and sold is exactly what it says: an entity that limits the liability of the shareholders, to the amount of their investment in shares and nothing else unless they have loaned the business money. The shares carried voting rights, meaning that the shareholders had the right to vote according to the number of shares that they held. One individual could, by those means, gain control of a company through purchase of over 50% of the voting rights. That was not the route the founders took however, as they preferred to see the investment burden spread widely. To help emphasise the revenue raising potential of the businesses, almost all professional clubs in those days had "& Athletic" tacked on to the company's name, as they had a nominal desire at least to use the facilities for other sports, such as cricket in the summer. Cycling tracks were often proposed at football grounds although in practice football dominated. It took until 1910, when Pompey were in some difficulty financially, for the first "Cycling and Athletic Festival" to be held at Fratton Park, to "help clear some of their adverse balance" according to the **Evening News**. The event attracted more than 5,000 fans on July 9, 1910. A flat cycle track of six laps to the mile was laid out on the playing surface and interestingly several of the team's players entered the athletics races. The 100 yards dash was a particular favourite, although they weren't quick enough and a professional runner from Peckham called Adam won the sprints. Simon Inglis (1983) in ***The Football Grounds of England & Wales***, confirms that at the outset, many of the limited companies set up were not just interested in staging football and their homes were all called "athletic grounds". By the turn of the century attendances were considered high if they hit the 20,000 mark but that wasn't necessarily sufficient to sustain a business and there was a public thirst for any kind of sporting spectacle, cycling, running, parades, pageants, and even baseball tournaments. However, Inglis notes that by 1914 most cycle and athletics tracks had gone so that more terracing could be added as crowds wanting to watch football grew.

The advert for the Portsmouth Football & Athletic Company's prospectus was widely publicised throughout May 1898. The intention to buy land near Fratton station from the Goldsmith family was formally announced: "The price to be paid for the land is £4,950, which amount includes the total liability of the Company towards the cost of making the approach roads leading to the ground from Goldsmith Avenue." The financing of that deal will come under scrutiny in due course. What is also fascinating to see was that the prospective directors were highly bullish about the costs of building a football ground. The prospectus went on: "It is estimated that a sum of £2,000 will be required to drain, fence, and lay out the ground and erect the necessary buildings, thus leaving about £1,000 for working capital." The new club would end up spending over double this.

This must have been a conscious decision rather than a naive overspend as Bone was an engineer, surveyor and architect by trade and Wigginton a builder. Brickwood would also know very well what buildings cost, given his business was, in part, constructing public houses. Yet they all agreed to quote a sum of just £2,000 - around £325,000 by today's prices. They should have known that this was never going to be enough to provide a ground with two well-appointed stands, so the reasoning remains a mystery that may never be solved. The prospectus also optimistically proclaimed: "Local Matches of interest are attracting large crowds of spectators, and it is considered that with the formation of a first-class Professional Football Team in Portsmouth the game would become equally as popular as in the Northern towns, where the attendance at matches frequently reaches from 20,000 to 30,000." Likewise, the success of the Southampton club was lauded: "The takings of that Club rose from £800 in the year 1893 to £3,300 in the year 1897, and for the season now closing it is believed the receipts will nearly double those of last year. These figures speak for themselves." It was clearly written to appeal to sports people of all persuasion: "The Directors trust that all lovers of football and other Athletic Sports in Portsmouth and surrounding districts would take shares, or at least one share, in the company, as, with a good cycle track and Cricket Pitch, the Directors reasonably expect that the principal Cycle and Athletic Meetings and Cricket Matches during the summer will take place on this ground," it trilled. The good intentions regarding cycling and cricket soon disappeared.

The **Evening News** reported on May 14 that "in our advertisement columns will be found the prospectus" and it commented favourably that "the ground is admirably situated close to tram and train, and it is hoped that in view of the great strides that have been made in football in the south in the past few years, the organisation of a good club, and the provision of such a ground as the company proposes, the game will become the most popular form of the winter recreation in the town". Four days later the same paper looked to cement its role in the foundation of the club for posterity: "When, a few months ago, it was mooted in these columns that the time was ripe for the formation of a professional football team in Portsmouth, the proposal brought forth an unexpected expression of opinion in its favour by local enthusiasts, and letter after letter was written supporting the idea. The signs of the times were not wasted upon some well-known local supporters of sport, and the outcome has been that the project has "precipitated", and the prospectus is now being advertised and the subscription list is open for 8,000 £1 shares." But it was confident the capital would be taken up by investors and, even in the event of the football business failing, investors would still have a parcel of prime real estate on their hands as the town began its urban sprawl to the east. It predicted:

> There should be no difficulty in getting the £8,000, for the promoters of the company have arranged the payments on very

easy terms, and their idea is that the shares shall be allotted in small numbers, so as to get as many people as possible with a direct interest in the concern. Five well-known townsman are the directors Mr. J. Brickwood, A.H. Bone, J.W. Peters, W. Wigginton, and G.L. Oliver. They have secured a piece of land in Goldsmith Avenue, and propose to lay out football and cricket pitches, and a cycle track, so that the ground can be used all the year round. There is no doubt of the wisdom of the choice of site. Land in the neighbourhood of Fratton Station is constantly increasing in value, so that should the new invention not meet with success, the shareholders would be sure of having a valuable asset left for realisation on the winding up of the company. From a football point of view, the company should be assured of success, if properly managed. The services of a good secretary and the engagement of a dozen or so players of reputation should give the venture a good start. Of course, there are difficulties about the commencement, especially as the Royal Artillery are now in the first division of the Southern League, but the point is that a good team is bound to make its way. It can enter the English Cup and similar competitions, and a couple of matches might be arranged against the R.A. When it has shown what it can do, the team may gain the coveted admission to the Southern League.

The point about the 'difficulties about the commencement' given the RA's place in the Southern League already is an interesting, if glossed over, one, which will be dealt with in due course. For the moment, just wallow in the parochial appeal to civic pride, sowing the roots of perennial rivalry: "If Southampton can run a team which is the pride of the South, surely Portsmouth can do the same? At all events, there is a very good prospect of success, for the company is in excellent hands, has a first rate asset in the shape of the valuable ground, while football grows every season more and more popular in the borough and district."

There was some early talk of games starting in the 1898/99 season but that was soon ruled out as impractical. On the day after the land purchase was completed in August 1898 and the club took possession of the field, the **Southern Daily Mail** carried an article stating that "it's a certain starter for 1899". Although 8,000 shares were anticipated to be sold, the share register shows the actual amount raised was initially substantially less. In fact, it took until 1905 to raise the full amount. The newspapers soon caught on that the sale was going slowly. The editorial of the **Southern Daily Mail** of August 31, 1898 said "the shares were not eagerly snapped up" although the paper remained positive about the initiative. Further proof that shares were slow to sell was contained in the club's first Form E in September 1898, which was the list of current shareholders submitted periodically to Companies House. It showed that only £2,112 shares out of the £8,000 offered for sale had been taken up after the first four months. Even by the December 1899 AGM only 6,772 shares had been issued, some 20 months after formation, leaving the club over £1,200 short of their initial target. An incentive of having a free season ticket for those buying more than 25 shares, which had been soon brought in to boost take up, still hadn't completely done the trick. The slow take up left the directors with three options: keep close tabs on the club's initial expenditure to ensure bank overdraft charges were not racked up, invest more themselves or find funds from elsewhere until the shares were fully subscribed. For the first time in the club's history and certainly not for the last, the choice was made to arrange an overdraft with the club's bank, with the one ledger we have from the time showing an agreed limit of £500. It wasn't used at once, as share monies were continuing to come in and providing enough cash to meet the day-to-day commitments. The cashbook states the balance at the bank each month and it only slips into an overdrawn position some two years later in August 1900. The bankers were the Capital & Counties Bank in Portsmouth, subsequently taken over by Lloyds Bank in 1918.

What is clear though is that by the time the commitment was given to buy the land, very early in the process, the new company simply didn't have the funds to buy the land and build the ground. The overall pessimism about football finances, seen in the previous chapter, had cast doubt on the automatic success of a professional club - its proponents were perhaps guilty of the sin of wishful thinking - and this had made it more difficult than anticipated for Pompey's founders to attract share capital throughout 1898 and 1899, meaning some sleight of financial hand would be needed to get the project off the ground...

THE MAKING OF MODERN POMPEY: KEY DATES

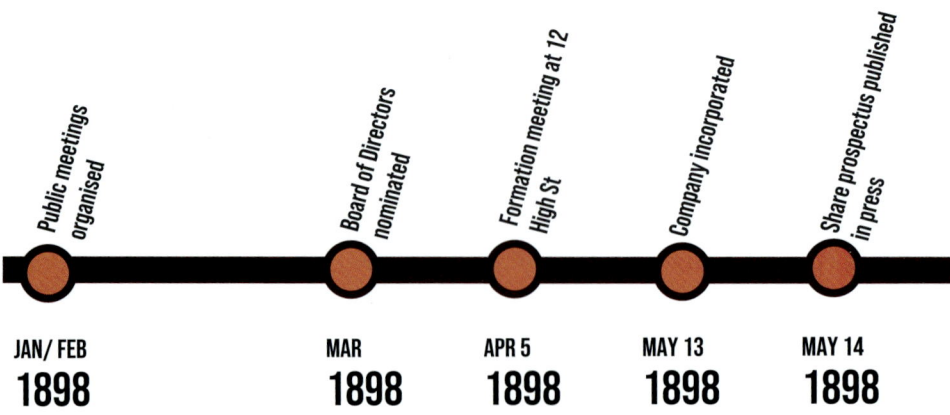

Chapter Three

RAISING CAPITAL

Following the meeting on April 5, the task was to quickly raise capital. The prospective investors would be, by and large, local people and the fact those leading the enterprise were well-known and respected would have helped drum up interest. The target investors were not wealthy. Many invested £25 - roughly £4,000 at today's prices - which would have been a substantial amount. However, it would entitle them to a free season ticket for as long as they held shares. For the most part they simply loved football and would soon come to love the club, a community club if you will, invested in by the people and a concept which would have more than a hint of an echo in 2013. The new club's share prospectus set the goal of issuing capital of £8,000 divided into 8,000 shares of £1 each. Football enthusiasts in Portsmouth were invited to subscribe and to encourage take-up they could be paid for in five shilling (25p) tranches, which was typical of the time. For most of the 1890s, professional football clubs were thought to be a decent investment, but that narrative, as has been shown, was on the wane. On June 13, 1898, after the initial offer period had closed, the financial secretary Percy Whitmey, recorded the first shareholders in the register. Disappointingly, there had been just 180 subscribers, and a mere 2,152 shares sold. The 'cup half full' version is that many of those people had invested substantial amounts for the time, even those 57 who had only bought one or two shares at a cost of around a week's typical wages. By the end of 1899, in addition to the founders, a further eight had each bought 100 shares. What is clear though, is that when the purchase of the ground went through at the end of August 1898, the directors did not have the purchase price of the land, set at £4,950, sitting in the club bank account.

Most of the founders purchased shares, but not in huge numbers. Those men might have had money and some might have been able to invest more, but no one took a majority share in the enterprise or would qualify as a major investor by today's standards. To be fair, company law meant they weren't allowed to draw a salary for their efforts, so any time they put into the venture should be seen as an intangible additional investment. Most didn't formally own the shares until 1899 according to the register. In that initial period 1898-1899, George Lewin Oliver took 200 shares - that would be an investment of around £30,000 today - but put them in the names of his family members, a typical practice, usually to minimise tax liability. He took 125 while his wife Elizabeth and children Margarite and Herbert were allocated 25 each. William Wigginton's family eventually took 205 shares again spread around, with him taking 50 and wife Emma 25. Their children Frank, Sidney, Robert, William and Percy were each allocated 26. Both of John Brickwood and Alfred Bone took 200 with Pink purchasing 100 initially, Windrum 50, Murtough and Jelks 25 apiece, Preston five and Percy Whitmey bringing up the rear with two. A full list of all those who invested £25 or more can be found in Appendix II. Investors were drawn from a broad spectrum of society from surgeons to a small number of 'gentlemen' and, more down to earth, one or two fishmongers. As an aside, one of Southampton's first directors, George Thomas, who built The Dell, was a fishmonger. However, the Portsmouth list had rather a brewing and beverage flavour to it. If there was any doubt beforehand that the good people of the town like a tipple, then the share ledger provides ample evidence it was so. Besides when sailors came ashore their capacity to drink beer and spirits is well-documented, so someone - Brickwood and Wyatt Peters mainly - had to supply them and the ships in which they sailed. When Whitmey sat down to issue said certificates, neatly torn from the pristine book bought by the club for £2 from a local stationers, one might have thought that he would give the honour of the first share to Brickwood, or one of the other founders. He could have even made himself the first. But no. He must have had a pile of applications on his desk in any old order and that seems to be his method. The investor issued Share Certificate Number One, when they were written out in 1899, was a Harry Whybro, from The Railway Hotel in Commercial Road but the investor recorded in the register as owning the first share bought in May 1898 was a Walter Finch Andrews, the superintendent of the Eastney Cemetery, now called Highland Road Cemetery. Wyatt Peters had the honour, such as it was, of being the first founder to be issued with his share certificate at number nine in the pile. Then again, only he had bought any...

The first shareholders meeting was held on September 2, 1898, at the Sussex Hotel near the town hall. The **Southern Daily Mail** reported: "Mr J Brickwood presided over a large attendance". What is interesting is that Brickwood did not, apparently, mention a £4,000 mortgage over the ground as it certainly doesn't crop up in any of the newspaper reports of the event. Shareholders, one would have imagined, might have been extremely interested in that fact, as it wasn't the original deal stated in the prospectus. All Brickwood seems to say is that "the ground has been paid for and the company were now in possession," which, as of August 30, was true. The club owned the freehold and could do what they liked with the land, subject to planning rules. It seems like there was more discussion at the meeting about the crop of potatoes and cabbages the company hoped to sell than the fact that it was now saddled with a substantial, potentially long-term, debt. Brickwood made it clear that "the meeting was simply held to fulfil legal requirements" but he gave the good news that building work on the ground was imminent. "It would shortly be turfed, fenced, and generally prepared for play," he was quoted. Brickwood also reassured the meeting about the appointment of a manager: "Already negotiations have been entered into with a view to forming a proper football team, and no doubt in the course of time the team would be a successful one. The directors hoped to succeed in making Portsmouth a big football centre, such as most of the big towns in the country were now." He added: "There would be plenty of room, not only for the football pitch, but for a cycle track, for the ground was four and a half acres extent, as compared with the three acres covered by the new ground of Southampton. The professional team would not, of course, be started during the present season."

The mortgage would only be brought openly into the public domain at the second AGM in July 1900, although this might not have been unusual. By the 1890s it had become clear that company law had been enacted in the interests of companies, in the belief that commercial and industrial development was dependent upon their freedom to organise and manage as they saw fit. John A Lapp (1908), writing in the ***American Political Science Review***, said that by 1894 the evils arising from such secrecy had led to a parliamentary inquiry. A committee, chaired by a Lord Davey, had been tasked to investigate what amendments were required to company law to stamp out fraud in relation to the formation and ongoing management of companies. The result was the Companies Act (1900) which, in the main, followed the recommendations of the committee. The act was essentially about shareholders being able to get information. From 1900, company accounts had to be available for inspection and any mortgages or charges registered with the Registrar of Companies within 21 days. It also needed a further act in 1907 to clarify and toughen the provisions. The first AGM in December 1899 didn't even put any figures in front of the shareholders, so they wouldn't have seen the debt there either. The first balance sheet and profit & loss account were sent to shareholders in July 1900, roughly a week in advance of the second July 1900 AGM. There was a legal requirement to send a printed copy to each member and the figures were widely reported, including in the **Sporting Life** nationally. The **Evening News** of July 19, 1900, assessing the balance sheet just sent out, stated that "a loan of £4,000 has been obtained as a first mortgage on the freehold land at Fratton Park" and yet all that Brickwood said at the meeting is that "they had a ground equal to any in the south of England at a cost of less than £900 and that was by no means a bad result." This was either the adverse balance on the profit & loss account from the first year's trading or the deposit for the land they had to find and not the full cost of it. So, it looked like the mortgage was again not mentioned at the meeting itself. Seeing as dialogue was always covered in great detail, the lack of any comment feels odd, but in keeping with the sharp business practice of the day perhaps. One could argue the directors had got away with it, even though they had done nothing wrong. It could also be the matter genuinely didn't concern investors or perhaps people simply deferred to their 'betters' more in those days. Whatever, the directors didn't have to tell investors until the balance sheet was due, although, in fairness, the Memorandum & Articles of Association gave them the power to create a mortgage leaving aside, as mentioned earlier, that there is some doubt as to whether the directors had been acting legally at all. Interestingly, the **Football Mail** of April 1, 1899, several months before even the first AGM, did carry a comment from *Sentinel*, who was well-connected as we know: "From what I can hear the undertaking has had several important alterations affected financially since the original prospectus was drawn up, and the concern is to commence operations on a sound basis." It could well be this was an oblique reference to the mortgage. A search of the National Archive at Kew and the club records revealed nothing, so unless a set of papers that were sent to shareholders before the 1900 AGM turn up in a personal collection somewhere the full story of the mortgage issue may never be known. However, there was no obligation for the directors to tell shareholders about the mortgage at the time it was taken out, but it is fair to say the corporate climate when the club was formed was not always one of full disclosure.

To get back to the story in reality the timing of the share offer, followed as it was by a quick purchase of the land for £4,950 plus costs, never really did make sense unless an alternative source of funding had already been lined up. The timeline of the process to buy the land from the Goldsmith family, was quick. Shares were offered from May 16, 1898, with applications having to be in by May 21. Payment was then in tranches, so if the board had allotted shares quickly, they could have, at best, got half of the 8,000, so £4,000, in the bank by August. That sum wouldn't have been enough to even pay for the land or other formation expenses, let alone start construction, so one is inclined to conclude the directors must have had another plan from the outset. For make no mistake, the directors were the crème-de-la-crème of business people in the area. To recap, Wyatt Peters ran a huge wine importers and brewery. He was one of Brickwood's main competitors in a town where public houses and hotels were incredibly important to the local economy. Bone was a top architect, Pink a respected solicitor, Wigginton a well-connected contractor, Murtough supplied the navy with mineral water and Lewin Oliver was running a top independent school most successfully. They would all have been well versed in accountancy, company law and governance and would have had plenty of experience of cashflow management and business practice in general. When Brickwood purchased a rival business from Edward Jewell in 1899, the capital of Brickwood's brewery was increased to £700,000. That makes it at least a £115 million business in today's money. Philip Eley (1994) in his **Portsmouth Paper**, 'Portsmouth Breweries Since 1847' recorded Brickwood's as owning 333 public houses, which could be found from the Isle of Wight in the south, Southampton to the west and even as far away as Fulham, where the company owned an off-licence. To give an idea of the footprint of Brickwood's in the greater Portsmouth area, the Gales of Horndean brewery was sold for a mere £115,000 in January 1899. We are not talking amateurs here.

However, the club's new shares didn't quickly sell, even with the £25 season ticket offer brought in almost at once, so a Plan B was clearly needed. The purchase of Fratton Park in August 1898 was barely commented on in the local press, other than a general statement in the **Southern Daily Mail** to the effect that "it was difficult." What is clear is that a source of funding had to be found, especially as it is likely that contracts had been exchanged on June 24, a legal commitment to buy, when the share monies didn't exist to pay for it. A mortgage or loan of some sort had to have arrived by August as the press reported that the club "entered into possession" of the land on August 30. Of course, the directors could have put up the money themselves, but there is no indication that route was ever considered. Instead, with Wyatt Peters leading the purchase, the directors chose to ask the wealthy Goldsmith family for a loan. To be fair, the mortgage would be at a good rate, as will be explained in due course. Looking at the evidence 126 years on, it is hard not to conclude that the intention was always to take out a mortgage. Company law, as it stood in 1898, gave the board the necessary cover to take that route. A fait accompli, one might say.

By early 1899 very little else had emerged in the press concerning the new club, but the silence was broken on January 14, 1899 when the **Football Mail** reported an unnamed director: "I should like you to mention that as a guarantee of good faith all the directors of the company have to invest in the new club – this ensures that every man will do his best for the club." The **Southern Daily Mail** followed up in February: "Although practically nothing has been heard of the new Portsmouth Football Club, it should not be inferred the promoters have in any way abandoned the scheme. True, the shares were not so eagerly snapped up as was confidently anticipated in some quarters but the directors have plenty of faith in the undertaking and believe that success must follow in the end."

The **Evening News** of February 18, 1899 even tried to give potential investors a nudge: "Some of the spectators seats will be numbered and reserved. In this connection it is as well to note that there are still some shares waiting to be taken up. Owners of 25 shares and upwards not only get free admission to the ground, but are entitled to a reserved seat for all matches except cup ties." The paper had reported as far back as May 20, 1898 that the directors had felt it necessary to offer this concession. Incidentally, Plymouth Argyle followed a similar model in 1903. For a sum of around £3,800 in today's money, shareholders got a 'free' season ticket for as long as the shares were kept. This goes a long way to explain why most of the investors were small ones, as they would have been fans effectively purchasing a lifetime season ticket. And Pompey's was a better deal than at some clubs. AJ Arnold (1988) in *A Game That Would Pay* notes that in 1908 Bradford City issued a prospectus seeking to raise £7,000 in £1 shares to relieve the strain on the committee who had individually guaranteed the substantial bank overdraft. £3,600 worth were taken up, but to get the season ticket perk, for the best seats an investor had to purchase 100 shares

The scheme, though, caused Pompey aggravation with the FA periodically for the next fifty years. In 1921 FA rules were changed to expressly rule out the giving of free season tickets to shareholders. It was felt in doing so an artificial market price, or value, for the shares was created. The new rule allowed only for a 5% reduction when a shareholder bought a season ticket. Whether by ignorance or deceit, at Portsmouth the rule change was ignored. In 1925, when a few shareholders tried to sell their shares and pass the benefit on to a new owner, the club, having taken legal advice, wrote to the FA to ask what it should do. The reply set out all the issues and helpfully reiterated what had happened 27 years earlier. It read:

```
The original Portsmouth Football & Athletic Company
Co Ltd was promoted to the public in May 1898. The
promoters entered into a contract to purchase the
freehold of the land at Fratton now known as Fratton
Park but the response to the appeal for subscribers
towards the share capital at first met with very little
success. As an inducement to the sporting public of
```

```
          the locality to put their money into the venture,
          the offer was made of a complimentary pass, admitting
          to the ground and stand for all club matches, to
          those who subscribed for 25 £1 shares in the proposed
          company with the right to transfer this privilege to
          the purchaser should the shares as a bloc be at any
          time disposed of. This appeal met with success and as
          a result the company was registered in 1898 and the
          necessary arrangements carried out so that the football
          started at Fratton Park for the season 1899/1900.
```

That was the preamble but, to cut to the chase, the FA insisted the club comply with the new regulation. Again Pompey put it on the 'too difficult' pile and they carried on as before. In 1951 the matter reared its head again and Sir Stanley Rous, the secretary of the FA, and later the sixth president of FIFA from 1961 to 1974, had become embroiled. In a letter to the Portsmouth directors, after a meeting with him in the FA's offices in London, the club were pointedly told to resolve the matter once and for all. The instruction was a "revival of an instruction given to your club in 1926 (following the initial misdemeanour in 1898 and then again in 1912) which instruction was in that year tactfully evaded." And the letter went on to say that "Sir Stanley made it clear that the FA's request is now being insisted upon". The AGM report in the **Evening News** explained that the practice was now outlawed, and the free tickets would stop, replaced by the regulatory compliant 5% discount on the public purchase price. However, it was a good marketing idea in 1898. The issue of free season tickets had been covered in the Articles of Association of the original club and was completely legal at the time under both stock market and FA rules. It helped generate much needed income for the club at the time of formation and it was clearly a good deal for the investors. With the capital now, by hook or by crook, in place, for what would the money be used?

OF CABBAGES AND (OTHER) THINGS...

The market garden site to the north of Goldsmith Avenue, which was to become Fratton Park, was purchased from the Goldsmith family in August 1898. The directors had chosen a parcel of land to the east of Fratton, but the other side of the railway line and away from the built-up area. It was situated adjacent to the lanes that people used to walk between Fratton, Milton and Eastney. Contemporary reports make it feel like the site had been earmarked a while, as the newspapers were mentioning a ground at 'Fratton' from January 1898. The 1835 Ordnance Survey map shows how sparsely populated and how rural most of the Fratton and Milton areas were in the mid-1800s. It also shows clearly the canal along where Goldsmith Avenue is now situated, running east to west to the end of Locksway Road. The western half of Portsea Island then urbanised quickly, including Fratton, but to the east was still largely undeveloped even in the 1890s. Even in August 1899, just before games started at Fratton Park, the locals of Fratton complained to the **Southern Daily Mail** and the RSPCA that they couldn't get enough sleep due to the noise of the cattle in the fields. Apparently, they felt the cattle must be underfed...

A postcard depicting the Stamshaw Recreation Ground, which opened in 1891.

Author's Collection

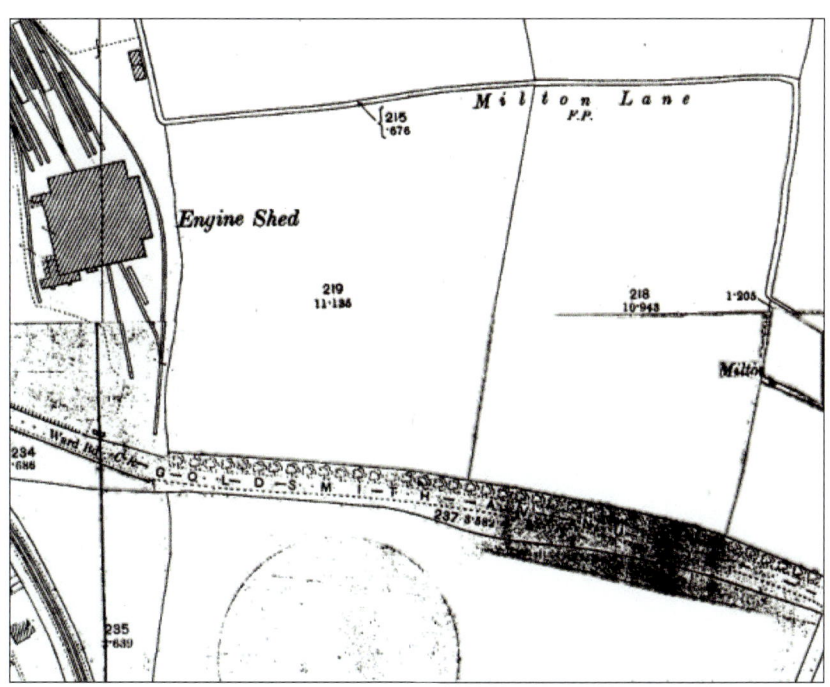

1898 Ordnance Survey map of land around Fratton station.

HMSO

The original North Stand at Fratton Park in September 1899.

PHS Archive

Fratton Park looking north in 1899. Note the earth-banked 'terraces' and the rural view beyond towards Milton.

PHS Archive

A view of the original South Stand (and the Southern League champions of 1902). Note the glass to allow back lighting.
PHS Archive

Tram tracks being laid in Goldsmith Avenue in the early 1900s. Fratton Park is top left. Note the word 'GROUND'.
PHS Archive

The 'Pompey' Hotel designed by Arthur Cogswell and built in 1901 for Brickwood's Brewery.

PHS Archive

A colourised team photo from 1903 illustrating the 'salmon' pink shade of shirt.

PHS Archive

The OS map from 1898 (on page 51) illustrates how countrified Portsea Island was still to the east. Villages, such as Copnor and Milton, pockmarked a rural idyll of market gardens, marshland and fields. The area on which Milton Farm sat, owned by the Goldsmiths, was central and convenient for inhabitants of any part of the island to get to. There are no records of how the directors found out the land might be available. No advert for the sale of that land appears in newspapers preceding the formation meeting in April 1898. However, it is known that Portsmouth AFC played on roughly the present site in a field loaned to them by the Goldsmiths. Wyatt Peters would have played on that land for P(A)FC, so playing football there was a known quantity and probate records show solicitor Pink dealt with some of the Goldsmith affairs, so the connection might well have come through him. The two ledger entries of income in that first year of the new company show the rural roots of the land, as they record the sale of the crops grown there during that autumn:

September - £16 8s 6d to E. Hall for the sale of the potato crop at auction

November - £3 for the sale of cabbage plants to J. Gage

At the 1929 AGM, on his re-election as director, Lewin Oliver emotionally recounted those early days. He said that the land on which cabbages were growing had been besieged by children trampling all over them but they agreed to "let them spoil them, as the potatoes were more valuable." This may well account for the small cabbage crop sold.

The plot of land that the directors chose is clearly shown on the 1898 OS Map. The canal referred to above - the Portsmouth extension to the original London to Arundel canal - had existed for some years. In the early 1800s it was decided to build an addition to the Thames, Wey and Arun waterways from Arundel across to Portsmouth Harbour and the dockyard, ending at a basin roughly where latterly Debenhams used to be in Commercial Road. Plans were drawn up by civil engineer John Rennie in 1817. This would provide employment and negate the need to take precious cargoes from the growing Empire for long, often dangerous, sea trips along the English Channel with goods coming into Portsmouth and bound for the port of London. After all, at the time war with the French was still a constant threat. The canal, built by the Portsmouth & Arundel Navigation Company, came from Arundel to Chichester, where a section still exists today, and then across Chichester Harbour. According to Ralph Cousins (2016) in *The Hayling Bridge & Wadeway*, the chosen route, going between Langstone and Hayling, where the road bridge is now, meant that the channels that existed around Hayling (apart from at the very top) had to be joined and the ancient wade-way between the Royal Oak and Northney severed and dredged to allow the passage of the barges. Since Roman times that had been the only way of walking across the mud. There is a plaque to this day explaining the building of the canal at the Arundel Street precinct in Portsmouth city centre. As rail transport began to expand, the canal became less important and besides it wasn't reliable, as it leaked. A section of the Portsea canal system in the Fratton area was sold in 1845 to the London & Brighton Railway for the construction of its main line from Brighton to Portsmouth. The present railway from Fratton to Portsmouth & Southsea station sits on its route and the canal eastwards from Fratton Station through to the end at Milton Locks was left derelict until Goldsmith Avenue was built. The redundant canal between Fratton station and the White House pub was filled with anything which could be found and a hard surface laid on top. Named after the farming family and 'Squire' Goldsmith, as he was locally known, the avenue opened to traffic in 1896.

The town also needed homes for its ever-growing population. A "For Sale" advert was placed in the **Hampshire Telegraph** on December 17, 1898, offering parcels of land in the vicinity of Fratton Park and they were quickly snapped up by developers. A **Football Mail** reporter in 1899 commented that "with cheerful optimism builders are erecting houses out amongst the fields around Fratton Park and I noticed one enterprising contractor within a few yards of the ground offers to put up 'houses to order'". The deal to buy the four and a half acres Fratton Park would sit on had been done less publicly, but prior to the completion date on August 30, the required monies were duly paid over to Mrs AH Goldsmith 'and others', as trustees of the Goldsmith estate, via her solicitors. Completion day was reported widely the next day. For instance the **Southern Daily Mail**, carried a "special" report under the heading "A Certain Starter for the Season of 1899 - 1900 - The Ground Secured" to show that the "negotiations have been satisfactorily concluded and the company entered into possession yesterday". Note, no mention of a mortgage... The Goldsmith estate still owned much of the area around the new ground. James Goldsmith was the original farmer of the land, known as Milton Farm. The main farm buildings were a little west of where the ground is today. In the 1891 census James is shown as the 'farm owner' aged 85. He died on September 16, 1892, and probate was given to his two sons, James Jnr and John. James Jnr or 'Jimmy' carried on farming on the remainder of Milton Farm. In the 1901 census he is listed as the sole occupant, aged 64. Records show that there were as many as six farms in the parish of Milton alone, even as recently as 1908. Jimmy Goldsmith died in 1911, and the Milton Farm estate was broken up. Portsmouth Corporation desperately required building land for housing so purchased Middle Farm, and parts of Milton Farm. The **Evening News** was full of complaints about the family trustees due to the price they wanted to charge and at one stage it looked like the council might pull out of the purchase. In response, public protests were organised in favour of the purchase of both parcels of land, which were the areas already known as Milton Park and land at Bransbury Road which was said to be a 'partially low-lying area running from Milton Road to the Eastney pumping station'. One of the dignitaries who led the campaign and who wrote to the newspapers exhorting the council to just get on and buy the land was the, by now Sir, John Brickwood.

During his time, Jimmy became known simply as 'Squire' and was owner of almost all the land and houses in the Milton district. George J Rogers (1985) wrote in **Memories of Milton** that James, just like his father, was a man to be respected and feared. He refused to sell any of his land for building, which is why the council had to wait until his death. He used to take the ballot box - in the days before secret ballots - around to each voter. Little wonder that he always got elected as squire of the parish council. He was a bachelor, living alone in the farmhouse which stood on the left-hand side of the present gate of Milton Park in Milton Road. The other son John is listed in all the census documents as a "Land Agent and Auctioneer" of West Street, Fareham. From documents that still exist, his widow Alice dealt with the new club when negotiations took place. Indeed, she is mentioned in the share prospectus as the lead for the vendors of the land. John Goldsmith was a long-time senior member of the Phoenix Lodge in Southsea, from 1867, well before Brickwood was initiated into the same lodge in 1879. However, they would have known each other well and, although he died in 1893, they would have had 14 years of certain contact at lodge meetings and social events. It is even conceivable the he might have known Wyatt Peters too, as it is known the family loaned Portsmouth AFC one of their fields to play on.

The site the present club now owns is registered at the Land Registry, so deeds are not required anymore. Attempts to find them have yet to bear fruit, but one lives in hope they may yet be. Should the deeds be uncovered, then it might be possible to work out who had what role in the transaction and if any interesting conditions had been placed on the club in their use of the land. At least a club accounts' ledger does exist from that early period in the History Society archive and there are also the club's liquidation papers from 1912 in Kew. Both agree that the mortgage had been given by the "Goldsmith's Trustees", and quote throughout "AE Goldsmith and others". That means either that Alice was one of the trustees of the original farmer James's land from the time that he died in 1892 or, more likely, she became a trustee a year later when his son, John, her husband, died and she took on the role of dealing with the land that he had inherited. The executors of John's estate, quoted in The Gazette following his death in 1893, are the same people who are mentioned in the club prospectus as agreeing to sell the land to the club, namely Alice plus her brother Bovill William Smith, a barrister-at-law, and Leonard Warner, a solicitor. There are various possibilities that might lead Alice to be the main signatory. One is that James Snr's will carved up the land into various parcels and gave some to each son. As a result, Jimmy, the elder, carried on farming the bulk of the land and John, his younger brother, became a land agent and, once he died, Alice and the other trustees decided to sell some of the land he had inherited.

To understand better the process back then, the **Evening News** reported, on June 20, 1898, the sale of around eleven and a quarter acres of building land, by the trustees of John Baker Goldsmith to the Joint Railway Companies. Trustees don't own an asset; their job is to look after it and carry out certain duties. It is also sometimes the case that the word 'trustees" could be used to describe 'executors' or the person or people responsible for distributing a person's estate on their death. Therefore the 'trustees' could have sold some land in their capacity as 'executors' and then took responsibility for looking after other land as 'trustees' until some event happened to enable them to discharge their duty. Alice, for instance, may well have had a lifetime's 'interest' in the land mortgaged to the new football club, given she received the interest payments, and would have been able to enjoy the interest she received. That could be one reason, apart from the club not being able to pay it back of course, why the mortgage was still in existence for so long. It wasn't until 1925 that it was repaid with an overdraft from the Midland Bank. Unusually for the time, the mortgage was interest-only, without regular capital repayments. Most lenders, understandably, required repayment of the principal debt, not just the interest. Interest on this loan was 3.5% per annum on the £4,000 and so a sum of £33 16s 8d, after deducting tax of £1 3s 4d, was sent to Alice's solicitors Goble & Warner in Fareham, every quarter. Interestingly, interest rates in the 1800s were fairly stable hovering typically between 4% and 6%. The bank base rate was about 3.5% in the middle of 1898, although in the early 1900s went as high as 7%. The bank or base rate, at which banks bought money in was 2.5% in June 1898 although the loan rate would be at least 1% above that. In consequence, a fixed-rate loan of 3.5% must be seen as a good deal for the club, especially as it seemingly had some longevity. It was still in existence, with no capital repayments having been made, until the new company was formed in 1912 and the old one liquidated. The 1912 club took on the existing mortgage and the ledgers show that the interest rate went up to 4.5% - still a good rate as bank base rate had climbed to 5% in the latter part of the year - when the newly formed Portsmouth Football Company Limited, passed a special resolution to take it on. It climbed to 5% in 1920 and 5.5% in 1921 as rates were rising generally. It was still in force in 1925 when the new South Stand needed financing. The club's bankers, the Midland, who took over from Capital & Counties in the early 1920s, loaned the club sufficient to pay it off and finance the new stand. The bank overdraft went from £1,790 in the May 1925 accounts, alongside a separate £4,000 debt, to one combined loan of £22,060 in May 1926.

In conclusion, the Goldsmiths ultimately got all their money back after 27 years, Alice having reaped a regular, if modest, return via the interest paid. She died in 1942. The founders of Portsmouth Football Club bought themselves time to raise further share capital and were able to do the deal by paying out just £122 in legal fees, plus the £950 deposit. It borrowed a substantial sum at a competitive interest rate, given the bank rate even went as high as 10% in 1914. With hindsight, that still looks a good deal for all parties, especially when it is seen what would be achieved when the money was put to work.

THE MAKING OF MODERN POMPEY: KEY DATES

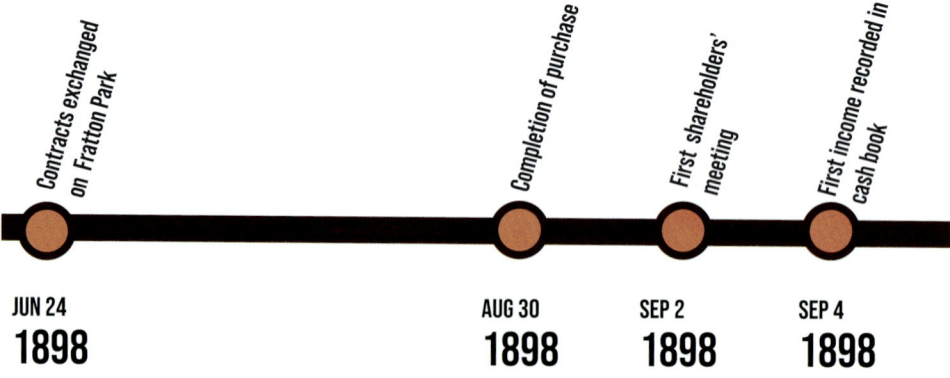

Chapter Four
BUILDING FRATTON PARK
WITH MICHAEL SAUNDERS

Not since the Romans, with their impressive amphitheatres, the most famous perhaps the Colosseum in Rome, had there been the need for dedicated structures to watch sport. In Britain, racecourses such as Newmarket had existed since the mid-17th century and cricket grounds such as The Oval had been built in the mid-19th century, however even these established sporting venues were, by modern standards, rudimentary. With the popularisation of association football as a spectator sport in the second half of the 1800s, the need for enclosed grounds to facilitate paying spectators and the construction of purpose-built stands to house the more affluent in relative comfort, had transformed football from a participation pastime into a leisure business. It therefore necessitated both raising finance and bearing the ever-present risks of financial loss and liquidation. Nevertheless, the football grounds of the clubs which formed The Football League in 1888 were still relatively primitive. Horse-drawn vehicles were often brought in to act as makeshift stands. Permanent grandstands were invariably constructed of timber, with few fans afforded cover from the elements. Most raised vantage points consisted of banks of earth often covered in clinker, that is to say ash from boilers. Where these banks were terraced, this was achieved using timber-supporting risers to form each step. By the early 1890s conditions had improved somewhat, but even the better grounds from this period, such as Everton's Goodison Park which opened in 1892, were still predominantly a field enclosed by a timber fence, with simple banks of earth and basic open-fronted 'sheds' to give a few fans some cover.

As the game continued to grow in appeal, so football grounds tried to keep pace. In the early 20th century one crucial innovation was crush-barriers, which reduced the pressure on tightly-packed terraces, and real progress was made in the era of the Scottish engineer Archibald Leitch. He almost single-handedly invented the football ground as we knew it from the 1900s until the 1990s, when stadia were transformed in the wake of the Taylor Report after the Hillsborough tragedy in 1989. However, Leitch's impact, which itself was a learning curve that included the Ibrox disaster of 1902, had yet to establish itself back in 1898. The proposed, but not yet named, new football ground for Portsmouth was laid out at a time when the requirements of a professional football ground were still evolving. Indeed, as Simon Inglis (1983) noted, the safety aspects of these enclosures was only just starting to be considered, following a series of accidents, as the art of crowd control was yet to be appreciated. In 1896 at Blackburn, part of a stand caved in injuring five people, while at Newcastle shortly after, a railing gave way and a boy lost a foot in the crush. Earth banks of open terracing were the most economical solution to packing people in and, at most grounds, the grandstand was often envisaged as a larger version of the pavilion structures which had precedent in cricket grounds. These were usually iron and timber structures which were then added to as demand dictated, beginning a piecemeal development strategy which almost all British football clubs adopted for best part of the next 100 years. Clubs improved their grounds gradually as finances and demand dictated, adding to and extending existing structures and making maximum use of the land within the club's control. Typically, clubs spent most of their budget on the grandstand and then eked out what money they had left to complete other areas around the perimeter of the pitch. Records at some clubs show they actively encouraged local builders to use their grounds to tip carts of spoil to help build up the embankments, with timber risers and clinker ash topping remaining in use well into the 20th century. At Fratton Park the first concreting of steps didn't occur until 1928, when the Milton End was terraced, and the Fratton End remained a timber and clinker terrace until the two-tier concrete structure was built in 1956.

Building a football ground in 1898 was a straightforward task but, nevertheless, a relatively blank canvas for any architect and the club had a couple of obvious choices to do the job. Arthur Cogswell is often credited with drawing up the plans for the initial laying out of the new football ground according to many sources, not least the now mandatory Wikipedia reference. He had trained under George Rake, who had been responsible for notable structures on Portsea Island such as Kingston Gaol, later known as HM Prison Kingston, and Milton Lunatic Asylum, later known as St James' Hospital. Rake himself had been a former partner of Thomas Ellis Owen, the architect and twice former Mayor of Portsmouth who had designed central Southsea in the mid-1800s. Cogswell had progressed to being a partner with Rake until Rake's death in 1885 and was one of the architects regularly used by the Brickwood's Brewery for its ever-expanding portfolio of public houses across the greater Portsmouth area. Often in the half timber 'mock Tudor' style, with glazed tiled ground floors and mosaic signage, the buildings became an intrinsic part of the fabric of the town, which remains to this day. The prominence of his works and his relationship with John Brickwood, the new club's founding chairman, would suggest Cogswell was always a strong candidate for the job. However, another of the directors of the newly formed Portsmouth Football Club was, of course, Alfred Bone who, as has already been seen, was an architect of some note himself. He was another of the brewery's favoured architects and had been chosen to design John Brickwood's new family home 'Brankesmere' in Queens Crescent, Southsea in 1896.

So, who did design the original Fratton Park? There are no listed payments in the meticulously recorded cashbook to an architect. However, it is known it was Bone who presented the plans to the town council planning meeting - then called the Roads & Works Sub-Committee - on August 29, 1898 under the heading of the new 'football field'. The minutes of the committee meeting "resolved that the plan drawn up and submitted by A.H. Bone showing the boundary of the football field in Milton Lane to be three feet from the growers be approved". The tender advertisement also states that "the plans and specification can be seen at my office" and then it is signed "Alfred H. Bone, Architect." It does not reference that he was also a director of the club. Given that Cogswell and Bone competed with each other for business at the time, it seems unlikely that Bone would go to such lengths to display and present a rival's plans, so the inference must be that it was in fact Bone who drew up the plans for the initial arrangement of Fratton Park. It would make sense on many levels. The club board would be utilising the skills within its own ranks to good effect and this would explain the lack of reference to architects' fees within the cashbook. Bone most likely gave his services without charge, in the spirit of the directors' common goal of setting up the new football club. That all said, Cogswell wasn't entirely out of the picture. Even though he was in ill health in 1898/99, collapsing at a meeting of the Surveyors' Institution in December 1898, which might also have cramped his style in terms of taking on a major job like designing a football ground, he recovered and was responsible for The Pompey public house, adjacent to the football ground's entrance on Frogmore Road, in 1900. The building, which still stands today and presently forms the football club's offices, was built at a cost of £2,848, more than was spent on the initial football ground. Planning permission was granted on August 9, 1900, with the application by Cogswell in the name of Brickwood's and not the club. Interestingly Brickwood's then took all the income generated by the thirsty football supporters and even charged the club for buffets and drinks supplied for every game and meeting.

Further evidence that Cogswell was not involved in the 1899 works can be gleaned from Andy Nash (1976) in his Portsmouth Polytechnic Architecture School dissertation entitled *AE Cogswell - Architect Within a Victorian City*. Assisted by prominent local architectural historians David W Lloyd and Deane Clark, Nash was given full access to Cogswell's records by Cogswell's son Douglas who had also been an architect in his father's practice. The dissertation includes a comprehensive list of the projects Cogswell carried out until his death in 1934. It is notable, whilst The Pompey is listed, including a photograph from 1905 taken by Cogswell himself (see page 54), that there is no mention of any involvement with designs for Fratton Park. It is also known that Cogswell was busy on the new Brickwood's brewery in 1898, as previously stated, and did not submit his usual volume of planning requests to the council that year. It seems safe to conclude that it was Bone who set out Fratton Park in its east-west orientation, which is uncommon in football terms. Usually a north-south axis was preferred, with the main stand on the western side facing away from the mid-afternoon sun. Instead, the boundaries of the market garden dictated an east-west axis, a fact no doubt rued to this day by goalkeepers, defending the Milton End goal with low autumn sun shining into their eyes. **Pearson's Athletic Record** announced that the new ground "will be made to hold 10,000 people with stand accommodation for 2,000." Although tenders were not issued until early December 1898, it appears from the club's records that enabling works had commenced prior to that, with payments for materials. The cashbook records various outgoings for items such as 'turfing' and 'timber'. The early December tender for building works was widely published over several days.

Bone's plans had been completed in August for the planning meeting which granted permission for the new football ground, but there is no record of a separate application for permission to change the use of the land for recreation purposes. In fairness, that was typical of the period. Unfortunately, none of the original planning documents exist, but from the minutes one application appears to have covered the whole concept. With the town wanting the club, director Pink soon to be the worshipful Mayor and with many other directors being so well connected, this almost certainly assisted a smooth passage. Only Bone's name is recorded on behalf of the club in the meeting minutes and within the lists of applications and their outcomes. What is also interesting is that the plan for the new stand - note the singular - followed later, submitted to the Road & Works (Streets) Sub-Committee on March 13, 1899. As a curiosity, the 13th is the date recorded in the original pen and ink version of the minutes, but the ninth recorded as the date in the typeset record of Council minutes. The application was submitted by Portsmouth builders, McCarthy Bros, who had won the December 1898 tender process. The plans were passed at the same time as for '29 houses in Frogmore Road' leading to the entrance of the ground but with a different builder to the McCarthys. The brothers did, however, have plans approved for 22 houses in 'unnamed roads out of Goldsmith Avenue' later in June 1899 so they were clearly busy.

Unfortunately, no record seems to exist of the actual ground plans. It is known that on July 27, 1899, the sub-committee noted in its minutes that the club were progressing works beyond what had originally been on the agreed plans: "It has been reported that the stands on the Football Ground in Goldsmith Avenue have been erected, but the W.C.s shown on the plan submitted have not been erected and also that a second stand has been put up without a plan being submitted for same." It was then ordered that the committee representative "immediately confer with the Football Club thereon". There is no entry in any subsequent council minutes - either full council or from that sub-committee - about the results of that 'conference' so we can only assume that it was agreed to leave the extra stand in place and move forward. It is likely Bone drew up the plan for the building of the simple 'Grand Stand' and then worked on it with the builders in January and February 1899. It was an uncomplicated task to lay out the pitch and the various structures around it, including enclosing the entirety with a boundary fence. After plans were approved in March 1899, the main Grand Stand was quickly erected by the McCarthys. The club prospectus stated that the intention was to drain, level and turf the ground and build "the necessary buildings" for £2,000. By the time the first game kicked off in September 1899 payments totalling £2,026, ascertained through cashbook entries, had been made. Of the initial £2,026, £764 went direct to McCarthy for work on the Grand Stand, and £600 to build the illegitimate second stand on the northern side. The rest was largely spent on loads of earth, ashes and clinker for the banks that fans were to stand on. Other items listed included turfing, fencing, wages and labourers' costs. The payments to the McCarthys recorded in the cashbook also illustrate the cost of various components such as turnstiles £80 and urinals £121. In some respects, the directors had achieved their prospectus budget. However, this soon rose to more than £3,000 midway through the club's first season. An uncovered wooden stand at the Station – these days called Fratton – End was added at once and by the end of 1900 the cost of building works had surpassed £4,500 so, in fact, the ground cost more than double the original estimate. The costs were comparable to many other football clubs in the country at the time. For instance, Everton, when they built their new stadium in 1892 - inflation in the seven years to 1899 was around zero so the comparison is valid - spent £552 draining and turfing - which is comparable with the £700 that Pompey spent. That club also laid out £1,640 for their three stands, one covered and holding 3,000 fans and two uncovered each holding 4,000 fans plus a few extras so around £2,500 in total. James Corbett (2004) notes there was little banking at Goodison, so this makes for a reasonable comparison.

What makes the speed of building Fratton Park even more remarkable is that the winter of 1898/99 was terrible and would have made the ground unworkable at times. A major part of the project was draining, levelling and turfing, things that could only be done when the weather was clement. The early part of the winter was very mild and extremely wet, but there was a cold spell in February, with severe frosts down to minus ten degrees Celsius. The poor weather – for building works at least – continued with a number of floods in the town during the summer, culminating with the inundation of July 22-23, 1899, when the press reported that "railway banks had been washed away". Three and a quarter inches of rain fell in a short period, with parts of Portsmouth under six feet of water. The official council records for 1835-1927, published in 1928 by William Gates, stated that in one hour, "347 million gallons" of water fell over the whole borough. Boys swam in Stanhope Road and many houses were damaged by lightning. A week later, though, the **Southern Daily Mail** reported that the thermometer recorded 120 degrees Fahrenheit – that's 48 degrees Celsius - in the sun. It reported that July 30 was a "record day for bathers" and "made us all forget the last few months". With such extreme weather events occurring through the entirety of the project build, having the ground ready for the start of the 1899 season was no mean feat.

The McCarthy brothers were John Henry and James Daniel. Both were freemasons with the inevitable links to fellow mason Brickwood. When John, by now living in Waterlooville, died in January 1962, his obituary in the **Hampshire Telegraph** revealed he was a past master of two lodges in Portsmouth, Temperance and Chapter. The obituary added that the brothers "were the contractors who laid out and built the stands at Fratton Park, when Portsmouth started as a professional club in 1899" and that they "started the building business in about 1895 and built a great many of the houses in Milton, Copnor, and other parts of the City of Portsmouth". Stephen Pomeroy's online database of Portsmouth history shows the McCarthy brothers as building much of Copnor and Milton.

James had been a Gunner in the Royal Marines Artillery and, although the name is not unusual, there is a J McCarthy recorded as having played cricket for the marines so it is certainly possible that he would have known Wigginton. It is known that it was a sizeable building company with 50 to 60 staff. In the early 1900s there are records of their staff outings in the press with one report of a very "enjoyable" trip started with the headline "45 go to Woolston". The McCarthys even "owned their own 'brick field' in what is now Winter Road" according to the **Hampshire Telegraph**. Brick making was a major source of employment for people in Milton, with thousands of the houses around built of McCarthy bricks. The clay was dug and mixed with fine ashes by barefoot treading during the winter - workers often died of tetanus from cuts to the feet - before being made into bricks by hand in the summer. That involved chopping the clay to size and shape and then drying and firing using kilns.

McCarthy Bros' offices were in Carisbrooke Road, to the south of the football ground. Pomeroy's database lists the company as being responsible for building houses on Goldsmith Avenue, Jubilee Road, Middlesex Road, Jessie Road, Castle Road, Frensham Road, Hyde Park Road, Pretoria Road, Wallace Road, Stubbington Avenue, Somers Road and finally Francis Avenue. Pomeroy's records, plus **Kelly's Directory**, cross-referenced with census data, also show both James and John living in Carisbrooke Road from when the first house was built in 1901. Number two, which is next door to the Pompey Hotel, looks like it was lived in by a Daniel McCarthy from Cork, their father. Kelly's shows the McCarthy family occupying 2, 14, 16 and 18 with number 16 being for "McCarthy Bros", presumably their yard as they built the houses around them. Today 14, 16 & 18 Carisbrooke Road are clearly larger houses, built in a slightly different style to the terraces either side so one can assume these may well have been the original houses built on the street when the roads were laid out in 1899. The 1901 directory shows only four houses or plots occupied, 2, 14, 16 and 18. By a year later they have built the entire north side of the road with half of the south side. The 1904 directory shows 2 to 44 and 1 to 35 all built, both sides of the road. Carisbrooke Road was built to follow the same angle and orientation of the new Grand Stand. The only report in the **Evening News** about progress of the ground to the end of 1898 seems to be on December 31 when it was reported that "fair progress is still being made with the ground and people are now beginning to ask about the team for next season." The article added: "A really good eleven and a professional team which gives good performances is sure to have a large following - although the men will need to be really class players". More of that in due course.

After Christmas progress reports became more frequent as works sped up. Back in October King & King had already been paid for timber for the Grand Stand and at the end of November, groundwork specialists Carter Brothers were paid the first instalment of £200 for the turf and fencing. By the end of February the pitch had been drained, levelled and turfed, thus avoiding the worst of the heavy frosts to come. The Milton area of Portsmouth – for that's where the ground was built rather than Fratton, which started at the other side of the railway – was considered to be quite marshy and the cashbook tells us that some 2,343 loads of earth and clinker were tipped on to the site in those first few months. The stands and the offices and everything else followed very quickly. On January 14 the **Football Mail** reported in an interview with a director that the "turfing process" was complete and he talked of the stands starting very soon. The plans had "been prepared some time back and are good roomy buildings which will give seating accommodation for two thousand". On February 18, it was confirmed the "pitch had been ready for some time". The **Evening News** carried a full column on the new club and the ground and manager. It reported:

> Just as people were beginning to wonder what the directors of the new Portsmouth football club were doing towards getting into working order for next season ... the ground in Goldsmiths Avenue has been drained, levelled, chalked, and turfed. The pitch has been complete for some time and is a very good one, of the "billiard table" variety, and is larger than the extreme dimensions mentioned in the rules of the game, so that there will be plenty of room. 10,000 spectators will be accommodated with ease when the preparations are finished. There is to be a covered stand 100 feet long, with seven rows of seats, and underneath and at the back of this will be the dressing rooms. Committee rooms, players' rooms, baths, et cetera. The stand will be on the south side near the entrance, and the bottom row of seats will be three or four feet above the ground, so that all the spectators will have a clear view of the game. There will be another covered stand on the north side, 240 feet long, and the spectators who do not patronise the stands will have the advantage of a wooden erection, with steps running in tiers round the ground, and affording good vantage points for watching the play. It will just be seen that the arrangement will be quite up-to-date. Turnstiles will be placed at the entrance, the press will be well looked after.

The article ended by commenting on an emerging rivalry with Southampton "The aims of the directors in lying out the ground has been to 'go one better than Southampton' and as the ground is larger than that on which the Saints perform, they have succeeded in one respect at all events the ground is very conveniently situated, as both tram and train run close by, and it is very likely that omnibuses will be run right up to the entrance when the time comes."

George J Rogers (1985) remembers that his father "as a treat" took him along part of the original lanes which led from Milton to Fratton to see the building work on Fratton Park. These routes had been used by the inhabitants of Milton village to get to St Mary's church in Fratton before the first church was built at Milton. The **Evening News** commented again on progress of the new ground on June 24, 1899: "The work in connection with the new Portsmouth football ground is now proceeding apace, and in another fortnight the bulk of it will be completed, and Portsmouth will be able to boast of one of the finest and most up-to-date private grounds in this part of the country. Some unavoidable delay has been caused owing to the directors of the company having found it necessary to make several alterations to the original plan. These changes will be found to add very materially to the comfort and convenience of the spectators at the matches. The banks will be completed within the next fortnight, and the large and commodious stand, which is also in course of erection, will then be well underway."

The name of the new ground was also causing some debate and amongst others, the **Evening News** weighed in "There has also been considerable speculation as to the most appropriate name for the ground, and although the choice has not been finally made, it rests between Southsea Park, Fratton Park, and Milton Park. We should think the first named would probably be selected." Other possibilities considered or proposed included The New Fratton Ground, Goldsmith's Avenue Ground and The New Portsmouth Ground. Choosing the name "Southsea Park" wouldn't have been as daft as that may sound today. At the time there was no other suburb between the location of the ground and Southsea and the directories of the time list roads such as Frogmore and Carisbrooke as being in Southsea. It was a well-known Victorian seaside resort that had a fast-growing reputation. Conan Doyle wrote in his memoirs in 1924 that "if I had to live in a town outside London, it is surely to Southsea, the residential quarter of Portsmouth, that I would turn". It had wealth and its own railway line, which ran from Fratton station and terminated at a station, now long-demolished, at the end of Granada Road. The line closed in August 1914, on the outbreak of war, but in 1899 the name might have encouraged fans to travel to the ground.

It was reported subsequently, in an undated article in **Hampshire** magazine, that Brickwood favoured the name "Southsea Park" as he lived in Southsea and felt that the name would give the ground a more upmarket feel, enabling it to compete better with rugby. However, this was an age where there were no cars and rail travel was exceedingly popular. Although the naming decision is not documented anywhere, with Fratton station a good 20-minute walk from the new ground, giving it the name "Fratton Park" made it feel psychologically closer perhaps, meaning it gained the final seal of approval from the board. Goldsmith Avenue was also still under-developed with no pavements or tramlines, so wasn't an easy stroll. Other clubs went through similar issues. Manchester United moved to Old Trafford in 1909 to be near a railway station and, famously, Arsenal managed to get the name of a London Underground station changed in the 1930s. As an aside, at the club's 1929 AGM there was an attempt by several "influential businessmen" to change the name to Portsmouth & Southsea Football Club - to match Brighton & Hove or Bournemouth & Boscombe - as "it would be worth thousands of pounds in an advertisement to the city as a pleasure resort", according to press reports of proceedings. The idea was thrown out. But we digress. On July 15, 1899, the **Evening News** reported on what we might these days call a press day:

The New Football Ground

At the invitation of Mr Brettell, the courteous secretary and manager of the Portsmouth Professional Football Club, a representative of the Evening News paid a visit to the new ground yesterday to see what progress was being made with the work. The Grand Stand with its admirably arranged and fitted dressing-rooms and offices underneath, is already completed, and is without doubt one of the best stands in this part of the country. The seats are built to give every comfort, and the 500 spectators the stand will accommodate will have a fine view of the Play. The visitors and members dressing-rooms are fitted and fitted with all modern conveniences, including five hot and cold showers and baths. At the south-east end of the ground there is a bank which, it is computed, will give room for at least 3,000. At the opposite end there is a similar bank estimated to accommodate about 2,000 spectators. The workmen have got the banks as far advanced as possible, and as soon as a good heavy rain come to set the banking properly down the whole will be finished off without further delay. Directly opposite the grand stand another stand, which will accommodate about 1,000 spectators, is in course of erection. This will be completed in a month's time, and by this time is hoped that the whole of the work will have been finished and the ground ready for play. With reference to the ground itself, this is also waiting for rain. When this comes all that the ground will require is to be properly rolled, and the grass, which is at present remarkably green and long, cut short. Near the main entrance to the ground two fine cycle enclosures are being built and these will be a great boon to cyclists. Although the ground will be complete a month hence, it will not be open to the public until the end of August, but before this several practice matches will be played. The players will all be in the town by the 25th inst. and active training will commence almost immediately. Up to the present, Cleghorn, Wilkie, Smith, J Brown (Sunderland), and Blyth have arrived.

On August 16, with anticipation building, the **Evening News** added: "The completion of the new ground is advanced as quickly as possible, but lack of rain still prevents the banking etc., being completed. Everything will, however, be in readiness by the time the first home fixture is decided. Supporters of the club will all regret to hear that while practising, Smith, the outside left forward, strained the muscles of one of his legs by striking his foot on the hard ground, and his injury will necessitate his laying up for some weeks". Three days later, the **Southern Daily Mail** recorded that there were to be "two commodious enclosures at either side of the main entrance" in Frogmore Road for bicycles and that they were proposing to make no charge for their use.

READY FOR ACTION

On the opening of the ground to the public in August 1899 from Goldsmith Avenue, the market garden to the north had been split into two parcels of land. The southern half was reserved for new streets of terraced housing, while the northern section was the new football ground. The laying out of the streets we know today as Frogmore Road, Carisbrooke Road, Ruskin Road and Apsley Road began around the same time the football ground was being built, but the football ground certainly can claim to have got there first. Patrons of the new Portsmouth Football Club would have walked through a semi-rural landscape from the more developed western side of Portsea Island along the newly laid Goldsmith Avenue and then down a designated track that had been earmarked to become Frogmore Road. They arrived at a football ground enclosed by a timber fencing of some six to eight feet high. Turnstile blocks were placed at the new entrance of the ground in its south-west corner at the point Frogmore Road met the ground. Once through the turnstiles - of which we don't have any detail but were most likely to be metal, housed in a timber construction giving shelter to the operator - the pitch would have been laid out to proportions not dissimilar to this day. Also in the south-west corner would have been a couple of bicycle enclosures, previously mentioned. To the right along the ground's southern boundary stood the Grand Stand, a predominantly timber framed structure, which was quickly enlarged. The **Football Mail** of September 16, 1899, a couple of weeks or so after the ground had opened, reported director Pink as saying "it had been decided to add a hundred feet to the grand stand, 60ft at one end and 40ft at the other" with the work to commence "without delay".

The initial 100ft-long stand would most probably have been nine structural bays long with ten roof-supporting timber columns. The front row of seats would have been set four feet above the ground with a vertically boarded timber-front wall facing the pitch. There would have been seven rows of bench seating with slatted backs accessed via staircases to the front. To the rear of the stand a line of windows provided natural light to the rear rows of seats, with the whole stand covered by a mono-pitch, corrugated-iron sheeting roof which sloped towards the playing area. The roof projected beyond the line of columns overhanging by eight feet. The roof-supporting columns had splayed bracing at the top where they met the roof trusses. The stand had dressing rooms, baths, committee room and players' room underneath. Once extended to its 200ft length in the autumn of 1899, it now had 18 bays with a roof supported on 19 slender timber columns with the two end columns forming part of the glazed screen ends which protected the stand from the elements. These screens were divided into six bays, each getting shorter as they were stepped in line with the stepped deck of the seating. Given how soon after the initial build the stand was extended it is unknown if the Grand Stand had similar screen ends in its opening day form. In front was a paddock for standing spectators. The stand was set well back from the touchline so that it backed on to the southern boundary wall of the ground. A 1906 Ordnance Survey map shows the stand at its 200ft length straddling the halfway line, stopping around at what today would be the edge of the respective penalty areas. A photo from 1902 shows the team lined up at the eastern end of the Grand Stand and the recessed opening which was to access the changing rooms below the stand can be seen in the fifth bay in from the end (see page 53). It could well be this is the end which gained five bays, the other end would have gained four adding nine in total to the original nine bays. Where the original access to the pitch would have been at the eastern end of the stand, once the extension was added it required a route to the pitch to be incorporated.

On the north side of the ground the originally intended 240ft-cover appears to have been amended to what was built. The actual North Stand straddled the halfway line and was built of 11 bays, again roughly 12 feet in width. This would have given a stand length of around 130ft. It had the same mono-pitch roof arrangement as the Grand Stand. The North Stand was much nearer the pitch, with spectators stepping straight into the stand through gangways which cut through its front wall, on to its steep terracing. This stand seems to have been very basic in terms of seating provision, with just timber steps to sit on as opposed to actual seats found across the pitch. At the ridge of the roof at the rear of the stand were placed advertisement boards, although these were not present for the first match. There was a small area of land between the stand and the touchline where an additional couple of rows of spectators could gain a vantage point. A photo from the first match shows its rudimentary nature (see page 52).

Either side of the North Stand were low earth and clinker embankments, seen clearly in a photo of 1899 (see page 52), to a depth of eight to ten people to stand on them. These stopped short of the North Stand structure allowing spectators only a couple of people depth to gain a view from these areas. These embankments carried around to the Eastney and Station ends of the ground, with room to expand behind in front of the timber ground enclosing fence. These embankments would have been built up of earth and spoil and topped off with clinker, which was the stony residue from furnaces. These were rammed on to the earth to provide a firmer footing and stop fans slipping on the slope. It was also possible to stand on the flat ground just in front of the North Stand. With very little beyond the ground other than fields leading over to the village of Milton to the east and the Portsea Island Union workhouse to the north, the backdrop to the ground was a rural one with just a few trees.

The clamour to improve Fratton Park further was immediate and unabated. The **Southern Daily Mail** of September 11, 1899, even felt the ground was potentially unsafe: "The Directors should make some alterations to the exits from the ground. There was a dangerous rush directly the whistle was blown and it was more by luck than good management that no one was injured." The **Football Mail** of September 16 revelled in a team which "has more than filled expectations" and "might even top the league come April." Playing success would mean many more than the 9,000 fans who had seen the first match attending in future. The directors apparently were "in a way alarmed at the success of the undertaking - pleasantly alarmed, it is true, but startled nevertheless. They lost no time in meeting to discuss the necessity of further stand accommodation." The subsequent extension of the Grand Stand doubled its capacity from 500 to 1,000 seats, a capacity that remained until it was superseded by the Archibald Leitch-designed new South Stand in 1925.

An advert for tickets for the English Cup game against Blackburn in February 1900 offers for sale seat tickets in both South Stand - at three shillings (15p) including ground admission - and North Stand - at two shillings (10p) including ground admission. There is also mention of admission to a "new uncovered stand at the west end of the ground" - the Station End - that was "being erected" and cost an extra sixpence (2.5p) on top of the ground admission of sixpence, which would have admitted you only to the paddocks and embankments. As a guide

10p is worth about £16 at 2024 prices. This tells us the timber open terracing was completed just a few months into that first season and that the better view it afforded commanded an additional entrance fee. There was a barrier in front of the upper section, so one assumes the only access to this terrace to control the additional fee was via the rear staircases. This raised terrace was accessed from the rear by two timber staircases which dog-legged to the upper most terrace. This can be seen in the OS maps from 1906. To the rear of this open terrace was a path with ground boundary beyond. On the rear wall of this terrace, painted in white lettering were the words FRATTON PARK FOOTBALL GROUND (see page 53), taken from The Talbot public house overseeing Goldsmith Avenue in 1909.

Such timber constructions became rarer in football grounds after the Ibrox disaster of 1902 where a similar, albeit much larger, timber and iron-framed standing terrace partially collapsed during a match between Scotland and England leading to 25 supporters falling to their deaths and a further 500 being injured. It was one of the earliest football structures to have been designed by Leitch. The quality of the wood used was questioned at a subsequent criminal case against the timber merchant Alexander McDougall but, although he was acquitted, Leitch's reputation survived. He subsequently was kept on by Rangers and his career in football ground design took off, although notably mostly using earth embankments as the de-facto method to support terraces from that point onwards. There was also an issue with missing iron loop-topped perimeter railing, which was supposed to be white, running the full perimeter of the pitch to keep spectators off the grass. An **Evening News** report, in November 1899, revealed that not enough had been ordered and it took a while to catch up. Whatever the trials and tribulations of getting Fratton Park up and running however, there is no doubt the directors did a magnificent job. From a standing start, in just two years the football ground in Portsmouth had become one of the best in the south. Now to create a club and, most importantly, a team to match.

THE MAKING OF MODERN POMPEY: KEY DATES

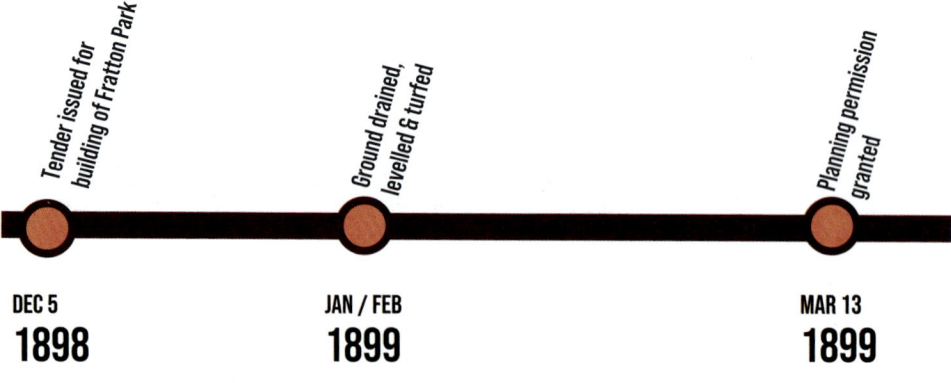

Chapter Five
CREATING A CLUB

With the works at Fratton Park in hand, attention also focused on creating a team worthy of the new ground and at a level consummate with the ambitions of all. The new club had been linked with players even before it had been formally launched. As early as March 19, 1898, over two weeks before the founding date of the club, **Pearson's Athletic Record** half let the cat out of the bag by announcing that a new professional club was to be formed "in an important seaport about seventy miles south-west of London and a batch of four players is likely to leave Blackburn Rovers at the end of the season to join the new organisation". It continued: "The players who are going Hampshire way are not on the public list yet and to the Rovers the defection is serious. As the new club is not a League club they lose the transfer fees." The Football League, mostly in the Midlands and North, had a transfer system which meant players could move south without clubs receiving any compensation, a cheap way for Southern League clubs to recruit. A month later, on April 16, the Record added: "The new club on the Hampshire coast seems to be gradually assuming more definite shape. At least four men now playing with the Bolton Wanderers are said to have been booked as far as they can be before the signing season arrives." It even named them - a half-back, Paton and Wright, J Miller and T Miller, all forwards. If true, and the publication was well connected, then it meant that the club was already commissioning agents. However, none of these players ever joined and it was decided fairly early on that the club wouldn't be ready to play for the 1898/99 season. And after all, since when did a football reporter ever let the facts get in the way of good story?

The real story began in February 1899 when the press fell over themselves to announce a real coup in the fact that the new club had recruited Frank Brettell who had been managing the team at Tottenham. He was almost certainly poached, probably by Freddy Windrum acting on behalf of the club, as the cashbook shows his expenses for meeting with Brettell. The **Football Mail** trailed the recruitment announcement: "...not a little surprise will be caused in many places when it becomes publicly known who have been appointed manager and trainer". Brettell immediately started to recruit the players. Cashbook entries show it didn't take him long to be claiming expenses for travelling to Liverpool, Preston, and other places in his quest. He also had to choose the colours that the new club would play in and get a trainer on board to help him run the team. He would have been helped by financial secretary Percy Whitmey, as there would have been a whole host of administrative duties to have undertaken in entering the league, not least registering the players. Brettell's job title was often quoted in the usual late 1800s way as 'manager/secretary' to ensure people realised he oversaw team matters. The **Football Mail** of April 1, 1899:

> This week has seen the new professional club in Portsmouth advanced another stage, and in a few days now we ought to be hearing news of probable players. All kinds of rumours have been afloat during the week, and I noticed that certain northern clubs have been complaining in the press that the Portsmouth agent has been at work already. For my part I cannot see why any grumbling should be caused by this trafficking in players. All professional clubs must approach men sometime during the season, and the sharp practices on the part of agents may, in a sense, be legal, but they are recognised for all that. We heard nothing of these complaints when a few years back the Northern league clubs were in the habit of poaching players in the South. But as I was saying, the new club is going ahead steadily and well, and on Tuesday the agreements were signed by Mr Brettell, the manager who is expected to take up his residence in the town shortly. From what I can hear the undertaking has had several important alterations affected financially since the original prospectus was drawn up, and the concern is to commence operations on a sound basis. No expense will be spared to secure the best possible talent, and with such a capable and competent judge of the head of affairs as Mr Brettell, shareholders may confidently rely upon having their money invested to the fullest advantage.

And on June 24, 1899, the **Evening News** commented further on the players, the colours of the playing strip, the potential nickname and the reserve team. Clearly good progress was being made to put a side together:

> The whole of the players who have been signed on are under orders to be at Portsmouth by the 22nd of July, and Mr F Brettell, the popular manager of the club, is now busy making arrangements for their lodgings here. As previously hinted, there has been a deal of discussion about the colours to be adopted by the club, but we are now able to state that the problem has been finally solved, and that the players will don salmon jerseys with maroon cuffs and collars and blue serge knickers. Now that these colours are known, it will not be long before the busy brains of the Portsmouth football enthusiast will involve some fitting nickname by which the club will be known. What about the "shrimps" for instance? With reference to the reserve team, Mr Brettell is anxious to get more names of local footballers who would like to play in the season's matches. He has already

received a great many applications and it is his intention to hold two trial matches as soon as possible to decide which of the men shall be selected to play. There are also a large number of open dates for the reserve team. This is owing to the Hants League being so small next season. Applications for matches with strong naval and military and civilian teams should be made without delay to enable Mr Brettell to prepare his fixture list. Mr Brettell has been given permission to issue an official programme as soon as possible, and it will be published under the title of "PP." He also intends to publish a handbook containing photographs and histories of the men, and a mine of other useful and interesting football information.

The colour of the shorts might have intended to be blue serge, that's navy blue, but they ended up white. By way of explanation, in those days it was very common to change 'knickers' as circumstances dictated. By the time the club's entry was printed in the 1899 Hampshire FA handbook the shorts were formally recorded as white. Socks were never mentioned in those days, but do look to be black, a popular choice at the time. Photos from the period also make the socks look a slightly darker colour than the edging of the shirts.

But why choose a shade of pink? Dave Moor, from the historicalkits.co.uk website – which is a comprehensive database of clubs and their kits over the ages – explains: "Pink was not an unusual colour for the late Victorian period but not a common choice." In fairness, the colour pretty much died out by 1915, as fashion changed. Trawling through newspapers, books and periodicals of the period doesn't help regarding the colours as there seems to be no reported rationale for the choice. However, there are a few scraps of evidence that lead us to a working hypothesis. Football kits in those days were not purchased from one big supplier, but were sourced locally, and manufacturing techniques weren't what they are today to ensure exact matches between batches of garments. Rudimentary washing processes would have also faded colours quite quickly, as dyes were far from colour-fast. A limiting factor was that the choice of colours depended, in part, on what others had not registered already. Given their late accession to the Southern League first division, Pompey were playing catch up. Tottenham, for example, were to play that season in their now traditional shirts of white with navy shorts so the old Royal Artillery (Portsmouth) colours weren't available. In addition, in 1899, Thames Ironworks, the forerunner of West Ham United, wore the old Portsmouth AFC kit of blue shirts and white shorts, so this combination couldn't be used either, especially as Millwall also played in the blue. No other team used pink, but it is interesting how contemporary reports stated specifically that the club were to play in "salmon" pink, which has an orangey tint; think salmon and shrimps when cooked or smoked. The first British Standard for colours, issued in 1930 and adopting what had been standard colours used for the previous 50 years, included a 'salmon' pink as standard number 447, clearly more orangey than the lighter, traditional pink created from combining red and white.

A contemporary colourised team photo from around 1903 (see page 54) exists in the Pompey History Society archives and is definitely similar to BS447. The Hampshire FA handbook from the 1899/00 season shows other teams recorded as playing in "pink" with Pompey the only "salmon pink". As Moor said, other clubs had used the colour previously, such as Everton, a fact mentioned by the **Hampshire Telegraph** in its review of the first league game at Chatham. The paper stated that Portsmouth are now "playing in the old Everton colours and have been christened the "Shrimps" although most of the papers, including the **Football Mail** and fans who wrote into it mostly called them the "Shrimpers", "Pinks" or the "Pink 'uns" from the start. The **Football Mail** in December 1899, when interviewing Brettell, made much of him and the choice of his old Everton colours. The colours that Everton played in 1890/91 had been salmon pink shirts with royal blue shorts, which were the colours the papers suggested in June 1899 that Pompey would adopt. The Everton FC Heritage Society's Rob Sawyer confirms the fact: "In Everton's final year at Anfield the club wore a shade of red, preceded by the salmon shirts, but switched to blue - paler than the current royal blue - for our first season at Goodison in 1892/93." Everton even issued a tribute salmon pink shirt in both 1992 and 2001 as change colours. Bolton Wanderers also turned out in salmon pink shirts in the 1880s, with Moor's online database recording them as wearing these in 1882/83.

Interestingly, Brettell had been at the Everton club as a player and served on their committee at some stage before joining Bolton. When his playing career ended he became a full-time newspaper reporter in Liverpool so would have seen these shirts used on many occasions, particularly as another Liverpool-area club, New Brighton Tower wore the same kit as Pompey's, except with black trim instead of maroon. It certainly feels too much of a coincidence Pompey ended up in this kit, given that Brettell was so familiar with the colour scheme, despite its uncommonness. In August 1899, the editor of the Southern Daily Mail stated that the colours were to be salmon jerseys and "unlike anything ever before seen in the South" adding "to the superstitious it may be interesting to know that the old Everton team fought their way to the final of the English Cup while wearing the same hues". The rationale behind the maroon trimmings is not recorded either, but the working hypothesis, until additional information is uncovered at least, is that they were inspired by the colour of the corporation trams in the town. This colour was used until the 1980s on city buses. Two other facts are possibly relevant. Firstly, we already know that 12 High Street, where John Pink ran his solicitors' business, had salmon pink wallpaper, which probably dated from at least the 1890s. Then, in July 1909, **Lloyds Weekly** ran an article stating that at Portsmouth "there had been a change in the directorate of the club" and as a result "it is worth noting that they have immediately decided on new colours for next season". The only director who resigned that year, was ... Pink. The minute he leaves, the manager Richard Bonney changes the shirts to white and the shorts blue, just like his old Royal Artillery team. A coincidence? You decide. Taken together though, the strong supposition is that Brettell decided on salmon pink as he was familiar with it and it was not taken by any other club, perhaps encouraged by the club's solicitor who shared the name and the decor.

That takes care of the shirt colour, but what about the team? After all, that's why Brettell had been hired. When the Evening News announced his appointment in February 1899, it was very positive about him and especially his experience working in the north and at Spurs: "Introducing northern ideas to the south, Mr Brettell improved the Hotspur team by securing such men as Cameron, Cain, Bradshaw, Smith, McKay, McNaught. In fact, he made the Spurs the famous team they are, and no doubt he will perform similar good offices for the new club. He has a strong belief in the future of southern football, contends that the Southern League will in time become quite as strong as the League proper, and intends to help it forward as much as possible. This is just this man to start the Portsmouth team. Add to his football qualities that he is a cricketer, billiard player, and a good shot, and that he is most genial, and a thorough businessman, and it can be seen that he is a genuine acquisition." Incidentally, the same article also hinted at the name of the new club: "The team will probably be known as plain 'Portsmouth', fancy additions such as 'United', et cetera, not being in favour."

At Spurs, Brettell's motto had been to "get the best players and give the public value for their money". At Portsmouth he would do likewise by persuading well-known professionals to move south from Everton, Liverpool, Preston, Bolton and Wolverhampton to join top-class military amateurs, drawn from the RA. Brettell recruited them without the use of substantial signing on bonuses. He used agents to help him, as we can see payments for this in the cashbook, although it also sounds as if he was good at keeping in touch with previous players that he had worked with. Bob Jack tells the story of the day he signed for Argyle in 1903: "Frank Brettell always kept in touch with me after he left Bolton, and although I had rejected his invitations to join the 'Spurs and Pompey, I was not surprised when my old friend Jack Fitchett brought me word near the end of April, 1903, that Frank wanted me for the newly formed Plymouth Argyle". His managerial tenure was from September 1899 until May 1901 and in that time, he managed 100 senior games, winning 63, drawing 12 and losing just 25. One can see why Tottenham wouldn't have been too happy to lose him and the **Football Mail** of September 23, 1899 noted that the Tottenham handbook for the season spoke about Brettell and Brierley, the trainer he brought with him, "in anything but complimentary terms".

One other advantage that the new club had was the connection with the Royal Artillery (Portsmouth). The fact that their leading man, Fred Windrum, had agreed to join the Portsmouth board should not be underestimated. He brought Southern League experience to the table. The **Evening News** of February 14, 1899 underlined the point: "The board of directors of the club has been greatly strengthened by the addition of Sergeant Major Windrum, R.A,. and it is not too much to say that that enthusiast's wide experience in connection with the R.A. team will be most useful ... On the one hand, it is hinted that the R.A. offers a good foundation for the defence, and some writers have even gone as far as mentioning Reilly, Turner, Hill, and Hanna." The timing of this announcement is significant. At that point the RA were, under Windrum and Bonney's stewardship, still fighting for their Southern League first division lives, while anticipating a big FA Amateur Cup quarter final against Harwich & Parkeston later that month.

The fact Windrum had been already seduced by the professional club project – and it was inconceivable that his best mate Bonney wasn't part of the package too – perhaps hints that the Gunners' amazing Icarus-style flight had already reached the sun, irrespective of the crushing FA ban stored up for them after that fateful quarter final. The army were clearly ambivalent about Windrum's association with the new club and the fact the RA's players were being publicly tapped up to join it. In his new role, Windrum often took the lead in speech giving at dinners and the like involving players and he was active in helping recruit players, along with Brettell, so he was, perhaps, the club's prototype Director of Football. Of sorts, anyway. He only lasted for about a year before being posted by the army to the west country, when he was replaced on the board by Bonney.

THE GOING RATE?
So how did Brettell go about recruiting the first squad? Agents were certainly used, even back in those days, to get the right players. In the first set of accounts 'Agents Fees' were £80 to three separate individuals in that first year. For 1899 it was a significant sum, although bear in mind that a whole team needed to be recruited from scratch so you can't blame the directors for getting some help. Professional players of the time were paid relatively well in comparison to semi-skilled workmen but less than others in the world of entertainment, according to AJ Arnold (1988). Even by the 1950s, footballers' pay was still only equivalent to that of teachers. The club needed to recruit a whole new team in the matter of a few months and without poaching other Southern League players so as not to upset them and scupper the club's chances of directly joining that league. That meant casting a net in the Midlands and North and even Scotland. But if anyone thought Pompey put together their squad by paying over the odds, the figures don't bear that out.

Firstly, Brettell and the directors were in a good position to poach some better than average Football League players on the cheap as the Football League and the Southern League didn't acknowledge each other's contracts, so there was no need for transfer fees, which usually applied between the northern clubs when a player moved. The northern clubs understandably got upset when poaching took place, but Football League clubs were also trying to keep wages down. A player could always earn more by coming south provided, after the introduction of the FA wage cap for all English professionals from 1901, they didn't get more than £4 per week and £208 per year. The cap didn't apply at first in Scotland and not having to pay transfer fees helped keep wages up in the south. Andy Kelly (2020), writing in his online history of Arsenal, said: "This meant a fairly wealthy Southern League team such as Tottenham could entice players from Football League teams knowing that they could pay them a much higher wage as it would be subsidised by the fact that they didn't have to pay a transfer fee. For example, if a player was on £4 per week at a Football League team and had a £400 transfer fee value, a Southern League team could offer him £6 per week as they wouldn't have to pay a transfer fee that another Football League team would have to pay if they bought him. Between 1897 and 1900, Tottenham Hotspur brought in at least 14 players from Football League teams, for which the Football League teams received no transfer fee." To be fair, Pompey weren't far behind... They could entice players from the Football league knowing they could pay them a higher wage, as it would be offset by there being no need to pay a transfer fee. Southern League clubs also wouldn't adopt the Football League retain and transfer policy until 1910, which was widely regarded until the early 1960s by the players union as the 'slavery' rule. It was abolished by Mr Justice Wilberforce in the High Court in 1963, when adjudicating the case of Arsenal's George Eastham. The judge, by coincidence, was a relative of the Wilberforce who helped to abolish actual slavery in 1807. The rule often kept players at their clubs against their will, so players often moved south simply for the ability to be masters of their own destiny.

David McArdle (2000) in *One Hundred Years of Servitude: Contractual Conflict in English Professional Football before Bosman* summarised the position at the turn of the century:

> If a player wanted to move clubs at the end of the season, he would need his old club's permission before being able to take up that new offer of employment. This provision applied if the player had refused to sign a new contract with his old club, and even if that club had no intention of playing him - or of paying him a salary - in the forthcoming season. Consequently, a club could in principle refuse to release a player's registration, and thereby prevent him from being able to play for another English League side. A player in such a position would be obliged to seek employment with a club in the (English) Southern League or (from 1890) the Scottish League, where the standard of play and the wages were lower but the clubs were not bound by the English League's punitive registration provisions.

A player could leave the northern club and move south and maybe – or maybe not – get a pay rise. However, getting a signing on bonus and the ability to easily move the following year made it an attractive move and they were in control of their own destiny. It wasn't all about the money. Southampton's experience is helpful to illustrate the point. Data compiled by Gary Chalk and Dave Juson, both historians of the club, about Saints' transfer dealings in the late 1890s gives several examples of players moving across the leagues. For instance, Southampton signed Everton player, John Tait Robertson in 1898, meaning there was no need for a fee. Robertson regretted the move so, the only Football League club he could go to was his previous one, unless a transfer could be arranged by that one. He ended up signing for Rangers, as the Football League and the Scottish League did not recognise each other's contracts either. Jack Robinson is another case in point. A regular England goalkeeper he walked out on Derby County in 1897 and joined New Brighton Tower in the Lancashire League. Tower successfully applied to join the Football League in 1898, and Robinson - so the story goes - was unable to play for them in Division Two. In consequence, he applied for the job of Saints' goalkeeper advertised in the **Athletic News**. A friendly tip-off probably helped. In Harry Woods' case, he was tracked down and signed by Saints' trainer Bill Dawson who, whilst in his native Midlands, had read in a local newspaper that the player was in dispute with Wolves because they were trying to sell him to Everton. One can guess that neither Wolves nor Everton were happy about the development as Wood was an exceptional footballer. Until a wage cap was introduced in 1901, it does seem the Football League tried to keep wages down and Southern League clubs would pay more. When Saints beat Brettell's Bolton in the English Cup in 1898 to get to the semi-final, Southampton players according to Bull & Juson (2001): "Each man was on an £8 bonus for a win and £5 for a draw."

As well as wages, signing on bonuses were also paid to Pompey's new players. This was in recognition of the fact the transfer might involve the loss of bonuses or other benefits from the previous club. In that first year Pompey paid a signing on bonus to the new manager, Brettell, of £50 - so roughly £8,000 today. That doesn't feel an excessive amount to prise Tottenham's manager away from them, although it was equal to twelve weeks' wages. In addition, the club paid between £5 and £10 per player in bonuses around May 1899 – remember matches wouldn't start for another three months - perhaps as an inducement to move house to the south or to compensate for losing an end of season bonus from their old club. Blyth got £10 plus £13 5s furniture removal costs, presumably as he was the only married player. McKenzie, Hunter and Struthers all got £10 with Struthers also getting a £7 furniture bonus and Clark, Turner and Cunliffe got £5, so seven players in total receiving a signing on payment. And Pompey weren't alone in the practice. Saints were more generous, paying a £30 signing on bonus that year to Robinson mentioned earlier and, likewise, Robertson got £50 to sign from Everton and Wood the same amount. The Pompey signing on bonuses seem equivalent to a typical annual bonus paid by most southern clubs of around a couple of weeks' salary. Woolwich Arsenal, for example, were recorded in the **Woolwich Gazette** in 1894 as paying signing on bonuses of £10 and Pompey's were mostly around that figure more than four years later. Interestingly manager Brettell, at the 1900 AGM, was quite negative about the amount he had had to pay out although this does sound like he was simply mirroring the mood of the AGM, which was concerned about the loss of £875 on the first year's operations.

Pompey were also helped by being able to attract players from the old Royal Artillery team. Negotiations, whether overt or covert, were underway with certain players for sure from early 1899 as the promise of higher wages and being able to continue playing senior football was dangled. RA were struggling as an amateur team in the top flight of the Southern League and their future was becoming increasingly compromised. One such player was star goalkeeper, Matthew 'Gunner' Reilly. The **Football Mail** of April 15, 1899 suggested that Pompey should sign him "as his time was up in September and he will be leaving the service". Cameron Pulsifer (2002) in the ***Journal of the Society for Army Historical Research*** shows that by the 1860s, whilst enlistment was voluntary, the "Queen's Shilling", which was the daily rate of pay accorded to private soldiers in the army of a young Victoria's time, had increased by a few pence although things like medical expenses were deemed a 'stoppage' from wages paid. By 1870, at least the deduction for food had stopped. The official rate of pay for a Gunner in the Royal Artillery would have been a little higher. So, now being paid

£5 a week - or around fourteen shillings (70p) a day, by Pompey, meant Reilly had increased his weekly wages by more than 1000%. It should be noted, he was paid wages by the club from May 20 so he either left the forces before September or the club paid him anyway to secure his services.

The club cashbook shows that 21 players signed on, with only two players earning £5, Reilly and Jock Hunter, another player signed from Preston like Bob Blyth. Hunter got no moving allowance, though, and his wage went down to £4 per week from the start of the second season whilst Reilly's stayed at £5. Then three players earned £4 10s; three players £4; two £3 10s; three £3; four £2; one £1 5s and finally two earned £1. Pompey's average individual player weekly wage works out as £3 3s. This was typical of the period for football clubs. The directors did go on record in the **Football Mail** in October 1899 stating that "no player would receive over £4 a week" with Brettell obviously feeling that he could cope within that budget, even though both Reilly, as a real star, and Hunter were exceptions to that rule. The Mail was also clear that "Mr Brettell did not follow the example of many of their rivals" in paying over the odds. The paper formally congratulated Pompey on that policy. It's also interesting to note from the club cashbook that bonuses were paid to all the players after a year in May 1900 at an average of two weeks' wages – based on total bonus payout divided by total weekly wage bill – with a spread of between £1 and £15 per player. End of year bonuses were much smaller the second year, from £1 to £8 5s per player and from the third year onwards, 1901, no bonuses were paid at all. This was due to new FA rules which scrapped all bonuses except for a maximum of £10 signing on payment.

However, to some it seemed obvious that Pompey had decided to throw money at players to get a team that ended up winning the most senior league available to the club in just its third year. Owen Arthur (2022), in *The World's First Superstar - The Life of Stephen Smith*, suggests that when the club recruited Smith, the England and Aston Villa forward, in 1901, he was paid well over the odds to come south, claiming "Smith could continue to earn £10 per week plus a £100 signing fee". After all, why else would he leave the league champions? However, the club cashbook shows that Smith, who was the brother of William already at Portsmouth, was paid £4 a week from the start, which, by then, after an FA rule limiting wages at all clubs, was the maximum that a player could be paid. At the time existing players such as Smith's brother William had their wages cut to the maximum allowed by the club and there is no evidence anywhere that under the counter payments were made. Fraternal company and the freedom to move clubs at the end of his contract seems the more likely reason. That was a common theme. In **West Ham United: The Making of a Football Club**, Charles Korr (1986) detailed the wages paid by the Hammers: "In 1906 the average wage for the whole team (a pool of 30 players) was £2 10s per week over the whole year. At least 12 were paid between £4 and £4 10s during the season and a minimum of £2 10s during the summer … Veterans who had been with the club since 1900 filled the reserve and third teams and their wages ranged from £2 during the season to as little as 15s per match. The directors insisted that all players earning more than £2 10s during the season should not take another job; they were full-time professional footballers and were being paid as such." There was little inflation in those days so using 1906 data is a valid comparison. When Liverpool won the first division in 1900/01 their AGM showed that their players were on £7, which with bonuses could reach £10. Besides, we have already seen Southampton paid higher bonuses than those at Pompey. The papers for Saints' AGM in 1899 show that three players got a bonus equivalent to two weeks' wages, two got three weeks' equivalence, two got four weeks and two got six weeks. The Pompey average bonus of two weeks' wages does not therefore feel excessive in comparison. To be fair, the Southampton chairman, at their AGM for 1898, stated that he thought that "perhaps they had paid too much in bonuses." Southampton's wages, recorded in newspapers at their AGM after the 1898/99 season show the wage bills of the two clubs were similar.

Reading FC, according to David Downs, a club historian, were recorded in their old directors' minute book as offering £2 per week in the playing season and £1 per week in the summer at the turn of the century. However, they paid bonuses on top. In January 1900 the players were promised a bonus of £3 each for a win or a draw against Newcastle in the English Cup and in September 1899 players were given a five shillings bonus each for a win against Millwall and ten shillings each for a win against Spurs. When they signed players in April 1900, they paid them around £3 in the winter and up to £2 in the summer, so again not out of line with Pompey's wage structure. And in early 1901 they were making bonus payments for an FA Cup tie versus Spurs - the eventual FA Cup winners - of £2 appearance, £3 for a draw and £5 for a win. At the 1900 AGM, the club's owners, like many other owners under the financial cosh from building the new ground clearly wanted to reduce the level of wages. It's also interesting to note that Chatham, another top Southern League team, said at their AGM in 1900, reported in the **Berkshire Chronicle** – as local papers always printed reports on their competitors' financial affairs – on July 14, that they were reducing their wages to £5 per week.

A comparison of annual overall player wage bills is also possible. In the year to April 30, 1900, Pompey's player wages were £4,033. At the Derby County AGM in 1899, reported in the **Sporting Life**, a list of player wages at other clubs was quoted as there was thought to be an issue with the level of wages that Derby were paying. The size of the squads is not given but Villa's wage bill was £5,300 for the year; Everton £5,000; Burnley £3,600; Derby £3,400; Sheffield Wednesday £3,900; Wolves £3,800; Sunderland £3,400 and Preston North End was £3,800. The article concluded that the Derby wage bill was not excessive and, clearly, neither was Pompey's. Villa had an average gate of 23,045 so far bigger than at Portsmouth, so one would expect that they could afford to pay more. Wolves' average gate for 1899/1900 was around the same as Pompey's as was their wage bill. In conclusion, the best word to describe Pompey's wage structure at that time is 'competitive', with bonus payments comparable with those paid by the Saints and others. One difference was that Pompey paid the same wage all year round, the cashbook shows this, while other clubs often paid players less in the summer, which would undoubtedly have helped recruitment and retention.

But how did footballers fare compared to other workers? According to the

National Archive, the average annual income at the turn of the century was around £43. Lee Jackson's Dictionary of Victorian London website wrote about the relative rates of pay in Victorian society generally. It is broadly agreed that the highest paid skilled working-class men peaked at £100 a year, but that wasn't widespread. There would also have been some regional differences in pay, of course. In December 1901 the **Evening News** reported that a tram driver in Portsmouth earned 25 shillings (£1.25), for a 60-hour week at 5d (3p) per hour. The article was saying that it really wasn't enough compared to others but on that basis a wage of £4 was a good wage for a professional footballer. There were a number of letters to the editor from drivers all saying they should get 8d per hour for an eight-hour day. According to Leone Levi (1971) in *Wages and Income of the Working Classes from 1885* (quoted in Pulsifer, 2002), £90 to £100 per annum would be typically earned by the highly skilled worker and above that was a middle-class income, with £500 a year being considered the beginnings of an upper middle class. The average yearly income of doctors at this time was about £300 a year or £6 per week, while between £20 and £200 per week would put one in the "gentry" class. Those earning more than £10,000 per annum were considered aristocracy.

It is difficult to translate this into today's figures, but a wage of £4 per week is equivalent to £34,200 per year and £5 per week is £50,500. These are not huge salaries by the standards of football today, but this kind of level persisted until the 1960s and the abolition of the maximum wage. Paul Brown (2013) states that "by 1900 footballers earned ten times more than general labourers with win bonuses common and other payments, with the average wage in 1900 being £7 per week, with less in the summer season". Korr (2006) shows in a comparison with other occupations that "in 1906 casual dockers earned between 5s 6d and £1 2s 7d for a 44-hour week. Tram drivers made £2 3s for a 60-hour week and men employed in the building trades averaged £2 8s for a 44-hour week."

The **Sunderland Echo** of September 1898 states there were 4,000 registered professional players across the country and added that "earning £3 per week during the season - with £2 out of season very common - was an excellent salary by working-class standards: very few skilled workers could expect to earn much more than £2 or £2 10 shillings (£2.50 today) a week. But as now, their playing careers were short and could be ended at any moment by injury. It was also a "dead end" job. There were very few openings at that time within the game for ex-pros and most had either to return to their old trade or, if they had none, find some other way of earning a living." In broad terms, the professional footballer in 1900 was earning, when all was included, up to four times the average wage and twice the wage of a skilled manual worker at the time; still pretty good despite the short length of the career. Some used some of their earnings to invest in a business, while others had businesses bought for them as a transfer incentive or when they retired. Many continued to follow their original trade, while still playing. Tony Mason (1980), in *Association Football and English Society 1863-1915*, a detailed social historical account of the players' lifestyle before World War One, does stress the widespread nature of part-time professionalism prior to 1914, adding that the maximum wage, from 1901, was not necessarily always paid to all players. However, Mason's view is that footballers' wages compared pretty favourably with those of industrial workers, and continued to do so even after the introduction of the maximum wage. Moreover, it was a more generally attractive life and that must have been an important consideration for the potential professional despite the lack of job security attached to the game.

Many became publicans after their career was over - Bob Blyth, took on the licence of The Pompey when it was built in 1901 and he continued in the trade when he left the club in 1904. A selling point for the move south for players would have been the number of public houses serving the navy in the district. Portsmouth once had more pubs per square mile than anywhere else in England, after all. And a footballer's life was not too hard in those days. Some clubs allowed players to get another job as, typically, footballers of the late 1890s began their working week on Tuesday and trained for just a couple of hours each day, starting at 10am. Pre-season training could be intense but after that it was fairly relaxed, many trainers terrified that their men would break down if overworked, something maybe to do with the poor working-class diet of the time. Players spent a lot of time out on 'brisk walks' dressed in jackets, waistcoats and caps. They then changed to jog round the pitch and do sprinting. Players rarely saw a football, purportedly to make them hungrier for it on a Saturday. Even in the 1940s this was the received wisdom. Pompey trainer Jimmy Stewart was a strong believer in only playing with the ball on a Saturday.

On the other hand, the hard-worked groundsman, Jack Trice, was on just £1 per week. Downs confirmed that the Reading equivalent was part-time and on six shillings per week working from 2pm until 5pm. Trice is recorded as playing on the left for Southsea Rovers, back in 1895. In one game against Havant, away, with both William Wigginton and his son Robert at the back, Southsea won 8-0 with Trice scoring four goals. A few years later Wigginton and Trice were both together again at Fratton Park. Trice was still playing for Rovers as on January 7, 1899, as he is recorded in the **Football Mail** as "preventing many dangerous attacks and keeping the play well away from the goal." He had moved back into defence as many older players did. He also played in a Pompey reserve friendly on December 16, 1899, against RMA. Pompey played with only nine men.

Brettell, the new manager, was paid £4 per week with all travel expenses and the trainer, William Brierley, who also joined the club from Spurs with Brettell, £2 per week. Brierley got no signing on bonus unlike Brettell. Bob Goodwin (1988) notes in ***Spurs A Complete Record 1882-1988:*** "The reason [why Brettell left] is simple. He was offered substantially more money to take on the manager's job at Portsmouth." The evidence is, though, the salary was in the ballpark for the time. By comparison, Liverpool's appointment of Tom Watson in 1896, cited by Kjell Hansen in an online history of the club, makes the point: "Liverpool pulled off a masterstroke by convincing the best manager in the country, Tom Watson, to leave Sunderland and join the Anfield brigade. Despite being only 37 years of age, Watson had already won the First Division Championship three times in four seasons at Sunderland in 1892, 1893 and 1895, finishing runners-up in 1894, as well as reaching the semi-finals of the FA Cup three times. Liverpool put together a handsome financial package for Watson with his annual salary said to be £300 – doubling what he had earned at Sunderland, reportedly making him the best paid football manager (or Secretary as it was more commonly called then) in England." In March 1898, the **Sunderland Echo** reported that Arsenal attempted to poach Sunderland's subsequent secretary/manager Robert Campbell, offering him £4 10s per week, a contract of three years and a signing on bonus of £50. Sunderland managed to keep him by upping his salary - although he did subsequently move to Bristol City in April 1899 - but Arsenal's offer and City's salary paid, were both more than Brettell received. The **Liverpool Mercury** in May 1899 quoted Everton's managerial salary at £253 including a few office expenses. Brettell's £250 annual salary was good, but by no means excessive.

Whilst Pompey's wages were not huge by the standards of the day, the club, like many others, was already sowing the seeds of future unsustainability. One key business ratio is staff costs to turnover or sales. It differs by sector, but many businesses would start to show concern if its staff costs to turnover ratio went above 30%. Football, where its staff costs went predominantly on highly skilled and, due to their scarcity, relatively highly paid players, inevitably tolerated a higher ratio. 60% wouldn't, and still does not, give undue cause for alarm. However, at Portsmouth, by 1901, due to falling attendances, wages were 87% of gate receipts. Whilst things stabilised, the ratio began to steadily climb again and was one factor in the club having to be re-constituted in 1911/12. Nevertheless, in conclusion Pompey's wages and bonus structure was on a par with their peers of the period. That the team Brettell built did so well was down to his undoubted skill as a manager. So, who were the players he recruited?

THE MAKING OF MODERN POMPEY: KEY DATES

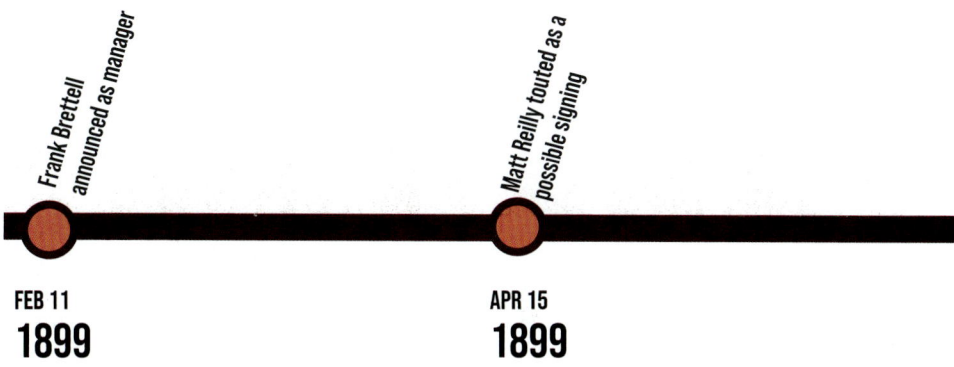

Frank Brettell announced as manager
FEB 11
1899

Matt Reilly touted as a possible signing
APR 15
1899

Chapter Five - Creating a Club

Chapter Six
PREPARING THE PLAYERS

Having established manager Frank Brettell had more than extracted great value for the club's investors to recruit a squad to compete with the best clubs in the south of England, who were the men who he would entrust with delivering on the field in Pompey's first season? The **Football Mail** of September 2, 1899 – the day of Pompey's opening match in the Southern League at Chatham – talked encouragingly about the new squad's blend of youth with experience:

> If names counted for everything, Portsmouth would be written down as below first-class form. There can be no getting away from this fact - the directors and Mr Brettell did not follow the example of many of their rivals and secure men who had made themselves a reputation of several seasons standing. Experience has shown that the old players, as a rule, are not to be relied upon so firmly as promising youngsters who have still to gain the premier honours of the football field. Several instances could be quoted of mistakes having been made in this direction. And the directors are certainly to be congratulated upon refusing to be tempted to invest more or less bulky sums in attracting what are generally known to footballers as stars. However, they very wisely introduced a few players of experience into the team, the idea, of course, being to give the younger men some confidence in themselves, as well as to furnish the necessary cool-headedness in times of difficulty or impending defeat. Taken all-round, though, Portsmouth will be represented by a set of clever youthful performers, willing and anxious to do their utmost for the club, and before the season is much older we shall be able to form an opinion as to their merits and capabilities. At present one has only other people's ideas as to what each man is worth in a playing sense, and unfortunately paper form is not always to be trusted.

Matt Reilly was undoubtedly the big capture, with Dan Cunliffe and Bob Blyth just behind. Reilly had been the goalkeeper for the Royal Artillery (Portsmouth) club throughout their short, but glorious, interlude. He had even found time, between the Gunners' fixtures, to make a couple of Southern League appearances for Saints during the 1895/96 season. He was firmly established as a hero around south Hampshire and it was a smart move by the Portsmouth manager to persuade him to sign on in the spring of 1899 after completing his army service. He was also clearly what these days we would describe as a 'character' in the dressing room. One of his first actions on joining the club was to teach a parrot to croak the words "Play Up Pompey". The parrot's obituary was published in 1934 in the **Hampshire Telegraph** after it spent 35 years supporting the team. It had been owned by John Cuthbert of Southsea, a dairyman. Reilly visited the shop each day to get his milk and soon taught the African Grey to shout not only the opening line to the chimes but "shoot, shoot, shoot" as well. Cuthbert brought the bird to Fratton Park in its cage "in all weathers" and it was described as the club's first ever mascot.

Reilly had already established a tremendous local reputation and was later capped for his native Ireland in Pompey's first season. However, on February 4, 1899, the **Football Mail** reported that he almost played for England. The FA selectors sent an inquiry to the town's Clarence Barracks to check on his nationality On learning he was Irish his chance of playing in a North versus South match disappeared. It would be Ireland's gain. Reilly was no shrinking violet either. In December 1898 he was recorded as playing for the RA at Wycombe and having just "patted" the ball out of goal, he was then heavily challenged by one of the opposing forwards. He went to fetch the ball and was heard to say loudly something about "getting his own back". He then squared up to, then struck, a spectator who came through the ropes to challenge him. A 14-day ban was his reward and Wycombe were also banned from playing at their ground, or even going within three miles of it, for a week. He didn't learn his lesson and repeated the misdemeanour in a match against Swindon in January 1904.

However, fans adored him. In *Soccer - The Ace Of Games* Alec Whicher (1940) recalled that he could still name practically all the players in the first few years of Pompey's existence, with Reilly making a particular impression:

> [He] was a grand player, and the most remarkable goalie I have ever seen. Never, to my mind, has a keeper been known to punch the ball like this ex Royal Artilleryman: his fist would emerge from a crowd of players and the ball would be returned almost to the half way line. In those days a goalkeeper was allowed to advance out of his goal provided he did not carry the ball over the limited number of steps. I have seen Reilly patting or bouncing the ball and dodging opponents to well past the half-way line, eventually passing to a forward to enable him to score. I never saw the ball taken away from him. He was unique in the art, and always delighted the home crowd with his antics. Another peculiarity was that he never wore gloves like the others and seldom did he sport a cap. He kept goal for Ireland against England on two occasions to my knowledge - I think 1900 and 1902. Reilly was responsible for an alteration in the laws of the game. His play was actually a mixture of both soccer and rugger, and his wonderful skill of bouncing the ball, caused the Football Association to prohibit the handling of the ball outside the penalty area. Truly a mighty goalkeeper was Reilly.

He was quoted in Athletic News in 1899 as being "head and shoulders over all" and a "public hero" in the town, perfecting the technique of "running a long way from goal, bouncing the ball in front of himself and clearing opponents every time". Goalkeepers were allowed to handle (but not carry) the ball anywhere in their own half and the technique was first used by Leigh Roose of Aberystwyth Town, who later played in England for Everton, Stoke and Sunderland among others. Spencer Vignes (2007) tells the remarkable story of 'football's first playboy' Roose in his book **Lost in France**. The tactic was also picked up and made popular by William Foulke of Sheffield United. In the Laws of the Game, issued by the FA in 1885, it was stated: "Rule 8 - No player shall carry, knock on, or handle the ball under any pretence whatever, except in the case of the goal-keeper, who shall be allowed to use his hands in defence of his goal, either by knocking on or throwing, but not carrying the ball. The goal-keeper may be changed during the game, but not more than one player shall act as goal-keeper at the same time, and no second player shall step in and act during any period in which the regular goal-keeper may have vacated his position." A clarification for umpires was issued soon after regarding this law, adding that the rule didn't apply if the keeper was in the opponents' half. Reilly's, totally legal, habit of bouncing the ball towards the goal gained widespread fame as his own fame spread. The FA eventually banned the practice by limiting the goalkeepers' handling to their own penalty area.

Most of the players were documented in the first handbook that club secretary Percy Whitney produced in summer 1899. Assuming it was he who penned the pictures he certainly pulled no punches when describing the players. His pithy paragraphs gave a real flavour of the men who would represent Pompey. Full-back Edward Turner, signed from Everton, was "fairly fast, a good tackler, and bound to improve" while outside left (or right) Harry Clark, another from Everton, was "a splendid and unselfish worker". Liverpool-born George Barnes was "fairly fast, and centres well" while a rare player signed from a southern club in George Hewitt, from Luton, was given with one hand and taken with the other: "...although on the slow side [he] never gives up". Inside left William Smith, from Hednesford, the brother of England international Stephen, was described as "quiet gentlemanly player, brilliant yet untiring" while centre-half Harry Stringfellow provoked "a regular crisis … in the Everton camp" when he signed for Pompey. The squad also had a distinctly Scots feel to it. Thomas Cleghorn, the 28-year-old full back was from Leith but had made his name at Blackburn and Liverpool, where he would have come to Brettell's attention. John Brown was a centre-forward who had played in a Scotland Junior international, and he signed from Sunderland. Centre-half Thomas Wilkie was from Edinburgh and signed from Liverpool as did another man from Leith, winger Robert Marshall. Then there were a couple of players both born in Glenbuck, in Ayrshire mining country. Sandy Brown (no relation to John) was a youthful 21-years old and described as "without a superior in England or Scotland as a centre" but it was another original from the village who caught the eye. Robert 'Bob' Blyth was at the veteran stage of his career when he signed from Preston. Whitney's words hinted at the future service he would give to the club when he described the 30-year-old as one who "has a perfect knowledge of the game and has already provided manager Brettell with great support." The 'White Heather' connection was completed when Whitmey noted even local boy Dave Halliday, signed from Ryde, was "of Scotch parentage".

Brettell's job would have been to use his football know-how to meld the group into a team which could collect points. So, how was football played at the turn of the century? These days, any self-respecting fan knows what wingers, centre-forwards, goalkeepers and full backs do. Those positions on the field still exist, even if sometimes adapted, in the modern game. However, for some it is less clear what half-backs and inside-forwards did. Half-backs were primarily defensive players, preventing any attacks from coming through and allowing the centre-back behind them to play long, ranging passes if required. The job of the half-back is simple - protect the defenders and keep the ball moving in midfield. Centre-backs or sometimes centre-halves are simply full-backs that defend the area directly in front of the goal. An inside-forward, left or right, usually play as part of a front three or five and from their wide starting position they look to attack infield with runs off the ball and by dribbling diagonally towards the goal.

The players would be organised according to the standard formation, which by 1900 was a 2-3-5 structure. The comprehensive ***Inverting The Pyramid** - the History of Football Tactics* by Jonathan Wilson (2014), is one of the best on the topic. Before 1880 all teams played a very attacking game and line ups reflected the all-out nature of these games. Most articles quote the Scotland versus England game on November 30, 1872 where England were said to have played an "attacking" 1-2-7 formation with Scotland playing 2-2-6. Newspaper reports of the game, such as that in **The Field**, *The Country Gentlemen's Newspaper,* in December 1872, show that apart from the three or four 'backs' the rest of the players were forwards. One or two players would always hang back but the rest would attempt to take the ball forward as far as possible by dribbling past opponents and only when they could proceed no further, would they kick it ahead for someone else to chase. The game then was all about long kicking and dribbling. Cooperation through passing and any real kind of organised defending was just not in the game at that time. In the Portsmouth AFC team, documented by Kevin Smith (2004) in **Sherlock Holmes Was a Pompey Keeper,** the 'backs' including Arthur Conan Doyle and Peters, were held up as shining examples of the game, mostly though for their kicking ability. No finesse was required, merely an ability to hoof the ball away.

The comprehensive ***Association Football*** four-volume series edited by Geoffrey Green and AH Fabian, (1960) records that by the 1880s, teams started to play with two defenders, one of whom would often stay close to the goalkeeper to prevent barging, with the other slightly further forward to break up attacks, and three 'half-backs' and five forwards, so in a 2-3-5. Wilson, and others, called it the pyramid. By the 1890s, it was the standard formation in England and for the first time, a balance between attacking and defending was reached. Wilson talks about how the spread of the 2-3-5 formation in England meant that the centre-half had become the fulcrum of the team - for Pompey this was Stringfellow, a player who could both attack and defend, could break up opposition attacks and start them. After he had moved on, he was mentioned in the Leeds Mercury, recording his debut at Bradford in September 1905. They recorded that he was 'a highly skilled centre, who fully appreciates his duties, both as to attack and defence." England had played a 2-3-5 for the first time against Scotland in 1884 - **The Field** once again showing the formation and talking of the "three half back arrangement" of the English before clearly listing the team as a 2-3-5 formation. The system was soon so common by that year that teams were commonly listed in the papers in 2-3-5 formation. This way of recording the team for the papers and match programmes continued until the 1960s, despite formations having evolved considerably by that time. The Pompey team that won the championship twice in 1949 and 1950 was always recorded in newspapers and programmes as a 2-3-5 but actually played using the 'WM' or 3-2-2-3 formation - think of outfield player positions as an attacking W on top of a defensive M with the goalkeeper at the base - developed in the 1920s and perfected by Herbert Chapman with the great Arsenal team of the 1930s. Green & Fabian (1960) cover the use of the "W" which is the front or forward element of the formation, in great depth. But the 1899 Pompey team lined up in a 2-3-5 and were described as such in the club handbook for the 1899/1900 season. Under this formation, which resembles a pyramid turned upside down, players stayed in their rough positions. The aim was to quickly pass the ball along on the run towards the opposition goal. When defending, the two full-backs would mark the opponent forwards, the half-backs would fill the gaps and the centre-half had a key role in both helping to organise the team's attack and marking the opponent's centre-forward, usually one of their most dangerous players. The team was very attack minded, with the wing players making their way to the corner flags before lobbing centres into the goalmouth for the rest of the team to try to push into the net. The basic structure of the pyramid allowed for greater width in attack while protecting against central counter-attacks. The skilful forwards were covered by half-backs or centre-halves. As possession was lost and teams moved into their defensive third, the centre-halves joined the full-backs to numerically account for the opposition's forwards. A 2-3-5 was originally used in order to achieve superiority in numbers and to cover the whole pitch with players. Teams attacked in numbers and five players allowed for lots of quick passing and then shots on goal. Then they defended in numbers. Nowadays it would be easy to play against - an accurate pass up to a single fast striker into one of the holes, for example at left back that were left by the other team in all-out attack. But then all teams played that way.

The **Evening News**, on May 6, 1899, talked in glowing terms about the building up of the team: "Local football enthusiasts have been on the tiptoe of expectancy for a long time past as to who would be the players for the Portsmouth professional team next season, but the whole of the arrangements which the directors of the club were making were kept so dark that although the rumours as to possible players were numerous, the real facts have never leaked out, till now, when they are announced officially." The paper added "at the beginning of the week" the manager Brettell had "left for the North" to sign on players. It "was known that he had certain men 'in his eye' but no one was really aware what 'stars' he would be successful in obtaining." It also congratulated Brettell on his procurement: "The policy of the promoters of the club has all along been a forward one, and since they have secured the fine ground at Fratton they have shown that they are thoroughly alike to what is required. The capture of Frank Brettell caused quite a stir in the football world, for he was one of the foremost men in his particular line of the day". They told us that the club had decided not to recruit from the other Southern League teams as "they wished to keep on the "best of terms" with them, unless of course the other clubs gave them permission to do so first. So with the exception of two players from the Royal Artillery every man has been chosen from 'First League' Clubs so that the inclusion of the new club in the Southern League is practically assured, although the meeting will not be held yet". Interestingly, the online history of Plymouth Argyle by Roger Walters (2016) revealed the majority of Southern League clubs would require financial inducements to vote to admit such an outpost. These were authorised by their board, but Portsmouth, Southampton, Spurs and Reading would not take anything. During Pompey's formation, there is no record of any inducements paid to other clubs.

As regards the players recruited, the News story is not quite true, as one, Halliday, was signed from Ryde, via Southsea Rovers. Much of the reserve team, who occasionally played, also came from local clubs. The article continued "foremost among the players who have actually signed on is the goalkeeper Gunner Reilly. "The club could not have made a better choice" and "is undoubtedly one of the best keepers the Army has ever produced". The paper told us how him playing Gaelic football in Ireland helped with the use of his hands and where he "picked up his "bouncing out" practice for which he has become noted". The other players were commented upon. Turner was to become "one of the best backs in the South", Marshall was "one of three men selected to play from English clubs for Scotland last season". Cunliffe was "head and shoulders above any other forward in the New Brighton team last season". It also waxed lyrical about the trainer Brierley originally from Bolton "who has trained the English International teams for the past five years and is at present at Dublin University."

The **Athletic News** of November 20, 1899 also noted another feature of the team's squad, namely how tall it was: "Amongst several other claims to distinction, Portsmouth have the very useful one of possessing the tallest set of players in the Southern League. Mere height does not count for much in football, but when, as in this case, it is allied with pace and general cleverness it is an important factor. So Bristol Rovers found towards the close of their English Cup tie with this club on Saturday. Then, when they began to tire, they often had difficulty in clearing their lines, owing to the skilful way their opponents used their heads." Players were often also good all-rounders. Stringfellow was described in the **Southern Daily Mail** in August 1899 as a good billiards player, "beating the best local amateur the evening before by 20 points in a match of 300 up at the Talbot Hotel". Some played cricket well, breaking up training in summer 1899 with games against the Saints ex-players for example. Blyth, meanwhile, is recorded as being the only married man amongst the team, so that probably meant the others socialised a bit more than they might otherwise have done.

Chapter Six - Preparing the Players

INTO THE LEAGUE

While the playing squad was being recruited during early 1899, the directors had another success when the club gained entry to the Southern League Division One without undergoing a trial run in Division Two. On May 29, 1899, it was ratified at the league's AGM, held in The Rainbow public house in London, that Pompey would play in its top division with the other new boys, Cowes, Bristol Rovers, Queens Park Rangers and Thames Ironworks, all of whom had been playing in other leagues. The **Evening News** had already announced on May 8 that joining the top division was "definitely decided" and the story added that the first team would also play in the English Cup and Hampshire Cup while the reserves would play in the Hampshire League and Portsmouth Cup. Make no mistake, this was a real coup. At the same AGM, the yin to Pompey's yang was this line in the minutes: "It was noted that Royal Artillery, having been beaten by Cowes in the test match, had retired." The promotion/relegation play-off with second division Cowes had been for a place in Division One the following season, but it is a moot point whether RA would have taken it up had they won. In March 1899, shortly after the FA ban had been imposed, The **Evening News** reported: "People are now asking whether there will be any R.A. team next season. 'Twill be a good thing when that long-promised professional team is established at Fratton. Folks will then have a right to expect a good exhibition from the players they patronise and the new professional club is expected to do well as it could pick from players all over the country and pay for the best." On April 8, the day of the RA's appeal against the ban on its players, the paper went further. With the headline 'Will there be a R.A. next season?' it indicated the end was nigh: "The Amateur Cup business has completely spent everyone connected with the club and even Sgt. Bonney seems to have become disheartened. Reilly of course will be leaving the service before the winter, Turner will be the only class man left as Hill and others follow suit. It will be sad if they fold but they have been outclassed this season and next season opens up a new era in Portsmouth football..." Quite. With several of its best players about to turn professional at the new club, the Gunners' brave defiance of football gravity was all-but over.

The first division of the Southern League was, for clubs south of Birmingham, on a par with The Football League Division One, a view endorsed by the players from the north signing for Pompey. Thomas Cleghorn told the **Football Mail** at the end of 1899 that the Southern League was harder in many ways and the southern clubs have levelled up "to a wonderful extent." In the ***Official History of the Southern League***, edited by Leigh Edwards (1993), produced for its centenary, it explains that in 1890, two years after the Football League was formed, "the first attempt to form a league in Southern England" was in order to "rival the Football League". At that time the Southern League was a real soccer power in England. Clubs like Southampton, Spurs, Millwall and Swindon could match many Football League clubs for skill and reputation. For instance, Southampton carried the Southern League banner to the English Cup final in 1900 and 1902. Pompey's policy of not poaching from the other southern teams – as Brettell's predilection for players from the north underlined - undoubtedly would have helped and the new club was careful not to use other team colours or upset them in any other way. Pompey's application was bold and ambitious and whilst it was unusual to go straight into the top flight without the usual probationary period in the lower divisions, the Southern League were clearly keen to see a professional team from Portsmouth join them. Bristol Rovers and QPR also went straight into the top division although both had served time in other leagues, for example Bristol playing in both the Western League and the Birmingham & District League in the previous season. Keith Allen, the current president of the Southern League, looked into the league's records for this book and concluded that some "serious strings were pulled".

Certainly, Pompey's election to the top division seemed assured weeks before it was ratified. Southern League secretary Nat Whittaker was reported in the **Southern Daily Mail** on May 1, 1899, as saying: "Personally, I think there is a great future for 'socker' (sic) generally in Portsmouth and if they can only do well next season the success of the club is assured. Help them? Of course I will, and anyone else who wants to make football grow in the south." Whittaker was a former player who understood the game. He sat on the councils of the FA, the London FA and the Southern League and also managed to find time to referee games, such as the 1907 FA Cup Final. He added: "[I am] confident that Portsmouth would be elected into the league by the other clubs at the next general meeting of the Southern League", which they were. The 1899/1900 season, which incidentally saw the introduction of neutral linesmen for the first time, also included some more unfamiliar names considering this was one of the premier leagues in England. Bedminster, a suburb of Bristol plus New Brompton, who would become Gillingham, Chatham and Thames Ironworks were arguably the lesser lights.

William Pickford (1939) was fulsome in his praise for the Southern League in his memoirs. He said that "in its heyday it was a powerful body and did much to enable clubs in places like South Wales, Bristol, Plymouth, Reading, Swindon, Southampton, and Portsmouth to organise themselves on a much stronger basis than would have been possible without its inception and incentive." He also remembers both Saints and Pompey fondly: 'I saw many of the leading matches of both Southampton and Portsmouth over a number of years. They were both remarkably well conducted clubs and gave very little trouble." High praise indeed from one of the most distinguished administrators in the game at that time. Pickford was the first secretary of the county FA after its split from Dorset, was considered "the father of football in Hampshire" and he became president of the FA in 1937. Incidentally, in 1902 he was responsible for the introduction of pitch markings for the penalty areas, the penalty spot and the goal area, which led to the demise of Reilly & Co's basketball tactics. He was also a great referee, writing in 1906 the first guide for referees giving advice on how to adjudicate each rule, according to Norman Gannaway (2009) in **William Pickford: a Biography**.

On June 12, 1899 the Southern District Combination fixtures were announced with the club scheduled to play their first game away at Tottenham on September 18. The SDC had been set up by the Southern League and was designed to give the bigger southern clubs a midweek game to boost income. The summer was giving way to thoughts of winter football with the club getting closer to fulfilling its intention of playing professional football. On August 1, 1899, entries for the English Cup (the FA Cup these days) were published. The **Southern Daily Mail** said that Pompey were "included in the tenth division" adding pointedly: "It will be noticed that of the clubs excused the preliminary rounds in this South Western district a weak club like Weymouth is included amongst the four selected, and Portsmouth is not mentioned. This means that Portsmouth will have to fight their way right through the competition from the start". As an aside, the paper commented that the familiar figures of the Royal Artillery (Portsmouth) appear in neither the entries for the Amateur Cup or the bigger national trophy. That club had basically shut up shop as regards first class football. The term "tenth division" referred to the fact that Pompey was being treated as a tenth-tier club for cup purposes and therefore needed to enter the qualifying rounds accordingly. The club having to play five qualifying rounds to reach the first round proper in January corroborates this view.

In the build up to the new season, a Pompey XI played cricket against the ex-Saints in Southampton, a full day match. In a "pleasant encounter" the Portsmouth men, captained by Brettell, succeeded in making it a drawn game. A return the following week at Stamshaw was scheduled but no record exists of the score. Then, on Tuesday August 15, 1899, a warm summer evening according to press reports, with the ground still being built and with Pompey yet to play a football match of any kind, a thousand spectators, among them the first Pompey players, walked along Goldsmith Avenue to the enclosure taking shape on the former potato and cabbage field. The 'Open Evening' was clearly a success and Kevin Smith (2012) in his e-book *The (Secret) History of Fratton Park* said: "those journeys were the forerunners of millions made by football fans, home and away, over the following decades." To show off the facility, an impromptu game, Whites versus Colours, was staged, refereed by Bob Blyth, the recently signed former Preston North End captain. The **Southern Daily Mail** reported the day after: "Considering the heat, long grass, want of practice and general swopping of forwards into backs and vice versa, the spectators had a capital hour's amusement". The teams which lined up for what must take the honour of the first, albeit unofficial, game at Fratton Park were, for the record, as follows:

> A team (White): Benger, Turner, Digweed, Rogers, Hiscock, Jackson, Hunt, Holbrook, Edwards, Thomas, Wells

> B team (Colours): Ruffell, Browitt, Smith, Holding, Cotton, Stonebridge, Hitchin, Griffin, Worsley, Webber, Dobson

The turnout for that ground-opening occasion in the final months of the 19th century convinced the **Southern Daily Mail** that the new professional club would be a success: "The most encouraging feature of the occasion was the evident enthusiasm and keen interest in the new undertaking by those present. And judging by the number who visited the ground yesterday, while the fare provided could not by any stretch of the imagination be styled attractive, professional football will be a success in Portsmouth." It was also positive about the ground being completed in time for the new season: "At present, the enclosure is now being completed and a second stand and a portion of banking are likely to be completed before the first home fixture is decided. It's satisfying to find though, that despite the tremendous spell of dry weather, the turf has not suffered to any appreciable extent and, with a little attention in due time, the playing pitch should prove to be in first class condition." For the **Evening News** though, on August 16, the summer weather was more of a hindrance: "The completion of the ground is being advanced as quickly as possible but the lack of rain still prevents the banking etc being completed."

On Friday August 18, trial matches started in earnest and Fratton Park would host three further games as the build-up to the club's Southern League debut gathered pace. The first game was, according to the **Southern Daily Mail**, "quite of a private nature" and "the directors merely taking the opportunity to see the men perform." News of it had spread though and at least a hundred people managed to watch and despite the "long grass and the uneven nature of the pitch" it went well. Regulars versus Reserves ended in a 2-2 draw. Pompey "clearly had a trio of heavy and powerful performers at the back and in goal and the directors were completely satisfied with the exhibition." The **Evening News** also reported on the next game, which occurred the following day, the 19th, between two teams of local players with the score unrecorded:

> Professional football has fairly "caught on" in Portsmouth was evident on Saturday night when a good crowd of enthusiasts assembled on the new ground at Fratton to witness a second trial match between teams composed of local players, the object of the match being to enable Mr F. Brettell to select a representative eleven to meet the Portsmouth reserves on Tuesday. Several of the players who had promised to attend failed to do so, and the vacancies had to be made up on the ground. However, a spiritedly contested game was witnessed, and the trial match tomorrow should prove interesting. With reference to the trial of the first team, on Friday last, the directors of the Club, Mr. Brierley, the trainer, and Mr. Brettell were all very favourably impressed with the form shown by the men and are confident that they will render a good account of themselves during the coming season. The next full trial match is to take place on Saturday, when the public will be welcome to view the game.

On the same day adverts started in the **Southern Daily Mail** for the publication of the new **Football Mail** from September 2. They boasted the fact that reporters would have a private telegraph line from the ground back to base, so could be first at sending news of the game. To cap a busy day all round, it also saw the release of the Southern League fixture list. The new club would start at Chatham, followed by a friendly against Southampton at home the following Tuesday to test the ground. Reading would be the first home league game on September 9. Even though it wasn't officially in use yet, Fratton Park was fast establishing itself as the football venue for the town. Excitement was growing in the town and on August 22, the next trial, a Reserves versus 'local hopefuls' to finalise the second team, ended in a 2-2 draw, was reported by the **Evening News** thus:

Interesting Trial At Fratton

Considerably over a thousand spectators assembled on the new Fratton Ground last evening, when another interesting trial match was played between the Portsmouth Reserves and a local team, for the purpose of selecting an eleven to do duty against Portsmouth in the public trial match on Saturday evening. Although somewhat scratchy at times, the game was very interesting. In the first half Brown (Sunderland) and Hanna (R.A.) scored for the reserves, but after the change over the "locals" gave a lot of trouble and mainly owing to some fine sprints by Cotton, the score was equalised before time was called. Benger kept goal very creditably, Dow, Hitchen, Cotton and Jackson put some specially fine work for the side.

The teams were:-

"Locals" :- Benger (goal); Pitt and Dow (backs); Holding, Smith and Digweed (half-backs); Hitchen and Cotton (right forwards); Jackson (centre); Thomas and Clay (left forwards).

Reserves. :- Ruffle (goal); Harms and E. Turner (backs); Walsh, Halliday and Hanna (half-backs); Coleman and Hewitt (right forwards); J. Brown (centre); Brazier and Barnes (left) forwards.

It was worth a couple of the 'hopefuls' turning up as Digweed and Cotton went on to play for the first team. Despite not being officially open yet, on August 24 the **Evening News** reported that the Portsmouth FA were from now on going to stop using the United Services' Ground – which the army was no longer going to use for football – and would use Fratton Park for their cup ties and the end of season cup finals. This would be a good money spinner for the new club. The new ground opened its doors for the first official public trial match on August 26 and the fans turned out in their droves to see what the new club was all about and see the first team beat the reserves 2-0. The **Evening News** reported:

Popular Football

Fully 5,000 were present on the new Portsmouth Football Ground, Fratton, on Saturday evening to witness the first public trial of the Portsmouth professional team, and, judging from the enthusiasm they displayed, they were very favourably impressed by the exhibition. The game was between Portsmouth and the Reserves, and the team lined out as under:-

Portsmouth:- Reilly, goal; H. Turner and Wilkie, backs; Blyth, Stringfellow, and Cleghorn, half-backs; Marshall, Cunliffe, A. Brown, Smith, and Clarke, forwards.

> Reserves:- Sergeant Harms (R.A.), goal; Turner (Southsea Rovers) and Dow (Field Artillery), backs; Sergeant Hanna, Halliday, and Digweed (Hornets), half-backs; Smith (Royal Artillery), Cotton (Naval Depot). Jackson (Southsea Rovers), Thomas (Southsea Rovers), and Barnes, forwards.
>
> Sergeant R. Bonney, R.A. held the Whistle. Immediately upon the kick off the "pros" who were wearing their salmon and maroon uniforms, attacked and throughout an interesting game they outplayed their opposition. The Reserves played a thoroughly plucky game but the vast superiority on every point of play of the first team men was most obvious. Their Forwards worked together in grand style, and their dash and brilliancy, general resourcefulness and clever tactics could not fail to excite general favour.
>
> And this was on rough, unrolled ground, covered with long grass, and against opponents, who try as they might, could not extend them. The back division also played with excellent judgement, and on a few occasions they were seriously challenged showed what they will be able to do when the necessity arises. Brown scored the first goal for the "Shrimps" (Portsmouth) soon after the start, and the only other point notched throughout the game was kicked by Clarke about ten minutes before time.
>
> It was only owing to the goalkeeping of Harms that a prodigious number of points was not scored, but it was very obvious that had the "firsts" decided to take matters seriously the result would have been far different. However, the reserves are to be congratulated upon the game they played, and will no doubt render a good account of themselves by-and-by.

It's interesting to note how many players came from Southsea Rovers, Wigginton's old club, which had been unable to join the Hampshire League as it had failed to find its own dedicated ground.

On August 29 the **Evening News** reported that Pompey had been drawn against Ryde in the English Cup with Cowes having a bye in the first round and Southampton being among the clubs excused from the qualifying rounds of the competition. Two days later, travel arrangements for the first game at Chatham were confirmed: A dockyard excursion to London left the Town station at 7.55am and fans would be able to buy cheap tickets to Chatham at either Holborn or Charing Cross for three shillings (15p) return. The train would leave Charing Cross at 1.25pm for Chatham and telegrams would be sent back to Fratton Park by manager Brettell so those watching the reserves' game versus the United Services could know how the match was progressing. On September 1, the **Evening News** reported that "today {Friday} was the official start of the football league but most clubs had postponed their games until tomorrow, Saturday 2nd so as to help its paying customers". Gate receipts would not have been huge on a Friday evening. They also covered the travel arrangements for the next day's game and stated that Sgt Maj Windrum, one of the directors, would travel with the team. The following day, the **Football Mail** excitedly announced that its new, private, National Telephone line to Fratton Park, would be up and running the following weekend. The paper also did a piece on each of the clubs that Pompey would face in their first season. Southampton had not made many changes from the team that won the league in 1899 and were seen to have "plenty of experienced men in the team." It was felt that this would "go a long way towards keeping them at the head of the table." Of the others, Millwall, QPR, Thames Ironworks, Reading, Chatham and Gravesend were seen to be challengers, with Spurs "likely to form, with Southampton, the keenest rivals to Portsmouth and be one of the best attractions at Goldsmith Avenue." It should be noted at this point that there was nothing other than a friendly rivalry between Portsmouth and Southampton in those early days. Dave Juson (2004) remains adamant that far from being upset that Portsmouth was now "treading on their turf", Southampton would have been very pleased that a club had at last been formed in the south the size of Pompey to help put the south on the footballing map and a "friend" that could help them attract crowds and drive up income and thus pay the wages.

The anticipation for that first ever league game in 1899 by now was at fever pitch. It could perhaps be compared to the wait endured by fans to return to Fratton Park, which remained largely closed during the 2020/21 season due to the Covid-19 pandemic. In the late 19th century football started in early September, but local league football didn't start until October. Football was truly a winter sport. But the newspapers were ready. The **Football Mail** proudly claimed that it could have the results for a game kicking off at 3pm back in the town and out on the streets by 5.15pm, a promise on which they were able to deliver, even at one game when the nearest telegraph office to the ground was two miles away. A (literal) runner was ready the minute the game finished to take the already dictated telegram to the office for it to be wired to Portsmouth. The "Shrimps" were ready in their smart salmon pink shirts with maroon cuffs and collar. The team was assembled, and presumably keen to get on with it. Let play commence.

THE MAKING OF MODERN POMPEY: KEY DATES

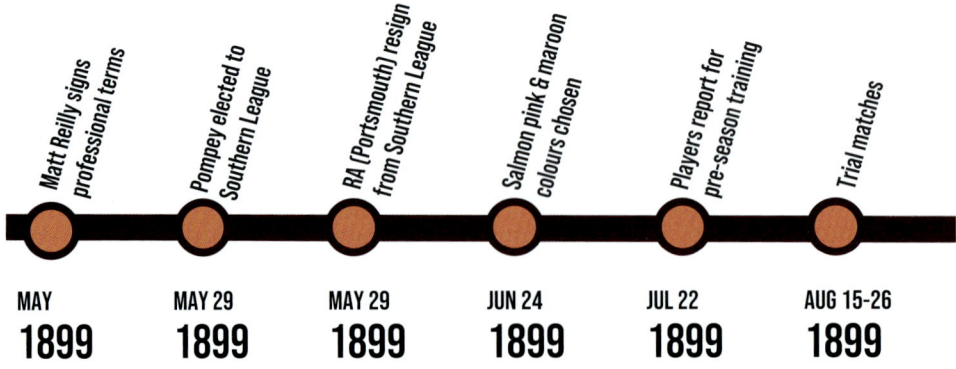

Chapter Seven
LET PLAY COMMENCE

Training was a bit different in 1899. A report in the **Evening News** on September 2, 1899, covered preparation for Chatham for that first game and the advice to the players from the trainer William Brierley had been: "Don't do too much and over-tax yourself. Have a kick about, eat what you like, but go easy on the beer before the match". He had been the trainer for the England international team for some years and also been at Bolton with Brettell in 1895. When the reporter from the **Evening News** called at the ground early in the first season to interview Brierley he "found him hard at work rubbing down his men after their morning exercises". He recorded that "all the players were extremely pleased with the way Mr Brierley was treating them – and no wonder." The article continued:

> Some trainers believe in a very vigorous course of treatment and when they are not giving their men hard walking exercise they are drilling them with clubs or dumb-bells, or sending them to the Turkish bath. Mr. Brierley is no believer in these methods. He believes that rest is a good nourishment. During the past week the team has done no hard exercises. Every morning they do a little sprinting and then they pass through the hands of Mr. Brierley, who attaches the greatest importance to the 'rubbing' of his charges. He gives them no walking exercise or clubs or dumb-bells but when he has finished with them he expects them to have a kick about - and this they all seem pleased to do.

The Pompey trainer said that hard, vigorous training takes a lot out of the men and they have a tendency to go stale. In his system this did not happen. He added: "I believe in my players eating what they relish and drinking in moderation until the day or two before the match." However outmoded Mr. Brierley's method would seem today, they certainly worked. The **Football Mail** in 1899 had a number of articles about training methods. The view was "reasonable diet and a reasonable mode of life" was considered important. "The lungs and heart must be equal to a series of sudden demands on them at three or four times the normal pressure and one match a week is almost sufficient if the player lives reasonably between whiles to keep himself in peak condition but it is not sufficient for the strain of competition matches". As "football was now a business", it was important to have a "professional trainer and some training as without him the teams soon begin to neglect regular exercise". However, the paper was clear that a professional trainer would be careful not to overdo it, especially as the eight months of football "put a considerable "strain and wear and tear" on the men". And "training should be stopped the moment a man tires". A few points that were seen to be important were - "a five mile sharp walk is better training than a file mile run; the skipping rope is the finest of exercise; few exercises beat running up long flights of stairs; don't do ball work, it's not needed; don't worry about diet and it's better to have a glass of beer than longing for one". They did however state that "the less alcohol the better and no smoking within two hours of a match". And the players "whole body was to be kept regularly clean by bathing, but not in hot baths". A different world, although, presumably after Brierley had left the club, baths continued to be a favourite of the players. The cashbook shows a club payment of £2 5s in March 1905 for "Turkish Baths".

Whatever the methods, the Pompey team had been duly prepared for the inaugural fixture and on September 2, 1899, Pompey's first league game ended in a 1-0 win at Chatham with the only goal scored by Harold 'Nobby' Clark. There was some dispute about whether it was his or not. In some reports it is given as an own goal, but the club ledger has Clark inscribed, so that is good enough for us. The **Hampshire Telegraph**'s take on proceedings was as follows:

A Capital Start

It was Pompey first serious engagement and a good victory at 1-0. We must congratulate them on the result and their entry into the world of professional football. The team left Fratton Station at 9.40am arriving at Charing Cross at about 1.25pm. A Dockyard excursion had already left at 8.05am for Waterloo packed with supporters. Telegrams were dispatched every quarter of an hour to Fratton Park showing the progress of the game. 1-0 does not give a true idea of the superiority of the Portsmouth team. Chatham played rough, scraggy and unscientific football throughout. All the Pompey forwards proved fitter, cleverer, speedier and several showed artistry, and with more games will gel together well. They worked hard but with little result at first. The game started at a leisurely pace. Praise can be bestowed on the backs and half backs. They dealt with the ugly rushes of the home team, coolly, cleverly and resourcefully and cleared effectively. Reilly, in goal, showed agility and cleverness of old. He handled several awkward shots in fine style. Chatham were firmly beaten. At half time the score was 0-0, but Clark scored in the second half. Pompey should increase the margin when Chatham visit us. For their return journey, the Pompey team left Waterloo on the 10.15pm train and arrived home at 35 minutes after midnight.

On the day, the **Evening News**, sister paper to the Telegraph, used those telegrams, the text of which were quickly typeset into the latest edition. Its 'on the whistle' report made for happy reading for football fans in Portsmouth who had long anticipated this day, although deadlines meant the second half coverage, including that of the goal, was scant at best...

The Season Opened

To-day the new Portsmouth Football Club made its debut in the football world, being entertained by Chatham in the Southern League, The team, looking thoroughly fit and well, left headquarters this morning in charge of Mr. Frank Brettell (secretary and manager), Mr. W. Brierley (trainer), and Sergeant Major Windrum, R.A., one of the directors, and proceeded to Waterloo by the 9.43 train. Thence they proceeded to Chatham, and their arrival on the ground was the signal for a loud outburst of applause from the large crowd of spectators. The teams turned out in dull and threatening weather. A heavy rain storm occurred about one but was without much effect upon the ground.

CHATHAM WIN THE TOSS - There were about four thousand spectators present when the Portsmouth men, led by Wilkie, took the field. They received quite an ovation. Chatham won the toss, and Portsmouth started off with a fine spurt, forcing a corner, from which Cunliffe centred. The Chatham defenders returned the ball but Marshall nipped in only to be grounded by Humphries. The visitors had the best of the next few exchanges, and Clements, who was possibly offside netted the ball. Just afterwards Reilly had to save a clunking shot from Collins.

EXCITING INCIDENTS - Portsmouth was penalised with a free kick through Smith charging from behind, and following pressure by the home forwards, Wilkie relieved fluidly. Chatham kept pressing hotly, but the Portsmouth forwards put in a fine bit at work, in the course of which Brown had his leg hurt. Continuing after a brief stoppage, Portsmouth did a bit of pressing, but the Chatham backs relieved in splendid style. The attack was persistent enough while it lasted.

REILLY CAUSES A SENSATION - Presently, well-sustained pressure by Chatham transferred operations to the Portsmouth end again, and the visitors had to exert their utmost efforts to clear. However, Marshall and Cunliffe got away nicely on the right wing, but Humphries stopped the centre, and the ball was once more returned to the Portsmouth goal, where Reilly caused quite a sensation by bringing off one of his patent saves from Kaye. The Chatham forwards, however, played a great game and another off-side point was registered.

At half-time the score was: Portsmouth ..... 0 Chatham 0

Play in the second half was in favour of Portsmouth, who opened the scoring from a centre by Clark.

The final score was : Portsmouth ...... 1 Chatham 0

A well-deserved win then, although the **Chatham & Rochester News** was also, albeit slightly more grudgingly, impressed and had a full description of the goal, which we will describe as a 'deflected cross':

A LUCKY GOAL GIVES PORTSMOUTH THE VICTORY

Disaster awaited Chatham on the ball being returned to their quarters. Eight minutes after the resumption, Clark received out on the wing, and running well in shot with terrific force. The ball struck Harper, who was in the line of fire, rebounded on to the crossbar and into the net. This was unfortunate, as the shot, which was by no means a difficult one, could have been easily saved by the custodian, who was waiting to receive it. The visitors were naturally in high glee over this somewhat unexpected success and they paid special attention to the defence of their charge after ... The visitors were an exceptionally smart team, and should the continue as they commenced, are likely to be nearer the top than at the bottom of the League table at the end of the season. They are a fine lot and triers every one of them.

Nearer home, the **Portsmouth Times** commented on how: "The Pompey team looked impressive in their salmon pink and maroon uniforms," but it would say that wouldn't it? The **Southern Daily Mail** on the Monday carried a comment about how good it was to have this team and told its readers: "After the match at Chatham on Saturday two visitors from Portsmouth were having tea at a restaurant, and their comments on the match were overheard by a gentleman sitting at an adjoining table, who good-naturedly inquired of one of the visitors, "well, and what did you think of the game?" "Pretty fair", was the reply. "But it would have been better but for the silly referee.". Judge the speaker's surprise, and the amusement of his companion, when the stranger observed, "I was the referee." The conversation then drifted to other subjects." Other games that day saw the following results in the Southern League:

Southampton	6-2	New Brompton
Tottenham	3-1	Millwall
Reading	3-0	Bristol Rovers
QPR	6-0	Brighton United
Cowes	2-1	Gravesend
Bedminster	2-0	Sheppey United

The **Evening News** also reported that the Royal Artillery players, who were declared professionals after the Harwich & Parkstone match the previous season, had been reinstated as amateurs, the FA notifying them via their barracks the day before. Too little, too late. However, it did manage to play some friendlies in the autumn of 1899, but it wouldn't be until the 1900/01 season that the RA (Portsmouth) club briefly reformed, using the core of the team drawn from the reinstated amateurs. The club was now playing at Hilsea as the army had, by now, decommissioned their United Services' Ground for football, to save it for cricket. To all intents and purposes they folded as a Portsmouth-based club in 1901, dropping out of both the Hampshire and United Services' Leagues. The Royal Artillery FC exists to this day and, incidentally, played a friendly against a Portsmouth XI at Gosport in September 2023 as part of Pompey's 125th anniversary season, to mark its crucial role in the making the modern club.

But back to the story. On the same afternoon, the reserves played what must be regarded as the first official game at Fratton Park against an opposition, albeit a friendly, when they played against the United Services. The game kicked off at 5pm in bright sunshine with Sgt Bonney as referee. The **Portsmouth Times** in its next edition reported on the outcome: "The friendly between Portsmouth Reserves and the United Services on the first day of the season attracted about 1,000 spectators, who witnessed a fairly interesting struggle. The local men chosen to play for the Reserves were Hanns, Harms and Coleman (R.A.), Dow (Field Artillery), Digweed (Hornets), and Thomas (Southsea Rovers), while the scratch team was a powerful one. The game throughout was even, but by no means exciting, and the Portsmuthians scored once in each half. Thomas scored in the first half and Brown also scored for Pompey in the second half, Cotton got one goal back for the Services, who were thus defeated by 2-1." The **Evening News** added that the United Services goalkeeper tried out a new method of play where he "dropped the ball over an opponent's head and ran round to kick it". However, "Pompey soon worked out how to play against this and scored only for it to be ruled offside."

The first team's first home game was a friendly against Southampton on Wednesday September 6 and Pompey won 2-0. Dan Cunliffe with a "clinking shot" in the first half and Clark with a "particularly fine shot" in the second scored the goals. Interestingly, the night before the **Southern Daily Mail** of September 5, 1899, had revealed how they relaxed before a game: "The members of Portsmouth are nearly all members of the Saxe Weimar Bowling Club, and some of them are adept players of the old English game". This exceedingly popular club was formed in 1895 and, as Southsea was a big tourist resort, a special rule was even introduced for tourists to play for 2s 6d a month. The bowling club is now called Southsea Waverley, but back then was in Saxe-Weimar Road. The road name changed during World War One to dissociate it from Germany. So, just like Arthur Conan Doyle, who took up bowls as his first sport when coming to Portsmouth, the Pompey players were aficionados.

The **Evening News** relished the start of a rivalry in its opening paragraph of its report of the Saints' game, which was attended by his worship the mayor, Alderman T Scott Foster JP, and watched by around 5,000 people who were "flocking" to the ground ahead of kick-off, according to the paper: "The first of what, it is hoped, will be a long series of historic football battles between Portsmouth and Southampton took place on Wednesday at Fratton Park, as the new ground in Goldsmith Avenue has been named. There has always been a deal of rivalry between the two towns, but Southampton long since took the initiative in securing the services of a good professional team. Last season when the Royal Artillery met "the Saints" in the Southern League there was a considerable amount of interest evidenced, and now that Portsmouth can also boast its own professional eleven that interest has been vastly increased. Today both teams took the field without knowing the sting of defeat, Portsmouth having succeeded on Saturday in vanquishing Chatham in their first engagement, and Southampton having succeeded in making New Brompton look small." The paper subsequently reported the Southampton contingent had been impressed by their Portsmouth counterparts:

Notes On The Game

'There is no doubt that you have got together a very fine lot'. This from one of the Southampton team at the conclusion of the first half of yesterday 's match to Mr F.E. Brettell. And the sentiment it is safe to say can be endorsed by every spectator who witnessed the excellent display. It was the first occasion on which the team have engaged in a serious match before their own supporters, and naturally they desired to create a good impression. Judging from the continuous round of applause which followed the various incidents in their display, they succeeded in accomplishing their desire. Some people are inclined to the opinion that Southampton were not trying, but anyone who saw the match and understands the game cannot but admit that after Portsmouth had scored the Saints exerted every effort to get up on equal terms. The home forwards, notwithstanding that they greatly missed Smith, work together in grand style, and were quite a match for their opponents, not only in style, but in passing and centring. And that they were a shade faster must also be conceded. The three half-backs also played a very fine game, and never once were they away from the ball when they were wanted. Both Wilkie and Turner also shone, and as to Reilly, he played a grand game. Portsmouth fairly won on their merits, and despite the threat wait till we meet again, everyone is inclined to think that Portsmouth will render an excellent account of themselves during their forthcoming league engagements. They have this on their side at any rate: they have only played together in two matches, and as they gradually get used to each other's tactics, they must improve on Saturday's and yesterday's excellent exhibitions.

The **Southern Daily Mail** commented in its next day's edition that "for some years the folk of Portsmouth had cast envious glances towards football in Southampton but those times had now passed away, never to return". An eyewitness report on that first game by Alec Whicher (1945), recalled: "My first introduction to a big soccer match was when I was taken by my father to witness the premier game Portsmouth played at Fratton Park. The ground was not then fenced, and there were ropes round the playing pitch. I was a mere kid, and had to be lifted on the shoulders of kindly spectators to see the game. I can quote the team now. Every youngster had his particular favourite, and my vote in those days went to Dan Cunliffe. He was a brilliant shot, and one of the finest specimens of manhood ever – just the ideal build for a forward."

Inside-forward William Smith missed both the Southampton and the Reading games as he was in bed with – depending which paper one read – an injury or influenza, which was often fatal in those days so people were careful when they got it. Without him Pompey still were able to win their first home Southern League match against Reading 2-0, a game attended by around 9,000. The match was played against a backdrop of rumblings about the coming South African, or Boer, war. Negotiations with the Boer – the descendants of Dutch farmers who had settled on the east coast – to try to avert conflict were ongoing, but the government still announced on that same day that 10,000 troops were being moved from India to Natal and the Cape Colony in preparation for war. Twelve new destroyers were hurriedly commissioned by the Admiralty, most to be based in Portsmouth. At least the football was a way to take the people's minds off matters. An early edition of the **Evening News** reported: "Today's game v Reading kick-off has been brought forward from 4.30pm to 4.00pm as the Reading team are desirous of catching an early train back." Moving kick off times is nothing new it seems. Reading had also been the first team to meet the Royal Artillery at the United Services' Ground the previous season and now did the "double" by becoming the first to play a competitive game at Fratton Park. In its match report the paper commended the secretary/manager on his work: "Mr Frank Brettell did not make mistakes in his 'fishing tour' up north at the back end of last season. Those who have witnessed all three of the games in which Portsmouth have participated cannot help noticing the greatly improved form displayed. Whereas in the Chatham match the movements of the forwards [had been] somewhat loose and scraggy, on Saturday they were quite the opposite, and the quintet gave a thoroughly clever display."

However, it seemed the weather – perhaps that east-west axis of the ground was having an immediate effect – influenced the result, although the consensus was Pompey deserved the win. The report continued: "There is no doubt that Portsmouth received very great aid from the sun and wind in the first half, and in all fairness, it should be said that the "biscuit boys" played up with rare pluck and spirit. They were, however, distinctly outplayed, and although at times they gave some trouble, the Portsmouth citadel was seldom in danger. When the forwards have got thoroughly used to one another and their combined work thereby becomes stronger, there is no doubt that other Southern League clubs will have cause to remember their visit to the Portsmouth ground." The Southern Daily Mail added that both stands were completely full some fifteen minutes before kick-off and crowds continued to wend their way along Goldsmith Avenue.

It reported: "it was to be hoped that fans would arrive earlier in future". The town band entertained the crowd. The "long drought had rendered the pitch tremendously hard, and the continued absence of rain rendered it inadvisable to cut the grass, so that the going was rough and uneven".

September 1899 would prove to be a momentous month all round. On the 30th, the club played its first English Cup tie and Ryde were the team to do the honours, travelling to the mainland from the Isle of Wight. They would return with their tails between their legs as Pompey romped to a 10-0 win, which remains Pompey's record competitive win. That day also saw a "football special" train appear for the first time, although things didn't all go to plan. Kevin Smith (2012) noted:

> The managers at the South Western Railway Company decided the opening English Cup tie to be held at the ground merited the one-off excursion. So they arranged for a train to leave Portsmouth Harbour station at 2.40pm bound for Fratton, a mere two stations up the line. True, the distance was only a couple of miles but the ambitious officials were quick to realise the pulling power of the cup a month into Pompey's debut season. What they hadn't reckoned on, however, was the complete lack of pulling power of one of their steam locomotives. The stuttering engine barely made it on to dry land before it came hissing to a halt … The Islanders' supporters must have greeted the prospect of a specially laid on service with pleasure. That was far from their feeling when they finally left their seats at Fratton station. It had taken them 55 minutes to travel the short distance through Portsmouth town centre. Their train had stopped five times in all - and they would have been entitled to wonder during that most fragmented of journeys if they were ever going to see any football at all that afternoon. It would have been quicker for them to walk than let the train take the strain. Having finally arrived; the fans were forced to make a dash along Goldsmith Avenue with the kick-off having just taken place - at 3.33pm - as they pulled in to the platform.

Smith also revealed the match was always likely to be one-sided: "A walkover had been predicted by the Portsmouth Evening News in its early match day edition that Saturday morning. The basis for this forecast was a friendly on September 11 which the two teams had played on the island. Pompey had fielded all their reserve backs, and made changes to their usual forwards, and still emerged winners by three goals to one against Ryde's first team. And the home side's solitary goal was a penalty."

The English Cup also aroused passions with the first report of crowd violence involving Pompey supporters. When Bedminster were conquered 2-1 at Bristol in a fifth qualifying tie in December, the cheers of 500 "enthusiasts" put the home supporters in a "bad humour". An eye witness reported: "When the boilermakers persisted in waving their large Portsmouth standard it was like holding a red flag to a bull and in the rough and tumble which followed the flag was torn from the staff, the pole shattered, and the standard bearers came in for a rough handling. In the free fight which ensued more than one Portsmouth supporter was then escorted to the police station." But things were going well in general. A month earlier, on November 4, the **Football Mail** sent their correspondent *The Veteran* along to see the ground and give his opinions of the state of play during the previous round of the cup against Swindon. He reported back:

> For a new team it is a very strong side, and distinctly one of the best in the South. The defence is very powerful, Reilly being a veritable host in himself. He has improved, too, and I noticed a little more polish. Everyone says that his patting down game is risky and will be useless in a first-class match but so far it is not true so the half-back line is particularly sharp and agile. Cleghorn and Blyth are distinctly of the artistic stamp. I'm afraid I did not see the front row at their best. Everyone says so-so that if I was disappointed and consider that their play was not so clever as that of Swindon and that Cunliffe and Smith individually caught my eye the most favourably, I am only saying what my impressions were. It is confidence that wins a big name for a team and will make Southern football the equal of Northern football, as it pretty nearly is now in theory. The Pompey Chimes were a novelty to me, jaded as I feel at times with a plethora of football, but what words do people use nobody can tell. It is a phase of enthusiasm that does nobody harm, but I am not in love with it.

Throughout that first season some comment was expressed about the spectators and their attitude to the players, particularly the forwards when they didn't score. The **Football Mail** weighed in:

> Recent correspondence on the behaviour of the crowd at Fratton Park has brought a new batch of letters - they are too long, and in some aspects wide of the real issues, and perhaps it would be as well to close the subject. I have seen all the matches at Fratton and have attended football matches regularly for the past twelve years and my experience tells me that the Portsmouth supporters are much below the average crowd in one-sidedness and partiality for their own team. They very naturally cheer their own players in preference to the other side, and no harm is done to anyone by so doing. It is only when a crowd loses itself entirely and attacks the referee under the mistaken idea that the unfortunate individual is not carrying out his duties fairly that any danger arises. Perhaps it would be wise to simply warn the Pinks more enthusiastic admirers that exceedingly grave consequences will arise if a referee was interfered with.

In December 1899, the club also hosted a team from South Africa. Overseas football was rare in Victorian times, but Pompey had the chance midway through their debut season in the Southern League to host the so-billed 'Kaffirs' which is these days a term banned in that country. The visitors, made up of 16 black players, were soundly beaten 7-3 by the reserves despite the South Africans' billing as 'first class players with great staying power'. Chris Bolsmann (2011) in *The 1899 Orange Free State football team tour of Europe: 'Race', imperial loyalty and sporting contest* cited several reports from up and down the country which suggested the goals scored by the visitors were effectively gifts from the home team to add to the spectacle. The team were touring England and Scotland under the auspices of the Orange Free State FA of Southern Africa, a nominally whites-only organisation. They had begun their tour against Aston Villa but when they stopped off in Portsmouth, the bad weather was ill-suited to football and only a small crowd gathered to see the game. Bolsmann concluded:

> On the eve of the South African War the Orange Free State football team travelled to Britain, and in four months played 49 matches in unfamiliar conditions and against first class amateur and professional opposition. This was the first South African football side to play abroad and despite the trying circumstances of racism, ridicule and humiliation reported in the British press, the team was fêted and well-supported throughout its tour. Although the results on the football pitch were far from encouraging, if we consider these in the light of the poor results all South African teams initially achieved against British cricket and rugby teams in particular, the footballers' tour followed a similar pattern, and this does not detract from its importance. Far from being insignificant in South African and British sports history, the 1899 touring football team deserves recognition for the pioneering role played in late nineteenth-century football.

As the new year turned, by February interest in the English Cup ended in the first round proper but only after two replays with Football League side Blackburn Rovers. In the end the team lost 5-0 in a second replay at Aston Villa's ground, but the fact Pompey had earned two draws previously underlined how close in standard the Southern and Football Leagues were. Besides, goalkeeper Reilly had heard just before the game the unexpected news that he was to be capped for Ireland against England and some reports blamed his shock for a poor performance and the loss of the game. Interestingly, both Reilly and team-mate Cunliffe were selected, the latter for England, with the game ending a 2-0 victory to England. There was even a bit of a financial schemozzle in March 1900, when the **Evening News** reported that the club were being sued by a contractor called Edward Bendell - who regularly figured in the club's cashbook as a supplier - for an unpaid debt. It was a major story and the paper outlined the case:

> The Portsmouth Football and Athletic Club Company Limited, was sued at the Portsmouth County Court on Thursday by Edward Bendell, contractor, of Kingston, for £12 and 12 shillings for goods supplied – the plaintiff said that last July he was approached by Mr Brettell, the defendant's manager who asked him to supply fine sifted ashes and clinker for certain

parts of the ground. Bendell said he agreed to supply them and he fixed the price at three shillings per square yard. After he had delivered a large number of loads he sent in his bill, and Mr Brettell then called him and asserted that he agreed to purchase the material at three shillings per load. Bendell disputed this and stopped his men from delivering any further loads. He delivered 133 loads, and Mr King explained the amount in dispute was the value of 16 loads. One of the plaintiff's men, named Richards, also said that the arrangement between the plaintiff and Mr Brettell was for yards not loads. The case was adjourned for a week.

When the case resumed, "The plaintiff, Bendell, urged that the clinker were supplied at 3s a yard but the defendants, the club, contended it was 3s per load and disputed 18 loads. His Honour, Judge Gye, gave judgement that the price should be 3s per load". The club had won and there are no further payments to Bendell from that time on.

In summary, on the pitch, the first season had turned out brilliantly for the "Shrimps" or the "Pinks" as the team tended to be colloquially known then. The nickname "Pompey" was still catching on. The top scorer was Cunliffe with 29 goals and the star of the side, as predicted, was goalkeeper Reilly. Tottenham won the league with 44 points, but Pompey were only three points behind them. Southampton finished third, six points further adrift and Reading were fourth. It was the first of three successive seasons that Pompey went unbeaten at home. Pompey won 33 out of 53 games, 20 of the 28 Southern League matches with a goal ratio or average as it became more commonly, if inaccurately, known – the number of goals for divided by the number of goals against – of 2.034, in other words twice as many goals scored as conceded. This method was used until the 1980s to decide placings if teams had the same number of points. Owing to the collapse of Cowes and Brighton United, four games were expunged from the records. The first team also competed in the Southern District Combination, and did well, winning eight and drawing two of their 16 matches to finish third. The reserves won 18 matches out of 31, scoring 103 goals against 40. Reporters were fulsome in their praise for the first season's activities. For the fans things could barely have been better – a whole new team, a new ground, finishing second in the league and having two players selected for their respective countries.

MONEY MATTERS

The first proper financial year to April 30, 1900 was not a total disaster. The **Evening News** damned the figures with faint praise: "It is not so bad as it might have been..." The club made a trading loss but the bank account balance was £983 in credit, at least that is what is scribbled inside the club's cashbook. No records exist to show exactly how they got to £983, but a rough calculation using figures extracted from the balance sheet elements that were published in the press, shows that this sounds about right. More than 149,000 people had watched home matches and without the Boer War this would have almost certainly been higher. In addition, tramlines had yet to be laid in Goldsmith Avenue to help fans get to the games. The club had 300 shareholders investing nearly £6,800, two stands had been built and the main one extended while two bicycle enclosures had been added near the main entrance. The only words of caution financially were that they had made a loss for the second year running and that the club had spent most of the money raised through shares on the ground, so the directors would need to be mindful about further expenditure. The paper added that smaller than expected attendances could be blamed on the fact that the garrison of the regular men was "depleted and the reserve regiments called up did not take much interest in football". The army increased in size by over 25% at this period - from 416,000 to 539,000 regulars and Britain mobilised unprecedented numbers of troops including reserves and volunteers. Many Royal Naval and merchant fleet volunteers kept the ships moving, but they were focused on war and often overseas rather than being garrisoned in Portsmouth.

The cashbook shows us every transaction for that first season and the resultant loss of £875. This is made up of gate receipts which totalled £5,948 gross, £4,596 net after payments to other clubs for their share of gate revenue, such as at cup ties, costs of £5,368 including the payments outlined below, interest on the mortgage of £135 and a few items of income such as advertising £32 and the sale of refreshment rights of £46. Gross gate receipts per game were anything from £4 - when the reserves played Southsea Rovers - to a more typical £200 for the bigger games like Reading and Tottenham, right up to £406 when the first team played Southampton in April 1900. Receipts peaked at £526 for the English Cup tie against Blackburn Rovers in January. Income was running at roughly £600 per month in the playing season, with costs running at anywhere between £400 and £800 per month. Money had been spent on the following:

Wages & Bonuses	£4,033
Hotel & Travelling	£72
Advertising	£80
Secretary's salary	£98
Kit, boots, footballs	£50
League Subs	£21

The first entry in the cashbook under "Gate Receipts" is for the reserves game versus United Services when £29 16s 9d was collected through the new turnstiles. When Southampton visited four days later the receipts were considerably higher at £121 11s 9d. When Reading came to town for the first home league game, receipts more than doubled to £252 10s 9d. The admission price to sit within the new Grand Stand was one shilling and sixpence - sixpence to enter the ground, sixpence to enter the enclosure on the South side and sixpence to sit in the "Grand" or South Stand. The normal fee to enter the ground and stand on one of the banks was sixpence or the equivalent today of just £3.25 to stand. As an aside, a couple of years later in December 1901 a letter to the **Evening News** complained about the admission prices increasing for the English Cup game against Small Heath. The fan wailed: "I normally pay one shilling and sixpence for my south stand seat. Next Saturday it is sixpence to enter, 18 pence in the enclosure (treble the usual) and two shillings for the Stand (four times the usual)." Supporters complaining about big match price hikes is nothing new, it seems. Anyhow, in September 1899 the directors would have been pleased to see the cash starting to roll in at last. In fairness, the admission prices compare well to others. AJ Arnold (1988) states that "for all clubs between 1890 and World War One the minimum admission fee was sixpence for men and threepence for ladies and boys with clubs charging at least an extra sixpence for entrance to the stands."

It was common practice among football clubs in the late 19th century to hold an Annual General Meeting of all the shareholders, quickly after the season finished in June or July and Portsmouth were no different. Details, including the profit and loss account and balance sheet for the previous year to April 30, were sent out roughly a week in advance of a scheduled AGM and then reported on in some depth in the local newspapers. The AGM concentrated on nodding through the accounts without too much discussion or challenge as those in authority seemingly weren't questioned too much in those days, but the reviewing of the playing season and the progress of the club overall was covered in some depth by the chairman John Brickwood. Then followed a question-and-answer session. In fact, Pompey had two AGMs in 1899/1900. The first was on December 7 covering the first full financial year to April 30, 1899, but with no balance sheet or accounts. To be fair to Brickwood, the requirement to publish an annual balance sheet to shareholders might have been a good thing to do but was only made law in 1900 and even then, there wasn't a template of how to do it' even if Francis B Palmer (1901) explained the Companies Act (1900) and its consequences in some detail in his book of the same name. It was only in 1907 that the act was amended, introducing the requirement to produce and file accounts at Companies House. The requirement for separate profit and loss and balance sheets didn't come in until after the first world war. In consequence, not putting accounts in front of shareholders for the financial year to April 30, 1899, wasn't the sin that it would be today. Then the second AGM, held at the Albert Hall, Southsea, after the season ended, was for the second full financial year to April 1900.

In the papers sent out to shareholders before the AGM were the balance sheet and the profit and loss account. Unfortunately, no copies seem to exist anymore, but the 1901 accounts, which do exist, provide many of the figures for 1900. Besides, the press always commented in full. On July 10, 1900, ahead of the meeting on July 18, the **Evening News** reported:

Portsmouth Football Club Loses Over £800 On Its First Year's Workings

The first annual balance sheet of the Portsmouth Football & Athletic Company Limited has just been placed into the hands of the shareholders, and it reveals the fact that had it not been for the directors being caught napping when they agreed to pool gates with Southampton and Tottenham there would have been a profit on the year's working. As it is, however, there is a larger balance than was expected on the wrong side of the ledger.

The nominal capital of the company upon starting was £8,000, divided into shares at £1 each. £6,779 was taken up, and a loan of £4,000 was obtained as a first mortgage on the freehold land at Fratton Park. The total capital of the company amounted to £11,732 13s 10d. On the opposite side of the account it is shown that the fine pitch known as Fratton Park, said to be the best ground in the Southern League, cost the company to purchase £6,533 11s 3d, the erection of the stands and buildings, turnstiles, heating apparatus, bathrooms, dressing rooms, et cetera, cost £9,372 10s 1d. Clothing, boots, and players' requisites ran away with £50 and after deducting various other expenses, a net loss on the working to date amounting to £875 0s 5d was shown. This will be a surprise to the majority of the shareholders, but when the effects of the war upon the dates and other things are considered, it is not so bad as it might have been.

Turning to the first item of the profit and loss account, the wages and bonuses paid to the team last season are shown to have amounted to no less than £4,033 6s 3s. Hotel expenses and the travelling expenses of the first team cost £440 15s 4d, and those of the second team £60. Special training absorbed £211 2s 6d. For sundries, £54 4s 3d is allowed, bringing the total cost of the teams up to £4810 8s 3d, which is exclusive of £142 15s 9d for wages, retaining bonuses, and agents' fees prior to the commencement of the financial year. Other expenses bring the total under this head to £5,413 11s 9d. Gate receipts from September 2 to April 28 amounted to £5,940 17s 7d, but from this satisfactory total has to be deducted the sum of £1,344 0s 1d, paid under the pooling arrangement previously referred to. Letting refreshment rights, rent of advertising spaces, et cetera, brought in £73 and 10s and this with three guineas interest from bank, brings the total receipts to £4,873 18s. A schedule of the preliminary expenses of the company shows an aggregate of £411 3s 6d.

This report does make it look like the building costs were nearly £16,000 but it has double-counted and the grand total in the audited accounts was £9,372, for both land and building. In today's money, that would be the equivalent of about £1.5m. The **Portsmouth Times** on July 21 reported Brickwood's regret at an "adverse balance" but that "shareholders had reason to be satisfied with the season's work, especially with the performance of the team. Good men had to be got, and, they being an unknown quantity, had to pay large sums in the way of bonuses, while as far as possible the pooling of the gates would not be done again. Next season the wages would be less, and special training would not be indulged in again." As already noted the club didn't pay large signing on bonuses and the wages were not any less in following years. It isn't believed that any items were missed from the cashbook as it is extremely detailed and these were Victorians, precise about recording every item properly, so perhaps it was just an excuse. Nevertheless the Times reported: "In conclusion he [Brickwood] said that the directors were fairly confident the next year they would be able to report a substantial balance. (Applause)." At least the club didn't have to pay transfer fees to get players or the loss would have been far higher. Besides, things were actually not as bad as they initially seemed. The auditor, E Edmonds, of Edmonds, Son & Clover, chipped in announcing that "a mistake being made in the accounts and the adverse balance was really only £699 16 shillings and threepence." Incidentally, an Edmonds played for Portsmouth AFC in the mid-1890s and is referred to in the match report on page 11, but it is not certain this is the same person. The report was adopted by the meeting and the board duly re-elected. Richard Bonney was nominated and voted in to replace the departing Windrum. Intriguingly, Brettell at the AGM hinted at a realignment of English football, that Pompey would have been part of referring to "the probable formation in the future of the National League, which they had been asked to join when the time was ripe." That time would be 20 years hence...

Finally the club's first retained list was also announced: "The men signed on for the coming season are: – Reilly (goal), Wilkie, Turner, Blyth, Stringfellow, Hunter, Cleghorn, and Digweed, Marshall, Lewis, Bedingfield, Smith, Clark, Joyce, and Goss, the latter comes from Notts County, with whom he made a big name for himself last season." As soon as the AGM ended, the press not only reported but commented. The consensus was that the directors had done a great job and took them at their word about future cost-cutting. The **Portsmouth Times** put it:

> The coming season is looked forward to with the utmost confidence. Although a deficit exists ... there is no reason why this should not be wiped off, and if it is possible, the shareholders can feel assured that Mr Brickwood and his fellow directors will do it. In many ways the expenses will be cut down, and, as Mr Brickwood pointed out, Fratton Park is an increasingly valuable asset, for it is situated in a growing district, which will at no very distant day be covered with houses, and, if the corporation fulfil their promise of lying down tramlines through Goldsmith Avenue, it will be a great convenience to supporters of the club ... A saving will be affected by doing away with special training, a course which will meet, we think, with general approval, and expenditure in inducing players to sign the forms has been nothing like so great, for men naturally hesitate in making agreements with an unknown club ... Summer pay must be cut down, for it is an encumbrance that few clubs can bear. The sooner something is done in the matter the better, for what with the war and other causes, many clubs – the majority, it might almost be said – are up to their ears in debt and cannot afford to pay the ruinous rate of wage that is now involved. The Portsmouth Club, happily, is better off than most of its neighbours, and the prospects of success are very bright.

There had also been mention at the AGM of a proposed informal tie-up with Clapton FC for the following season, which came to pass. Clapton were one of the original founders of the Southern League in 1894 and provided the first chairman of the league, Robert Clark. The club were one of the few amateur teams in the league and of course they struggled, resigning at the end of the 1895/96 season. They were the first English team to play on the continent in 1890 and founder members of the London League in 1896 and the Isthmian league in 1905. They should not to be confused with Clapton Orient, out of which Leyton Orient were formed. All in all, it had been a cracking start for professional football in Portsmouth. Brettell's astute team selection was certainly justified, and he proudly wrote in the club's official handbook in 1900: "Nothing in the history of football can compare with the phenomenal rise and extraordinary performances of the Portsmouth club." The **Evening News** added: "Despite the fact that the financial results have turned out indifferently the shareholders have every reason to be proud of the season's working." And the Directors had done what they promised. They had shown ambition by encouraging the best players and building the best ground possible at the time. A whole new ground had been built in double-quick time, funds had been attracted, the company registered, one of the country's best managers appointed, who had built a great team. By 1902, they would be champions. All credit is due to the founders. The period of roughly seven or eight years that had now just begun should be looked back on as a golden age for south coast football. Both Pompey and Saints were regarded as being amongst the country's elite clubs, fighting for and winning honours. The founder of The Football League, William McGregor, quoted in *Association Football & the Men Who Made It* by Alfred Gibson and William Pickford (1906) went so far as to say that as his competition lacked the likes of Portsmouth, Southampton or Tottenham then it couldn't be "said to be truly representative of the elite in the country" adding for good measure "Hampshire can claim to have been stronger at football in this period than the capital". Football had arrived in Portsmouth. Modern Pompey had been made.

THE MAKING OF MODERN POMPEY: KEY DATES

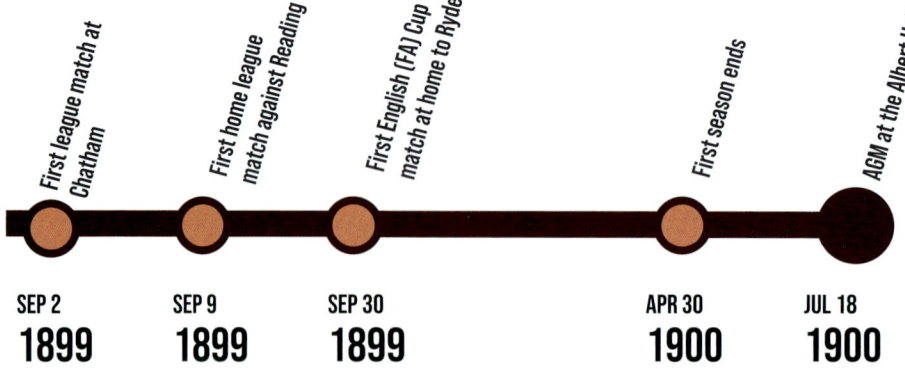

SECTION TWO
THE MEN WHO MADE IT

I - THE MOVERS
George Lewin Oliver, William Wigginton & Bernard Murtough

With any major undertaking, a core requirement is people to not only have the vision, but also bring the drive and determination to see a project through. The three men featured in this section had all those qualities and more. George Lewin Oliver ran a successful school, while William Wigginton was both a sportsman and engineer. They were friends with Bernard Murtough, who defied prejudice against the Irish, to become a major figure in Portsmouth politics. Without them, modern Pompey would almost certainly not have taken the form that it did and a professional club in Portsmouth may well have ended up a completely different beast to the one we know today.

GEORGE LEWIN OLIVER: OF SCHOOLING AND THE CHURCH
Invariably described as a "schoolmaster", Lewin Oliver has a fascinating back story and how he came to become involved in the running of a professional football club has largely been overlooked, but there are some clear dots which can be joined up which meant the man who would become known as the "father of the Club" ended up at Fratton Park. Born in 1854 in Portsmouth, his father was Thomas Oliver, originally from Cambridgeshire, who was recorded later in the census as a "Millwright" in the Dockyard. In the 1871 census George lived in the town with his father, mother Eliza, sisters Cecilia, Eliza, Mary and Rose. A previous census also records a brother, Arthur. George was married to Elizabeth Ann Hamlin in Bromley, Hertfordshire on Christmas Day in 1876. Elizabeth was 25 years old and also born in Portsmouth. The couple had found themselves in Herts as he was visiting schools to learn the trade. In the 1881 census he was recorded as a "schoolmaster, private" and it clearly ran in the family as his sister, Cecilia, was recorded in the 1871 census as a pupil teacher and she later ran her own school "Beach Road Middle Class School" as 'Principal First Class'. George and Elizabeth had five children but Lilian and Lewin, the first and the third, died after a few months. Their second son Herbert (1881-1914) became a schoolmaster and worked at his father's school. Lewin Oliver was known as "Skipper' to his pupils and every year the students gave him a birthday gift, which was reported in the press. For example, the **Evening News** in 1891 reported an "interesting presentation took place" on Oliver's birthday. The gift "took the form of a travelling and dressing bag."

Lewin Oliver acquired his interest in education having been an assistant at a school run by a Mr Barber in Lake Road. After his tour of the country learning about how schools were run he returned to Portsmouth in 1876 and set up his own school, according to the **Hampshire** magazine in a retrospective of his life published in 1957, above a saddler's shop in Lake Road. It was called "Olivers Academy". In 1878 it was reported in the **Hampshire Telegraph** that the school suffered a bad fire and whilst depressed about the knock back, Lewin Oliver got it up and running again by 1879 at 384 Commercial Road. Two years later the school had moved to 406 on the same street. It was listed in directories as a "Gentlemen's School" in 1887 and, being so successful, would have attracted a large number of fee-paying pupils, often coming large distances to attend. One advert, and it wasn't the only one, in the **Evening News** was asking for accommodation for a school pupil from Leith in Scotland.

It was clear that he was respected for his school's success. An advert in the **Hampshire Telegraph** in January 1898 cited 106 successes in one "competition", for the Naval and Civil Service Exams. Lewin Oliver's pupils had successes in various topics, including the 'South Ken' system as explained in the **Evening News** in July 1891. The system referred to was a syllabus for the teaching of art across the country. By the 1880s courses were governed by the South Kensington School in London until it became the Royal College of Art. This fits well with the 1871 census which records that young Lewin Oliver was an "artist/school teacher". He also had great success in delivering Civil Service, Dockyard and engineering exam results, a report on May 26 1893 in the **Evening News** saying that "Mr. Oliver's pupils have again obtained nearly one third of the vacancies available for engineering students across the country". Mile End House School was considered one of the best and most respectable schools in the town according to William Durman (1942) in *Portsmouth Education*.

There is no record of Lewin Oliver's hobbies, studies and qualifications nor is there a record of him receiving a degree, unlike others such as Bone, but there would have been very little governance of private schools at this time and degrees were often only for those with private means. However, he was clearly keen on sport. His obituary in the **Evening News** in 1934 calls him a "great sportsman" but there is very little record of him playing to a high standard himself. The only direct record that can be found is a reference to him running the All Saints' cricket team in their parish magazine and, of course, his school sports teams feature prominently in the press.

While clearly one of the leading founders of Portsmouth FC, Christianity was also important to him. Unfortunately, in 1897 he had a falling out with church authorities in the town and often appeared in the press complaining about what he saw as the decline of the church. The **Evening News** of April 23, 1897 talks of him saying that there was "no church in Portsmouth where matters were so strained". According to him "things" had been introduced into the service which had upset people and the congregation had got smaller and smaller. The post of churchwarden had also been devalued by the new vicar and Oliver would have had a big interest in that, having been one for many years. This probably goes some way to explain why, in January 1934, just after he died, apart from the line under "deaths" simply recording his name and the date there is no mention of his service to the church in their parish magazine. What is clear is that when he knew that he was going to be busy with the new football club, he stated that he didn't want to be church warden anymore or take on extra duties. This was reported in the **Southern Daily Mail** on April 14, 1898, presumably clearing the way to concentrate on Pompey. Incidentally, one of his acquaintances was a Dr Watson, also a close confidant of Arthur Conan Doyle, and the man whose name Doyle took to use in his writings on Sherlock Holmes. Both Watson and Lewin Oliver have numerous mentions in the All Saints Parish magazines of the 1880s and early 1890s for their good works of all kinds.

It is also known that Lewin Oliver was a freemason and the record exists of his regular attendance at the Carnarvon Lodge in Havant. He was initiated into freemasonry in January 1891, strangely choosing to join a lodge in Havant when regular attendance was required and travel was not that easy. There were at least 16 other active lodges on Portsea Island according to the History of Portsmouth website. Lewin Oliver was one of the key financiers of the group alongside Brickwood and Wyatt Peters. He was a man who loved his sport, was a great administrator and someone who excelled in the world of academia. Keeping the finances on the straight and narrow would have been a priority for him. Percy Whitney said in 1906 that Lewin Oliver always worried about the finances and the club ledgers that exist from this period have all pages signed off by Lewin Oliver personally as the director responsible for finances.

In summary, George Lewin Oliver was well-known in the city, believing passionately in the promotion of sport. He had money and was a good administrator with connections. He was the perfect person required to get the club going and he would have a key role down the line in ensuring it survived when the financial train hit the buffers in 1912. Not many photos of him exist and he hardly ever stood in the team photos when many of the other officials and directors did. This may have been through diffidence or more likely because he considered himself more of an administrator than someone involved in the playing side. Whatever. Pompey fans should be thankful he came on board.

WILLIAM WIGGINTON: THE SPORTING ENGINEER
Born in April 1843 in Great Marlow, Buckinghamshire, Wigginton's father, also a William - a practice very common in those days - was listed at that time in the census as a coal merchant and timber dealer in Worminghall. His father would be declared bankrupt in 1859. His mother was Mary Ann (nee Lee) and he had one brother Edward and three sisters Jane, Emma and Mary Ann. William Jnr was married in Portland, Dorset to Emma Adams, in March 1871. Emma was from Portsmouth and travelled by train and carriage to Portland for the wedding. This might explain why the family ultimately settled in Portsmouth but at the time they were married in Portland as he was stationed at one of the army barracks nearby. The couple had eight children. Two of the sons, William – should he be called Jnr Jnr? - (1872-1903) and Robert (1878-1927) both helped him with his business, Wigginton & Sons. Of the other children, Edward (1876-1937) was later listed as a grocer in Albert Road, Southsea. William and Edward and another sibling, Percy (1874-1966) were all born on the Isle of Grain in Kent when the family lived there. Robert was born on the Isle of Wight along with Effie - who died at age of two - and Frank (1884-1961) who, as we will see, was

a great sportsman like his brother Robert and his father. There are also sons Sydney and Rodney both born in 1883 on the Isle of Wight, possibly twins. The elder son William, who died young in 1903, was probably the Wigginton referred to in the **Southern Daily Mail** when they announced that the Southsea Rovers' centre-half, was to leave England, after being ordered to live abroad for the sake of his health. He was almost certainly suffering from tuberculosis. The On The Ball column reported: "It's a serious matter for Southsea Rovers as Wigginton is by far the best half; indeed, it may be doubted if he has a superior in centre in the Portsmouth district."

Our Wigginton's skillset, which he would bring to Portsmouth FC, had been forged in the military. In the 1861 census he is recorded as being a "sapper, Royal Engineers" and in the 1871 census he was a "sergeant lodging in Chatham" which like Portsmouth, was in those days a naval dockyard. He ended his military career as a Sergeant Major in the Corps of Royal Engineers, serving in India with a distinction, although for what is not recorded in the army records. He also served in North America and in Bermuda. He had enlisted in 1860 and was discharged in September 1884 at the age of 42. In the censuses of 1881 and 1891 he was recorded as living in Brading, Isle of Wight formerly as a "military foreman of works Royal Engineers department (soldier)" and in 1891 as "contracts man for Royal Engineers". By 1901 he was simply listed as a "building contractor" in Portsmouth living at London Road, Landport and was, at one stage, neighbours with Arthur Cogswell, one of Brickwood's two retained architects.

The database of Portsmouth people and history, maintained by Stephen Pomeroy, has records of builders and other trades and lists any of their works that were published in newspapers and other sources. Wigginton is recorded as having been responsible for building at least one house in Frogmore Road, two houses in Twyford Avenue, near Walden Road, a window bay for a house in Kingston Avenue near Kingston Cross and a shed for 8 Stubbington Avenue. He was hardly a prolific builder, as houses sprang up all over the north and east of the town. However, town council planning meetings and War Department records show him undertaking much bigger works, with a number of dockyard building contracts.

As well as his engineering and construction prowess, what is also clear is that he was a great sportsman. As "Sergeant Wigginton" he was recorded in the **Portsmouth Times** in 1875 and 1876 as playing cricket for the Royal Marines first XI so was clearly no slouch in that sport. The **Hampshire Telegraph** recorded in 1895 that he was still playing cricket reporting that he won a silver medal in a match along with son Robert. More pertinent to our story is the fact Wigginton was also heavily involved with Southsea Rovers, a club formed in 1889 according to Hampshire FA records. He was at Rovers for at least three years to 1898 when the **Southern Daily Mail** reported in August that "the annual meeting in connection with the Southsea Rovers was held last night at the Speedwell Hotel under the presidency of Mr W Wigginton. His son, Bob, was elected as captain of their first XI." However, Wigginton's obituary in 1918 goes further, stating he founded Rovers, so his tenure seems to be more than three years. He did a good job. Rovers were quoted in the papers in 1897 "as having proved themselves at this time to be second only to the RA in local footer." The **Southern Daily Mail** in September 1897 called Rovers, "Pa Wigginton's little lot". He was recorded in the same paper as being at all Portsmouth FA meetings in 1897. At one, it reported in December, there was a referee's report discussed, which complained about Southsea Rovers' conduct. Wigginton stated that he felt that the official had "overdone the matter". Rovers' secretary Wells was also present and said "the disturbance was not sufficient to justify a referee's report." How unlike a club to defend itself. A couple of years earlier, Rovers were recorded in the **Southern Daily Mail** as wanting their own ground as having one was important if a club wanted to bring in the revenue needed to sustain a sporting business. Of course, they never found one but, what is clear, is that Wigginton had a desire to take them forward and was skilled in running a football club. He was also a leader, so it was an obvious next step to get involved with the formation of the proposed professional club. When one of the papers said that the new Portsmouth club would be run with men with experience of doing so, they clearly meant the likes of Wigginton, with his connections to the Portsmouth FA. Wigginton was also a good cricketer – receiving a silver medal from the Portsmouth Cricket Association in December 1895 and was recorded as playing against Arthur Conan Doyle's Southsea team on various occasions.

As well as being president and chairman of Southsea Rovers, Wigginton clearly also moved in the higher football circles of the town. In 1894 he was asked by the Portsmouth FA to select a representative team. Wigginton's son Robert played to a good standard, and is recorded as playing as a back for Southsea Rovers against RMA in 1896 and also being included as a 'back' for a PFA representative side in April 1897. That team was made up of a few servicemen, but mostly players from Southsea Rovers and the Portsmouth Grammar School side, proof that the Rovers were one of the better teams in the town then. In March 1895 there is also a report of the Southsea Rovers game with brothers Bob and William both playing in the same team watched presumably by their proud father, and the fraternal pair won the Portsmouth FA Junior Cup in 1897 playing together. In 1898 Frank also played for the Mile End House School football first XI and there were numerous reports of Southsea Rovers playing that school first XI. The **Evening News** records one such example in September 1894 so it seems inconceivable that Wigginton and Lewin Oliver would not have met regularly both before and during Frank's attendance at the school.

As a man who had much experience of running a substantial local football team, Wigginton would have been the perfect consultant and, quite possibly, supplier of materials for building the ground. He was a wealthy individual and had a profile in Portsmouth. In those early days, of course, directors didn't get paid, so needed to have private means. With Lewin Oliver one of the main movers and shakers in the setting up of the new club, his connection with Wigginton made him an obvious person to add to the project. What is clear is that "Pa" Wigginton had the desire and the means and the skills to run a professional football club and clearly wanted professional football in Portsmouth. He was an ideal addition to the board.

BERNARD MURTOUGH: THE POLITICAL ANIMAL

Murtough was born in 1836 in Armagh, in what is now Northern Ireland. It is not clear exactly when he came to settle in Portsea. It could be that he decided to stay here at the end of his service in the army or returned here due to the potato famines of the time in Ireland. The timing fits. In his wife's obituary it says she came here 50 years before her death in 1926, so around 1876, which is when a famine was taking place. They started in around 1845 with the last one recorded in 1879. A potato disease was at the root of the issue, but matters were not helped by the British Government's unsympathetic economic policies, absentee landlords and single-crop dependence. Millions of people left Ireland in this period. The Murtoughs were staunch Catholics and had an "extremely large family" according to the News in December 1960. He became a JP and was the first Catholic councillor on the Portsmouth Borough Council. He was also elected to, and then served on for many years, the Portsmouth School Board alongside Bone who was their architect. In those days, Catholic schools had their own representative.

The **Hampshire Telegraph** of December 28, 1889 stated that Bernard was one of those businessmen that "were starting to do rather well" and that he was "rapidly coming to the front in public life". Murtough was elected as a Liberal councillor to the town council in 1891. The **Evening News** of January 17 reported: "Mr Murtough won a good victory yesterday in St George's Ward. We cordially congratulate the electors on their choice. Prejudice dies hard in England, especially those which have reference to nationality and religion". In the same edition, Murtough placed an advert thanking the voters for electing him.

He became a leading Liberal in the district and in December 1883 there was a "Great Liberal Demonstration At Southsea" reported in the **Evening News**. They sang "stirring Liberal songs" with the meeting led by Alderman J Baker, JP, president of the Liberal Association. Murtough was described as being prominently in the front row. John Pares, the father of the Pares brothers who started Portsmouth Sunflowers and were renowned in Portsmouth football, was sat next to him. In 1890 he was recorded as a vice-president of the Portsmouth Liberal movement at their annual meeting on March 6. Bernard was not only there, but he also made an impassioned speech in favour of Irish home rule, although in the early days at least he was keen on Ireland remaining within a United Kingdom with Great Britain. In those days Ireland was part of the UK with representation at Westminster and the country made up 30% of the population and supplied 42% of the soldiers in the British army. There was much angst from Murtough, described as the leader of the Irish community in the district, and directed at the British government for not helping solve the continual crisis of famine in Ireland. He had been chairing this group since at least 1886 as the **Evening News** in November 1886 advertised a meeting of the group with him in the chair, and with a Mr. Sweeney delivering a lecture on "Ireland, as it was, as it is and as it should be". His twin passions of Liberalism and Home Rule did fit together. The Liberal party supported the idea of home rule within a United Kingdom and it was the Liberal government of William Ewart Gladstone which introduced the first Home Rule Bill in 1886, which was defeated in the House of Commons only after a split in the Liberal Party.

Apart from politics, Murtough had profile in the business community through the Chamber of Commerce, working alongside Brickwood, often with Wyatt Peters involved as well, from 1894 onwards. In the directories of the time, Murtough was listed as a "mineral water manufacturer" at 11 St Georges Square. In 1886 the business moved to 42-46 St Georges Square as it expanded and the business also acquired 19-20 Kent Street in the late 1880s. Murtough was the President of the Portsmouth Mineral Water Association. It was big business in those days and, according to the **Evening News** in 1893, had set up the first collection and recycling scheme across the district for the carbonated drinks bottles, which used the pressure from the gas to push a marble to seal the opening. As well as through membership of the Chamber of Commerce, he also knew Brickwood and Wyatt Peters from Licensed Victuallers' association meetings and of course the ever-present freemasonry connection. Murtough was in the Phoenix Lodge along with Brickwood. Murtough liked sport, although there is little mention of him as a participant, but he is mentioned a few times in meetings of cycling clubs. For example, he was a judge for the cycling events at the North End Rec at the opening of the new pavilion in May 1893 and he was also recorded as being president of Cosham Bowling Club. In terms of his involvement with Portsmouth FC, he clearly had money and was well-connected, notably with Brickwood and Wyatt Peters. He was a councillor, helping run the Roads & Works (Streets) Sub-committee which adjudicated planning applications. He also took shares in the company early on.

The original formation minute that hangs to this day in the South Stand records for posterity the five businessmen and one solicitor who set up the club, but there were several others who very much should be regarded as being part of the founding team. One such is Bernard Murtough. He organised, with George Lewin Oliver who he would have known well through his work with the School Board, one of the two initial meetings in the town in early 1898, to ascertain the desire for a professional club. He also knew Brickwood well. He didn't make that meeting at Pink's offices to inscribe his name for posterity and we can speculate why that might be, but the list of directors shows him on the board by 1899 and he was sat next to Brickwood at the club's first full AGM at the Albert Hall in December 1899, described by the papers as the first "proper" AGM because an earlier one didn't put any financial figures in front of the shareholders. He was recorded by the **Evening News** as the first to speak after Brickwood's opening remarks and the financial report had been adopted and seconded. He was also formally elected to the board at the end of the meeting, so he had clearly been heavily involved throughout the whole formation period, despite missing the formation meeting.

II - THE SHAKERS

John Wyatt Peters, John Brickwood & Alfred Bone

While our first three men who made Pompey were drumming up popular interest in a professional club, this was a project on a scale which would require the brightest and best Portsmouth could offer. Our next trio were at the beating heart of the town: the brewery industry. If the army marched on its stomach, the navy sailed the seven seas on beer and rum. Still, on the face of it, John Wyatt Peters forming an alliance with John Brickwood to create a professional football club seems unlikely. The pair were business rivals and while Wyatt Peters loved his sport, Brickwood was far from an enthusiast. However, as shall be demonstrated, this odd couple proved to be two of the core pillars which supported the new club, along with an architect who helped design it, Alfred Bone, who knew the former two well, professionally and socially.

JOHN WYATT PETERS: THE BACHELOR BREWER

Despite studying law, Wyatt Peters never practised and instead became chairman and managing director, of George Peters & Co, then one of the biggest wine importers in Portsmouth. Wyatt Peters was also a military man. In January 1890, the **London Gazette** recorded his promotion from lieutenant to captain in the 3rd Volunteer Battalion, Hampshire Regiment. Through this commission, Wyatt Peters would have come to know another founder, Alfred Bone, along with GE Kent, who was the man who lent the old Portsmouth AFC their first field to play on back in 1884. Kent's son also played in that team along with Wyatt Peters. At a regimental dinner in April 1886, Lt Peters sat next to both his captains, Kent and Bone, and at a shooting competition at Fort Cumberland in Eastney in 1896 he was reported to have donated some of the prizes.

Pomeroy's database shows that in 1857 the company was listed as 'Cigar Importers' in Queen Street. Built up by John's father George, in 1867 the company added "vinegar manufacturers" to its description and in the 1881 census George was a "wine merchant" of Kings Road, Southsea. He died in March 1887 with his funeral being reported in the **Hampshire Telegraph**. It was a large affair as he had been an alderman and "would have become Mayor if he hadn't been taken ill". There were 55 wreaths and many carriages to transport the mourners, attended by three of Pompey's founders: John, obviously, but also Bone and Pink. The business was inherited by George's two sons, and his brother George Henry, decided to sell his half of the business to John for £6,721 in August 1895. The contract listed 18 properties of which 11 were mortgaged, with those loans totalling £24,050, so it was a sizeable business. In 1889 Wyatt Peters was, like so many other up and coming people in the town, initiated into freemasonry, namely the United Brothers lodge.

One of a family of seven, born in 1864, Wyatt Peters was a good footballer, playing for Portsmouth AFC, alongside Conan Doyle, who was on his way to becoming a very successful doctor in Southsea. As we know, he called himself 'AC Smith' when playing soccer but used his real name when playing for Southsea Bowls Club or Portsmouth Cricket Club. The **Evening News** reported in January 1886 that "the full backs, particularly AC Smith, did what work devolved upon them so satisfactorily that the office of the Portsmouth goalkeeper was quite a sinecure [a position with no work]." In that game they beat Portsmouth Sunflowers 2-0 at North End with the half backs including a 'Peters' who was seen as a "useful acquisition for the club." It is almost certain that this is our Wyatt Peters. In newspaper reports he was often called 'J Peters' although sometimes they listed him as 'W Peters', and once as 'G Peters', after the name of the family firm. All three Peters played in the same position and this misidentification was a common mistake in newspaper reports of the day. Kevin Smith (2004) also records that 'Peters' played eight times that season and nine times the next, in addition to running the line when not playing. The **Evening News** in January 1886 reported: "AC Smith and his fellow full-back, J. Peters, were so safe in their dribbling and tackling they were never once passed so as to put the Portsmouth A.F.C. citadel in danger". Even when they lost a game later that season the paper commented that "consolations for the beaten home team were hard to find. AC Smith's heavy kicking was among them, along with Kindersley's distinguished display and hard work and hard kicking of the Reverend Norman Pares and Peters at full back." Peters and Doyle were both called out for special praise in winning 2-0 in the semi-final of the Portsmouth District Association Cup against Southampton team Freemantle: "The backs proved a difficult nut for Freemantle to crack, the flying kicks of Peters and the heavy punting of A.C. Smith were invaluable." Peters was also picked to play for Hampshire against Dorset in March 1887, but he never got to play as several of the players dropped out, including him. Wyatt Peters stopped playing for Portsmouth AFC at the end of the 1886/87 season, which fits with the timeline of the death of his father, meaning he may well have had to dedicate more time to run the family firm.

An original director, the company's prospectus named him as the man delegated by the board to negotiate the purchase with the Goldsmiths and subsequently, if somewhat clandestinely, take out a mortgage with them to pay for it. There are no records of him doing anything else for the club in those early years but, in fairness, the ground was a big project in itself. Despite their business rivalry, Wyatt Peters and John Brickwood knew one another well. They were great friends and reports place them together in many places such as Chamber of Commerce meetings. The rival breweries often tried to outbid the other. For example, when Brickwood's acquired Bransbury Hyde Park Brewery at auction it was up against George Peters & Co, but the tables were turned in 1884 when John's firm outbid Brickwood's for the Kingston Brewery. The two companies even came close to a merger in 1896 but talks broke down and Wyatt Peters ended up buying Shaft's Brewery for £17,000 instead.

There are no club minute books or records of that nature from 1898 until the end of Wyatt Peters' time with the club as a director in 1906, when he resigned to give full attention to his business, so we do not know exactly what role he undertook subsequently, but he was clearly a successful and well-respected businessman and his friendship with Brickwood and association with football in Portsmouth from its organisational infancy would have clearly lent credibility to the fledgling club. Wyatt Peters never married and at the time of setting up the club he lived in Lennox Road South, Southsea with his three servants and a butler.

JOHN BRICKWOOD: THE PUB MAGNATE

Born in Arundel Street, Portsmouth on June 23, 1852, Brickwood's father ran the Cobden Brewery in the town, but he died when John and his brother Arthur were both young. John went to Trafalgar House School Twyford near Winchester and eventually the business passed to the pair. They would quickly set about creating what would become one of the biggest businesses in the region. Brickwood's first marriage in January 1881 was to Eliza Miller, at St Mary of the Angels in Westbourne Grove, London. They had a daughter, Madeline, born the following year. Sadly, Eliza died in Lisbon in February 1889 after being taken ill at sea and having been "carried ashore to die". He re-married in September 1893 at St Mary's Church, East Molesey to Jessie Cooper in a "bright and hearty" service and received "numerous presents", according to the **West Middlesex Herald** which also records that the best man was John Wyatt Peters. The couple honeymooned in New York and San Francisco, sailing on the 'Paris' out of Southampton.

In 1896 John and Jessie moved to 'Brankesmere' on Queens Crescent in Southsea, which caused some excitement in the press due to the transportation and transplantation of a twenty-ton cedar tree, which was moved across Southsea on a trolley pulled by a traction engine. "The cost of moving will probably amount to £100" reports exclaimed. This house went up for sale in 2020, and **The News** reported how it had been updated, but one could still imagine what a fabulous abode it would have been in the late 1800s, complete with the Brickwood's public house-style turrets. The couple had two sons: Arthur, born in November 1896 and Rupert in February 1900. By the time of the birth of Rupert, Brickwood had already become the club's first chairman. He clearly had energy to burn. In addition to his family and business he pursued interests such as literature, archaeology, astronomy, architecture and Egyptology. He loved talking in detail with either Arthur Bone or Arthur Cogswell about the plans for the next pub and would have relished the challenge of building Fratton Park.

Brewing became a major activity in Portsmouth from the 1700s, not least because of the substantial dockyard and army garrison. Many houses turned their front parlours into a bar to accommodate visiting sailors and billeted soldiers. Portsmouth was the leading naval port in the British Empire, and according to Paul Brown (2018) in *The Portsmouth Dockyard Story* by 1813 it was "the world's largest industrial complex". Members of the Brickwood family had been brewing in Southwark and Whitefriars in London from the late 16th century, but latterly, it was a Fanny Brickwood who bought the Cobden Brewery

II - The Shakers

in 1851, which was based in Arundel Street in the building originally designed to be the toll house for the London to Arundel canal, which used the route we now know as Goldsmith Avenue. On her death in 1854 it passed to her son Harry, later Sir Harry, and on his death in December 1862, at just 34 years old, it passed to his two sons John and Arthur. The business was put into the hands of trustees - Messrs Nash and White - pending the brothers' respective 21st birthdays. Between 1862 and 1874 the trustees acquired at least three more breweries. In 1874 John inherited his half after an apprenticeship at the Mitcham Brewery and was joined by Arthur in 1875. The business plan was to grow by acquisition. The Hyde Park Brewery (1881) and the Portsmouth Brewery (1887), the oldest in the town, fell under its control, then in 1898 the Saint Catherine's Brewery, with 72 licensed premises, was bought for £265,000 – a multi-million deal by today's standards. The by-now Sir Arthur had died in 1894, but John – he would have to wait ten more years to get the same honour – was continuing the good work. By the time Brickwood's was sold to Whitbread in 1971, there were 675 pubs in the chain, many built by Bone or Cogswell in the highly recognisable mock-Tudor style which is Fratton Park's trademark to this day. The Brickwood's brewery in Admiralty Road – now demolished – was also rather grand, and the business was moving into it at around the time of Pompey's formation so all credit to Brickwood for taking on both projects simultaneously.

Brickwood's influence in the Portsmouth area in the 1890s was huge and his name alone would have opened many doors for the new club. He was variously leader of the national Country Brewers Society, chair of the Port of Portsmouth Chamber of Commerce and chair of the National Trade Defence Association. He was also an active freemason and would have known most of the other founders through this connection. He was a senior freemason through the Phoenix Lodge, which he attended alongside Pink. He had initiated Conan Doyle into the same lodge and would have been at meetings along with him and Conan Doyle's long time secretary Major Alfred Herbert Wood. Wood played football for Portsmouth AFC, was the secretary and sometime auditor of the Portsmouth and the Hampshire FAs, and also in the Duke of Connaught Lodge with Bone and Pink.

As one of the most prominent businessmen in the town, the other founders would have valued his leadership and Brickwood would have been an obvious choice as chairman. Yet, extraordinarily, his interest in football was apparently negligible. The **Football Mail** on September 2, 1899 - the reporter obviously knew Brickwood well - said as much: "John Brickwood tells us that he has never seen an Association football match in his life. He doesn't know anything about football, he says, and whilst he has good friends who do know the game well apparently, the interest he takes in the club is a purely business one. This is perhaps as well, for he is a giant among business men, and his presence on the directorate will be a guarantee that the club is run on business lines. He has however surrounded himself with men who do know the game well."

Despite his reported ambivalence towards football, it is inconceivable that Brickwood would not have recognised the commercial possibilities of the game for his business. Several brewers had already become involved in football, using the game to market what they produced. The book, *The Rise of Fan Ownership* by

Jim Keoghan (2014) gave the example of "Manchester City [who] became known as the "brewers' club" because so many early benefactors, such as local beer magnate Stephen Chester Thompson, were involved in the trade". And after all, very few places had as many pubs as Portsmouth...

One of the aforementioned men who 'know the game well' was undoubtedly Wyatt Peters, but Brickwood moved in other soccer circles in the town. He knew Conan Doyle, not only initiating him into masonry but attending many meetings of the Portsmouth Literary & Scientific Society of which Conan Doyle was secretary. According to Geoffrey Stavert (1987), in his book *A **Study of Southsea***, Brickwood and Cogswell also attended the farewell dinner that was held for Conan Doyle attended by many of Doyle's sporting chums from the worlds of soccer, rugby, bowls and cricket in December 1890. At this were also other football "greats" from the town including Lancelot Pares from Portsmouth plus Wood and William E Grant the secretary of Portsmouth AFC in 1888.

ALFRED BONE: ARCHITECT EXTRAORDINAIRE

Born in 1846 in Portsea, Alfred's parents were John - in the census a retired "retail brewer" - and Sarah, a housewife. He married Eliza Bell in 1873 in Portsea and in the 1891 census is recorded as living with her at Hanover Street along with daughter, Frances, and a son Alfred Jnr. In 1901 the family moved to a much bigger house at Clarendon Road, presumably on the back of his successful practice and his profile as director of Portsmouth FC.

When the club was formed in 1898, he was living at 148 High Street, just down the road from Pink's offices. He already had a successful career as an architect, engineer and surveyor, designing several of Brickwood's pubs, competing for the business with Arthur Cogswell. Whilst it looks like Cogswell designed and managed the build – architects tended to do both in those days - for the majority of Brickwood's pubs, some of the best examples of Bone's work that stand today are The Nell Gwynne and The Fawcett Inn. They were both designed by Bone using the Brickwood mock-Tudor house style of the time. Bone was extremely busy for Brickwood in 1898. A search of the planning committee minutes shows the many times he submitted letters or plans for Brickwood.

He was a member of the town council and went on to hold the prestigious position of the 'permanent architect' to the Portsmouth School Board and would have been involved in the building of any school in the town. He almost certainly came to know Lewin Oliver well. He also designed most of the wards at the Portsea Workhouse – with its 1,612 inmates in 1897 - at the time when Conan Doyle was chief medical officer of that institution. To be appointed to a lead role such as architect to the workhouse was an honour as they were big businesses in those days providing poorer and disadvantaged people with accommodation in return for work. Bone was clearly a man at the top of his game. He was also a military man and freemason, initiated into the Duke of Connaught Lodge Portsea in September 1879. It was not unusual at that time either for professional men to join a volunteer battalion and wait for the call to go overseas or undertake a posting in Britain. Alfred joined the 3rd Duke of Connaught's Own Volunteer Battalion as major in July 1898 and there is a record of him serving in this battalion alongside Pink in August 1900. His obituary in the **Hampshire Telegraph** in December 1919 also puts him in the same regiment as Wyatt Peters. Bone's military records show him as a major during the Boer War, serving in the Portsmouth Garrison "due to the dearth of officers." The volume of his submissions to the council for planning certainly reduce, probably due to his military duties and perhaps explaining why Brickwood went with Cogswell to design The Pompey public house in 1901. He ended his army career as a colonel.

Although it can't be confirmed, Alfred was very probably a sportsman. A 'Bone' was playing bowls and rowing for Southsea Rowing Club and importantly, played for the very first Portsmouth Football Club in 1875, the original team which only lasted a year. Census records indicate it wasn't a very common surname, so there's a strong chance it is the same man. Bone took the lead for the new company in the planning and design of Fratton Park, as he was the director who on August 29, 1898, submitted his plans to the town council. A man who made Pompey in more ways than one.

Percy Whitmey

PHS Archive

John Pink

Courtesy Portsmouth Museums

George Preston

PHS Archive

Bernard Murtough

PHS Archive

The Men Who Made It

George Lewin Oliver

PHS Archive

John Brickwood

PHS Archive / Colourised by Ed Emptage

William Wigginton

PHS Archive

Frederick Windrum

PHS Archive

Richard Bonney

PHS Archive

Frank Brettell

PHS Archive

III - THE ADMINISTRATORS

John Pink, George Preston, Percy Whitmey & Alfred Jelks

If Wigginton, Lewin Oliver and Murtough were the prime movers of the project it was Wyatt Peters, Brickwood and Bone who were using their good offices to encourage the participation of Portsmouth people with the skills required to make a professional club function. It is not a surprise they turned to men who they knew and could trust to do a good job, which brings us to the legal and administrative framework for the new club to thrive. John Pink was the solicitor used by Brickwood and he, in turn, needed his confidential clerk, George Preston, to support the process. Percy Whitmey fulfilled a similar 'trusted' role for Brickwood and Alfred Jelks was Wyatt Peters' lieutenant at George Peters & Co: a group of men, widely respected for their professional skills, who were essential to the success of the project.

JOHN PINK: A SPLASH OF COLOUR

Born on June 6, 1866, Pink was baptised at St Mary's Church in Fratton on July 27. His father, also called John, married mother Fanny, nee Towsey, in February 1863, in Southampton. He had one younger brother, George, who eventually emigrated to Australia. Pink was a student at Diocesan Grammar School in Southsea in 1880 and by the 1891 census he was living with his uncle Thomas King, an auctioneer, at Pembroke Road and was listed as a solicitor with Blake's, a firm of solicitors in the town. John married Jessie Frances Wink in Hampstead, London on June 17, 1893. They had three children, Stella, Marjory and Frederick.

The Pink family came from Fareham and were "coach and saddle manufacturers" and then "stable keepers", employing at one time 15 men and six boys. The family was also prominent in the St Peter's & St Paul's church community in Fareham. There is still a family memorial inside the church. The stables were in the High Street and they were suppliers of saddlery to royalty, so clearly well connected. Pink's father John was listed as running a hotel at Kings Terrace, Southsea in 1871 with his wife Fanny. He was involved in court proceedings over the bankruptcy of his father-in-law William Towsey - as reported in the Portsmouth Times in December 1863 and June 1864. As well as hotels, Towsey described himself as a keeper of many "posting horses for railway and steamboat passenger usage". He stated that "he attended to that side of the business whilst his wife did the accounts." The reports mention the transfer of the ownership of the hotel from Towsey to Pink, probably to avoid the loss of it to the creditors. John the elder died in 1873 and Fanny in 1872 - both are buried in Kingston Cemetery - so our Pink was orphaned at the age of seven.

Pink was in the reserve forces all his life. The **Reading Mercury** reported on June 4, 1892, that a young Lieutenant Pink was presented to the King by his battalion commander (3rd Volunteer Battalion, Hampshire Regiment). His promotion to Second Lieutenant was recorded in the same **London Gazette** entry as 'Peters' who became a Captain in the same battalion. He became an Alderman in 1899. The **Southern Daily Mail** commented that he was popular and there would be no opposition to his candidature for St Thomas' Ward when polling took place. He would then become the youngest Mayor of Portsmouth in 1903, aged just 37. Another member of the school board, so with clear links to Bone, Murtough and Lewin Oliver, he was initiated by Brickwood into the Phoenix Lodge in 1892. The records show him as a member in various town lodges for many years.

Pink was undoubtedly the linchpin of the club's formation. Lewin Oliver, Wigginton and Murtough all went to Pink to get help to set it up. He may well have brought Brickwood on board too, given their connection outlined in the previous section. From the off, Pink was the company solicitor although he only became a director of the club in 1905, replacing Richard Bonney. Pink himself resigned in 1909. Incidentally he was also a solicitor for Sir Arthur Conan Doyle. Although there is no record of a previous sporting interest, once involved with the new club Pink threw himself into sports leadership in the district. He became the vice president of the Portsmouth Schools Football League in 1898 - the **Southern Daily Mail** in September 1898 lists the officials - so he clearly liked football and was keen for it to do well in the town.

GEORGE PRESTON: ALWAYS THERE

Preston was born on August 7, 1875 in Portsmouth. His father was Alfred and his mother Sarah Angus. He married Sally Gibbs in December 1898 at St Thomas's Church and they had two sons. All solicitors have a team to support them, and Pink was no different. As Pink's 'confidential' clerk, Preston - working in the practice he joined straight from school in 1890 - was his boss's most trusted advisor. The room on the ground floor of 12 High Street was the first port of call for clients and it was there that Preston worked. He would have escorted the guests up to the main office and meeting room on the first floor. His obituary in the **Evening News** in 1950 noted: "[Preston] quickly gained promotion and became the managing clerk" while club chairman John Chinneck added he was: "With the pioneers of the club in 1898 and served the club right to the last."

George was in the same Battalion as his boss Pink but in the cyclists' section and played football at left-half for both the Portsmouth Wanderers and Southsea Wanderers Football Clubs. He was reportedly pretty good. In 1894 he was also on the committee of Portsmouth Wanderers, attending their AGM as an official. He, almost certainly, organised that formation meeting in April 1898 and he would become the club's second financial secretary after the first, Percy Whitmey, died in 1907. His presence qualifies him as a 'founder', especially as he was well known and respected in the Portsmouth football community. The 1948 Golden Jubilee handbook said of him, as he was by then a director of the club, after his retirement as secretary: "No one alive to-day has had a longer or more intimate knowledge of the financial ups and downs, successes and failures, of Pompey, than Mr. Preston, and his services have been invaluable. He would probably be the first to admit that in the early days of the Club it was often a nightmare for him to contrive ways and means of obtaining sufficient money to meet the wages cheque and pay other current expenses." 'Twas ever thus for the club secretary, but nevertheless, a fitting tribute to a fine club servant for more than fifty years.

PERCY WHITMEY: CODE SWITCHER

Born in Droxford - not Botley as his obituary stated - on December 9, 1866 the son of James Whitmey, a former stationmaster and timber merchant at Bishop's Waltham and Botley, he married on November 27, 1887 to Bertha Julia Batchelor and they had one daughter Frances in 1889. Whitmey's early sporting passion was rugby. He was also secretary to the Hampshire Rugby Union and the **Evening News** of September 1, 1893 shows him as vice-captain and secretary of the Portsmouth Rugby Club when John Brickwood's brother, Arthur, was re-elected president. He resigned the role in 1895. In addition, he served the Hampshire Rugby FA until 1898 and played as a forward for the county several times. In the first PFC handbook for 1899/1900 Whitmey is introduced as follows: "Mr. P.G. Whitmey needs no introduction to the football section of the public, for ten years Rugby Football in Portsmouth owed a great deal to him, and the promoters of the new club can rest satisfied that the duties of Secretary could not be in better or more able hands." He was paid a salary of £25 in that first year, around an eighth of the players' wages. Typically the 'financial secretary', according to Dave Walters in the Argyle online history, had "to keep the company's books, deal with all matters of finance, take the gate money, and act as the directors' secretary". The job title distinguished it from the title of 'manager/secretary' that was applied to the team manager role.

Whitmey was the club's first secretary right up to his untimely death in 1907. He even had his photo printed in the club's first handbook in 1899, although he almost certainly wrote and produced it himself, so perhaps we shouldn't be too surprised. In his day job he was employed by Brickwood's – 22 years as their chief delivery clerk - but Brickwood used him far more widely than that. These days we would call him a 'go-to' man to get things done. The **Evening News** in July 1897, talked of Whitmey as "Brickwood's right hand man", stating that "Brickwood would never move without the accompaniment of Whitmey". Whitmey would have likely been present at the formation meeting as effectively Brickwood's PA, although his presence wasn't minuted. However, he was one of the first seven legal founders of the club quoted in the Memorandum & Articles of Association. At the time of the club's foundation, he was not a freemason, but soon after, in 1904, as his influence grew he was initiated into Portsmouth Lodge 487 and rose to be its senior deacon. Another military man, with the rank of Colour-Sergeant, he was in a familiar-sounding regiment - the 3rd Hants Volunteer Brigade – frequented by some of the others.

ALFRED JELKS: BEHIND THE SCENES

Jelks was born in Islington London in 1844 and married Sarah Aynsley in February 1871 at Kingston Church, Portsmouth, moving to Portsmouth to be with her. In the 1881 census he was recorded as living at Claremont Terrace with his wife and children Harold, Archie, Ethel, Eddie and Gertrude plus an aged aunt and her servant/nurse and another domestic servant. An advert placed by him for a servant in the **Evening News** in 1882, stated that "a good salary would be paid" so he wasn't doing too badly for himself.

He was recorded as a "beer retailer" and the licensee of The Queens Head, Fratton Road from 1879-1887. In December 1886, the roof caught fire whilst Jelks was "in occupation". He went on to the Duncan's Head public house from July 1887, and then became the licensee of the Gunwharf Tavern, Gunwharf Road in 1891. In that year he moved to a new pub, The Stag in Buckland, leaving it two years later. All these public houses were George Peters & Co-owned properties so Jelks either ran the pubs or was the brewery's named licensee. In the 1881 census he had been recorded as being a "book-keeper (clerk wine merchants)" so it is likely he combined both roles. He certainly lived in the Gunwharf Tavern for a period. In March 1887, he was recorded as being at George Peters' funeral accompanying Wyatt Peters. Jelks was in the "fourth carriage" of a long line of carriages so was clearly important to the family. In 1891 he moved to St Andrews Road and was recorded in the census as being a "Wine Merchants' Manager". Unusually, there is no record of membership of the Freemasons.

Described as 'managing clerk' it was his links with Wyatt Peters which brought him to the table. It is known for example that, together with Wyatt Peters, he liked cycling. In the **Hampshire Telegraph** in January 1882 he was recorded as being in the Portsmouth Bicycle Club. At their annual dinner at the Bush Hotel, Southsea, there is reference to a Bicycle Club football team with him in it, and in March 1894 he was at the annual dinner of the Southsea Cycling Club along with Wyatt Peters. There is no record either of Jelks playing team sports, other than the bicycle football team, of course.

As Wyatt Peters' right-hand man, Jelks was almost certainly present at the initial formation meeting on April 5, 1898. The first legal documents, including the Articles & Memorandum of Association, are all signed by him but once involved with the new club he quickly became a shareholder, buying five shares in the initial offer and then a further 20 when the free season ticket offer kicked in the following season. While he is rarely to the fore subsequently, it seems highly likely he was doing plenty behind the scenes. These facts more than qualify him to be in the list of the men who made Pompey.

IV - THE FOOTBALL MEN

Frederick Windrum, Richard Bonney & Frank Brettell

To create a football club from next to nothing in 1897 to be competing at the highest level of the game just two short years later clearly takes vision, drive and, above all, people with the credibility to give investors confidence. In the likes of John Brickwood, John Wyatt Peters, Bernard Murtough, George Lewin Oliver and William Wigginton, the Portsmouth Football & Athletic Company had those qualities in spades. The administrative backbone was also in place, through John Pink, George Preston, Percy Whitmey and Alfred Jelks. However, football has always been a particular industry and to properly succeed meant it needed to be right on the pitch. That's where our final trio come in. Fred Windrum, Richard Bonney and Frank Brettell were the men who, in football terms, by the late 1890s had been there, seen and done it. They were just what was needed.

FREDERICK WINDRUM: SOLDIER SOCCER PLAYER
Born in Dover on June 26, 1862 Windrum, according to army records, enlisted in 1880 at age 18 on his birthday and was 5ft 7ins tall. Until enlisting, he had been a clerk since leaving school at 14. He served in Malta from 1880-1882 and in Gibraltar from 1882-1886. He became Sergeant Major in 1894; Regimental Sergeant Major in 1895 before being commissioned as a Lieutenant in 1900. He married Elizabeth Bailey in Dover, five days after his promotion to the officer ranks. Windrum was also a freemason, joining Ubique - a lodge for Gunners - in February 1893. Much of his career was devoted to army football and in particular the Royal Artillery (Portsmouth) club which had such success in the FA Amateur Cup and Southern League. He had founded it with Bonney, becoming treasurer and trainer. Windrum was clearly a leader and quickly gained positions of responsibility in both the army and football, for example being elected vice-president at the Hampshire FA and presiding over the United Services League annual meetings in the late 1890s and subsequently chairman of the Devon FA.

  Although not directly involved in the foundation meeting on April 5, 1898, when Windrum, by now a Sergeant Major, joined the new club's board in February 1899 it was clear he was already deeply involved in the new club. He would have smoothed the path to recruit RA players, like Reilly. In addition, he had current experience of the Southern League, its teams and players so could provide recruitment support to the team of directors. One of the first entries in the cashbook is a payment to Windrum for 'Brettell's expenses' followed by a payment to Brettell for 'bonus on signing'. Windrum would have known of Brettell from when the RA competed in the Southern League Division One for the only time in 1898/99, playing against Brettell's Tottenham twice that season. Effectively, Windrum acted as a prototype Director of Football or, at the very least, took on the task of recruitment until a manager was secured.

The **Football Mail** in September 1903 calls Windrum, and his friend Richard Bonney, who we shall meet in due course, club "founders". The **Dundee Courier**, in September 1934, celebrating "Great Football Clubs and Their Stories", under the headline 'A Sailors Club Started By Soldiers', said that "Freddy" was involved from the very start and "the first step was to seek the aid of the two soldiers before the meeting on April 5 took place". Windrum was said to "have played a very big part in the formation of the Pompey club". Similarly, **The People** in 1944 reported that the club was started by two soldiers Bonney and Windrum, adding: "Just over 40 years ago men of the Royal Artillery, stationed in the town developed a really fine footballing team. It attracted such a big following that a few of Portsmouth's leading personalities decided that it would be of great use for the town to have its own club. They talked the matter over with Sergeant Major Windrum and Sergeant Bonney and formed the club." The **Evening News** in November 1904, underlined that Windrum was "one of the moving spirits in the formation of the Portsmouth Football Club". He probably has a greater claim to be in the list of founders than Bonney, but the pair were inseparable, always quoted as being together. When Freddy went to Plymouth, Bonney travelled to meet him on several occasions. Windrum was named in the **Evening News** of September 1, 1899 as travelling, and claiming expenses, with the Portsmouth team to Chatham for the first game, which is arguably significant as not all directors automatically went to away games. Charles Korr (1986) noted that most clubs at the time had one director who was charged with attending each game.

In the regiment, he rose from the ranks to be commissioned as a Lieutenant (District Officer) for the Royal Artillery Garrison, Plymouth in March 1900 meaning he would be posted to the West Country. There he would play a major role in the establishment of the Argyle club, again helped by Bonney, who would by then be on the Pompey board as Windrum's replacement. Bonney even attended Argyle's board meetings on several occasions to offer his advice. The **Evening News** in March 1900 said that: "The many friends of Mr. F. Windrum will be glad to hear that he has been promoted to the commissioned ranks, last night's **London Gazette** containing the announcement that he is to be a Lieutenant (District Officer) on augmentation. Mr. Windrum who has for a considerable time been the Regimental Sergeant Major of Royal Artillery at Portsmouth is very popular throughout the district, and his general manner has gained him a whole host of friends both among the officers of his corps and the men. Mr. Windrum is best known however in the town in connection with his interest in all matters pertaining to the promotion of sport - football particularly. He was one of the principal supporters of the old Royal Artillery team and one of the most popular directors of Portsmouth Football Club".

RICHARD BONNEY: STITCHING IT TOGETHER

Born in 1865, according to his army records and death certificate, in Skerton, Lancashire, the same village from which pioneer Pompey players Nobby Clarke and Ted Turner came, Bonney's father was Edward and his mother Betsy Whittaker. He married Emily Jane Chapman in Battersea on April 5, 1890 and they had Richard in 1893, who died aged five weeks, followed by a daughter, Lily, born in 1901. He started his professional life as a 'tailor and cutter', apprenticed to a Mr Simpson in Lancaster for six years, after leaving school at 14. He played rugby for St Mary's, the big club in his town and after a year in Antwerp he joined the Royal Artillery as a tailor at Fort Rowner in Gosport in July 1885, aged almost 21. He initially signed on for "short service" of 12 years. He was another freemason, recorded as being in two Portsmouth lodges, and was eventually discharged in the army records as a "Sergeant (Master Tailor)" at age 40 "at his own request" after 18 years, "with a view to pension". Army records showed he never served abroad. He was appointed Master Tailor soon after enlisting and posted to Portsmouth, doing that role for the Royal Artillery for 16 years and had an "exemplary" conduct record. His only medals were for long service and good conduct; however, he did return to the army when World War One broke out, serving in France.

Bonney and Windrum led the RA (Portsmouth) FC to several trophies. In their first season, 1894/95 they won the Army FA Cup and won it again in 1897. In 1896 they won the Hampshire Cup and were losing finalists in the FA Amateur Cup. Bonney twice personally went up to collect the Army Cup on behalf of the players. According to the **Evening News** in 1904: "When the idea of having a regimental team for the Royal Artillery was first thought about, he threw himself into it with great interest and energy." From its formation in 1893 through to its demise, he was secretary/manager. He was also chosen to be on the executive of the Portsmouth FA in 1896, being secretary for two years before being elected vice-president in 1899, then president in 1904 alongside becoming a vice-president of the Hampshire FA. Somehow, he managed to combine all of his duties, including of course his full-time army activities. Bonney was, according to William Pickford, "the key figure, a master tailor by trade who knew a good player when he saw one, an intelligent man and 'straight'". He was willing, however, to engineer a commission into the RA for a player called Clarke, a promising forward, from Southsea Rovers so that he could play for the RA in 1898/99. This was the same Clarke who played a big part in Pompey's first season. Bonney also received help from Quarter Master Sergeant Manley to enable him to cope with the extra work involved according to Tony Mason and Eliza Riedi (2010). Bonney joined Pompey as a director in the first half of 1900 - he was formally appointed at the AGM on July 14 that year - with his address recorded as 'Clarence Barracks'. The **Portsmouth Times** editorial on July 21, congratulated the shareholders on the election of Bonney remarking "he made the establishment of Portsmouth Football Club possible". He was the club representative at meetings of the FA, the Southern League and the Western League and "his advice and opinions are always greatly valued" said the **Evening News**.

FRANK BRETTELL: CLUB BUILDER
Born in 1862 in Smethwick, Staffordshire, the 1881 Census shows Brettell's listed occupation as a 'Pupil Teacher', son of William, a widower and retired nut and

bolt works foreman, and living at 62, Aughton Street, Liverpool. He married Lavinia Spearman, from Devon, a year later and the couple subsequently had ten children. He played as a full back at the St Domingo Cricket Club in Liverpool which was formed into a football team in 1878 to keep the members together during the winter months. He also played cricket in the summer. From the St. Domingo club, attached to St Domingo Methodist New Connexion Chapel in Breckfield Road North, arose Everton Football Club and Brettell played for them too. He is mentioned, for example, in the **Liverpool Mercury** report of a game on January 13, 1880, against Birkenhead Association where he is recorded as a full back, but apparently after he broke his leg playing in 1886 his career petered out. Reports have him down as also working for the same paper while with the club. In an Everton match report from 1884, he was listed as the umpire. The Everton Heritage Society website records Brettell as "a founder member of Everton Football Club", one of their first players and 'secretary' or manager, instrumental in the formation of the Liverpool & District FA in October 1883. When Everton moved across Stanley Park in Liverpool to their new home, Brettell stayed at Anfield where he performed a number of duties. Although he is not listed as a Liverpool manager, he possibly has the honour of being the first first-team coach. According to *Pilgrim* in **The Cricket and Football Field** of August 1, 1896, quoted on playupliverpool.com, at the end of the 1895/96 season, Brettell not only had "charge of the team" but his reference from the previous Liverpool manager John McKenna "spoke flatteringly on his behalf, specially commending his judgement of the players and his placing of them in the field". A **Football Mail** of 1899 also references that "he played a prominent part in the new Liverpool team and was given sole charge at various times".

Brettell then moved to Bolton to become secretary/manager in 1896. Dave Juson *et al* (2004) states that Brettell wasn't desperately successful at Bolton, his time there ending soon after their 4-0 defeat by Southampton in the FA Cup in 1898. From there he went to Tottenham Hotspur before coming to Portsmouth a year later. **Pearson's Athletic Record** reported that when he joined Spurs he was given a three-year contract and a salary of £225 a year and at Fratton Park he was on £4 a week plus a signing on bonus of £50. He got no annual bonus, so the contract was not worth substantially more to come south. Perhaps he just liked building teams. At Tottenham he signed several players from Bolton and other northern clubs including John Cameron from Everton, who took over at Tottenham after Brettell left them. He resigned from Spurs in February 1899. When announcing his appointment on the 10th, the **Evening News** called him the "best conductor of the modern go-ahead club in the UK and his genial and persuasive temperament should go a long way with the new Club". He would manage Pompey from 1899 to 1901 but was sounded out about the move during the final months of 1898. The first payment to him in the cashbook was in February 1899 just after he resigned from Tottenham Hotspur.

He set about the task of building a team to make Portsmouth proud with typical gusto and, that his scratch squad managed to finish second on the club's first season in a highly-competitive league was a testament to his abilities. Of all the things that had to be got right in the new club, it was the team. In doing that job so well, he makes the cut as a founding father of the club. Ironically, his managerial roles at all his clubs were successful though generally brief, stepping aside to hand the reins over to someone else, as if his job were done. So it was at Pompey, as he left in June 1901 according to the **Evening News** "by mutual agreement" as the directors could not agree with him on "certain rather important matters". However, he left with a job very much well done.

FELLOW TRAVELLERS
There are, of course, others we must add to the team which made the dream of a professional club for Portsmouth come true. Two future directors also were around and about, including Stephen Cribb, the Southsea photographer whose library of images are a fascinating window into the world of an Edwardian football club, and Sidney Leverett, who helped greatly during the formation, especially in signing players. The 1948 handbook summed up his role: "Soon after its inception Mr. Leverett, who was then in Admiralty service, became unofficially associated with the Management and earned the confidence of the Directors. In those days a lot of work regarding the signing-on of players had to be done *sub-rosa* ['in secret'], and Mr. Leverett was entrusted with many delicate commissions which he invariably performed satisfactorily and secretly. He travelled thousands of miles, often at his own expense, in his quest for players, and he secured many valuable captures so quietly and unostentatiously that rivals in other Clubs were often not only disappointed but thoroughly mystified." However, they have not quite done enough to be considered a founder. Unlike, say, Whitney, Windrum, Bonney and Brettell neither had any profile whatsoever in the newspapers of 1897-1900 or subsequent accounts of those years. Similarly, Bob Blyth, the senior pro and team captain, played an important role, but his primary contribution to the fabric of the club was still to come. We must also acknowledge the various journalists who had their part to play, in particular the very first *Sentinel* who reported for the **Evening News**, latterly unmasked as Frederick James Harry 'FJH' Young, who also wrote the club souvenir handbooks in 1927 and 1948 and knew all those first players and directors so well.

In conclusion, the founding fathers of Portsmouth Football Club stretch somewhat beyond the 'six businessmen and sportsmen [who] formed themselves into a syndicate' as Mike Neasom *et al* (1984) in ***POMPEY The History of Portsmouth Football Club*** described those present at 12 High Street on April 5, 1898. Chairman-elect John Brickwood, directors-elect Alfred Bone, John Wyatt Peters, William Wigginton and George Lewin Oliver, along with solicitor John Pink have traditionally grabbed the glory and with understandable reason. To them, though, must be added the contributions of driving force Bernard Murtough who soon joined the board, the club's first secretary/manager Frank Brettell and the first 'director of football' and board member from the outset Fred Windrum, who was ably abetted by Richard Bonney, who succeeded him as a director. In addition, the club couldn't have thrived in those early days without the administrative skills of George Preston, Alfred Jelks and Percy Whitney. A baker's dozen of good men and true who made the modern Pompey. What a debt is owed to them.

V - LEGACY MATTERS

What happened next to Pompey and the men who made it?

There is no doubt the first season of Portsmouth Football Club was an unqualified success. Even by the standards of the time, where professional football clubs sprang up and then quickly faded into obscurity as the financial reality of the industry bit, to have gone from a more-or-less standing start to being one of the leading clubs and grounds in England in less than three years remains a remarkable achievement. The demise of both Brighton United and Cowes in the same Southern League first division as Pompey in 1899/1900 underlined the fact. The challenge for the fledgling club was to ensure it didn't go the same way. It would be one to which Pompey would rise, but it is fair to say there were some bumps on the road in the years which followed, and our thirteen founders, their fundamental mission accomplished, would see their respective paths diverge, some continuing to give long and loyal service but, in the case of others, the torch would be passed on. On the football side, secretary/manager Frank Brettell, who had melded the military roots of the Royal Artillery amateurs with the more itinerant and mercenary professionals from the Midlands and North so well, was one of the first to get itchy feet, but his wanderlust was perhaps fuelled by the enforced resignation of Freddy Windrum from the board after his posting to Plymouth in 1900.

In the meantime, in the 1900/01 season Brettell guided Portsmouth to third place in the Southern League and a Western League title but in May 1901, as Neil Allen *et al* (2023) in the **Official History of Portsmouth FC** put it, Brettell "reportedly amicably left the club ... however there were some rumblings of disagreements". The **Evening News** of June 3, 1901 reported: "Portsmouth knows Mr Frank Brettell no more. Only a question of terms remains for settlement ere he takes his departure to fresh woods and pastures new. At Portsmouth, matters between the secretary and directors have not run smoothly, and from both sources complaints are heard. Whatever be the conditions under which he leaves, Mr Brettell has certainly done wonders for football in the south. It is but a little more than three years ago that he left Bolton, yet in that time he built the foundations of the team [Tottenham Hotspurs] which now holds the English Cup, and started an entirely new club in Portsmouth, which has in its first attempt finished second in the Southern League competition."

There had been rumblings for some time that not all was well, so this was not internally the big surprise it was to the public. The paper concluded: "The directors could not agree with him on certain important matters and a mutual arrangement was arrived at by which he consented to resign". In June, Brettell got a payment of £50 "balance of wages" so roughly 12 weeks pay, which sounds very much like a compromise agreement/severance payment. In June 1901 at the AGM Brickwood was reported in the **Evening News** as saying: "Amicable negotiations had been concluded by which Mr Brettell had terminated his engagement with the company, and while thoroughly appreciating the effort their late manager made in starting and establishing the team and their reputation, it had been decided that for the present at any rate the vacancy should not be filled. In answer to one question it was mentioned that the three years agreement with the trainer had been cancelled, as well as that of the late manager, and nothing would be done with regard to the engagement of his successor until about August. Another shareholder wanted to know whether it was proposed to still further cut down expenses in the future, and Mr Brickwood said that they would continue to be as economical as possible, but it would not be possible to cut down expenses to any appreciable extent without starving the concern." The trainer, William Brierley, was also "allowed to terminate his engagement" according to the **Evening News** in August. To replace Brettell, the directors turned to veteran Bob Blyth, who became player-manager and guided the team to the Southern League and Western League double in his first season in 1901/02.

Returning to Windrum, the **Western Evening Herald** in September 1901 thought that Windrum could give a great fillip to local football and should be given a position on the Devon FA executive. He then became county chairman in 1902, but didn't stay in post long. Richard Walters (2011), in his online history of Argyle, reports him as being deposed in March 1903, in his absence, due to his links with the new professional club at Plymouth. The committee favoured someone with a greater liking for the amateur game. He was clearly well trusted by Argyle though, after his experience at Portsmouth, and Windrum was quick to draw on his Pompey contacts. Indeed Richard Bonney, who had succeeded him on the board at Portsmouth, even attended a meeting of the new Argyle company in February 1903. All recruitment of staff and players was passed over to him and at that meeting Windrum was put solely in charge of the recruitment of Argyle's first manager, recruiting - perhaps it was the plan from the start – Brettell at a meeting in Portsmouth in March 1903. According to Walters, Windrum had "the full trust of Clarence Spooner, who really owned the club, and the others". Albert E Webb, the manager of Chubb's Hotel where many of the formative meetings of Plymouth Argyle Football Company Limited took place, is quoted thus: "Lieutenant Windrum was outstanding. His zeal and wide experience were a tower of strength to the infant club."

Argyle were elected to the Southern and Western Leagues for the 1903/04 season and had an immediate, if unexpected, impact on football in Portsmouth, which had been following progress of the new club avidly it seems. Walters notes: "The arrival of Plymouth Argyle on the professional league scene was eagerly anticipated and its developments reported widely in the press, so much so that new clubs soon began to spring up with "Argyle" in their name, particularly in Portsmouth, home to Point Argyle, Portsmouth Argyle, and Palmerston Argyle." By that year at least seven Portsmouth clubs had added 'Argyle' to their name. The new club made their first visit to Fratton Park in September for a Western League fixture. Brettell included two Pompey 'old boys' Cleghorn and Digweed in the side and proceeded to win the game 2-1. The Mayor of Portsmouth, Sir William Dupree, along with mayor-to-be John Pink, entertained the directors of both clubs after the game to "celebrate the links between the two cities." Attendees included Brickwood and Windrum plus their fellow directors and most of the players of both clubs. Brickwood toasted the new Plymouth team, thanked them for sending a message of condolence after Pompey lost 2-1 to Saints the previous week. He also referred to the connection of Windrum "as he did at Portsmouth, with his help the new Plymouth club would have a successful career". Spooner responded and acknowledged the help that Argyle had had from Bonney and his co-directors. Windrum toasted Pompey and said that "Plymouth in its initial stages, had much to thank Portsmouth for and (he) heartily returned thanks for all they had done". Windrum's connection with Argyle ended in January 1907 when he was promoted to Captain and posted to Gibraltar. He died in 1952 after being taken ill during a meeting of the committee of, aptly perhaps, the Royal Artillery Mess at Woolwich and his memorial service was held in the Tower of London. The **Evening News** in its obituary said: "those who were associated with the club in the early days would be saddened to hear of his death".

Like at Portsmouth, Brettell's tenure at Argyle was short and he resigned at the end of the 1904/05 season, although according to the online history of the club he accepted a position on the board. The **Sunderland Daily Echo** in March 1903 commented that he had "unfortunately almost been forgotten about in the time between his jobs at Portsmouth and Plymouth" although "at one time was as well known in Lancashire as the president of the Football League himself" and it was going to happen again, this time definitively. For a couple of years, he ran the Golden Fleece pub in Plymouth but after 1911 the trail largely goes cold. According to Walters he ended up in Dartford, where he died in 1936. It seems though that by 1930 he had become involved with the Vickers-Armstrong (Erith) Athletic Club. His funeral in Crayford was attended by members of that club who laid their own wreath. It had been formed in 1916 by armament factory workers and during the First World War they had a very strong side, including seven Arsenal players. It seems likely Brettell helped run the club. As a postscript, he also has the distinction of being both the Tottenham and Portsmouth manager with the highest win ratio at 58.73% and 63.64% respectively. In October 1931, the **Daily Mirror** reported that Brettell returned to White Hart Lane to see Spurs play Plymouth. The reporter clearly knew him well and described him as "one of the best judges of a player's worth I ever knew" but "Frank today is an old man, stricken with rheumatism".

The men who had made Pompey were beginning to drift away but constants remained. In 1904 Brickwood was still chairman and Whitmey secretary. Lewin Oliver, Bone, Wigginton and Murtough were still the core of the directors, now with Bonney amongst their number. Indeed, Bonney would become manager of the team in December 1904. The club had been without a manager since May when Blyth resigned after he had returned, but without much enthusiasm, having been suspended by the FA for – and this was disputed – making illegal approaches for three Liverpool players in 1903. He moved, temporarily at least, into the pub trade, having run the Pompey Hotel for several months to tide him over during his suspension, but his story still had a few more furlongs to run. Bonney had already retired from the army when he stood down from the board to become Pompey's third manager. The **Evening News** carried the announcement of his appointment in November 1904, Sentinel reporting that the club had been "like a fine ship at sea without a hand on the tiller". However, he acknowledged that Bonney had pretty much been doing the job from the boardroom and his appointment was a formality. Bonney managed the team to runners up spot in the Southern League and third in the Western League in 1906/07, probably his most successful season as in January 1907 he also oversaw a famous 2-1 win at Manchester United in an English Cup first round replay. The original game at Fratton Park, which ended 2-2, had been watched by more than 24,000 fans.

In 1905 John Pink, the club's solicitor, at whose offices the meeting to formally set up the club had been held in April 1898, finally joined the board at the AGM in July but at the following year's AGM John Wyatt Peters resigned as a director, with the **Evening News** at the time reporting he was struggling to devote sufficient time to both the club and his brewing and public house business. Wyatt Peters' connection with the club pretty much ends at this point, although he continued to patronise sport in the town. In 1914, the Hampshire Telegraph records him presenting a trophy for use by the Portsmouth Swimming Club and states he was on the committee. He also loved his bowls, just like Arthur Conan Doyle did when he was in Portsmouth. There are a number of references to Wyatt Peters and bowling and in 1923 when the Portsmouth & District Bowling Association set up a new league, the paper reported that he presented them with a "very handsome silver cup" to be used as the trophy. Wyatt Peters never married, living alone with his servants and butler and splitting his time between his houses in London - he received the freedom of the City of London in April 1920 - and Southsea, working right up to his death. He travelled extensively, going round the world several times – the records are littered with details of countries he travelled to - and when he died, he left £100 to every employee in the firm. It is telling, perhaps, his obituaries in December 1938, after he died at home in Southsea aged 74, went to town on his distinguished business and military career but made nothing of his connection with the club. Only the **Sussex Gazette** referenced sports incidentally: "One of the older generations of Portsmouth's successful businessman, he was a well-known personality and great sportsman in the city, and his passing has been received with great regret." There was no obvious representation from Portsmouth Football Club at his funeral, Pink sent flowers and there were several of the Brickwood family in attendance. George Peters & Co kept going up until the late 1950s, a financial struggle ending after being bought out by Friary Meux around the same time Pompey's stay in the first division was ending with relegation.

A major shock was the news in May 1907 of the sudden death of the club's financial secretary Percy Whitmey, aged just 41. The cause of death was typhoid, most likely contracted by eating contaminated shellfish from Langstone Harbour, which was regularly polluted. The Medical Officer of Health at the Town Hall for many years, Andrew Mearns Fraser, even wrote to the **Evening News** shortly afterwards to impart "some valuable advice to consumers of cheap shellfish. It appears a large number of the cockles sold in the borough are picked off the mud in the neighbourhood of sewage outfalls and are therefore likely to be polluted with disease producing bacteria". The **Hampshire Telegraph** announced his death in its May 18 edition:

Painfully Sudden End

[The death] occurred with painful suddenness at his house 1 Playfair Road, Southsea, yesterday. Mr Whitmey was taken ill a little more than a week ago and was found to be suffering from typhoid. He at once took to his bed and succumbed this morning. Mr Whitmey, who leaves a widow and one daughter, had for 22 years been in the employ of Messrs Brickwood and Co-Ltd the Portsmouth Brewery, where he was greatly respected. In his younger days he was a prominent member of the Portsmouth Rugby Club, for which he used to play. At the formation of the Portsmouth Football Club Ltd, he was appointed financial secretary and in this capacity was well known throughout the country. The late Mr Whitmey was also a vice president of the Hants Football Association and a keen and enthusiastic sportsman. He was an active member of the Portsmouth Lodge (number 487) of Freemasons. Cut down in the very prime of life, he was only a young man, with singularly useful temperament, appearance and spirit and his death will be greatly felt by a large circle of friends. Mr Whitmey was the son of the former stationmaster of Bishops Waltham and Botley, and we believe was born at the last-named place.

As mentioned previously, he was actually born in Droxford. The funeral was, according to the **Evening News**, an "impressive affair" with "many mourners". The cortège was followed by all the vans of the Brickwood's company, showing the esteem in which he was held by Sir John, who had been knighted in 1904. The club donated the proceeds of its Western League match with Plymouth Argyle at Fratton Park on November 13 that year to his widow Bertha. After he died, William Pickford, writing in the **London Morning Leader**, commented that the world of referees would miss Whitmey: "When being paid by most club secretaries after a home match was lost they were usually grumpy and threw the money at the ref whilst he was still in the bath. Whitmey was a breed apart and still paid them in a "genial and business-like" manner, having waited until they were robed and had a cup of tea". George Preston succeeded Whitmey and, impressively, he would remain in the role until 1946 when he stepped down around the same time as manager Jack Tinn, who had guided Pompey to an FA Cup win in 1939. Preston stepped up to become a director, and was replaced as secretary by Dan Clarke.

MOVING ON

The club was evolving, the shock of Whitmey's death notwithstanding, and

Lewin Oliver was concerned as ever for the finances of the club. In his report of the club's balance sheet for 1906, *Sentinel* referred to Lewin Oliver as the "Chancellor of The Exchequer". He was also the only director recorded in the ledgers as lending the club money when cashflow was a challenge. For example, in February 1902 a sum of £75 for "signing on bonuses" for players had been noted in the club's cashbook and 14 months later the book noted he was putting his hand in his pocket again: "Money advanced for 8,300 loads of earth for new banks April 18, 1902 - £133". In 1909, Lewin Oliver would introduce the so-called 'sporting parson', the Rev Bruce Cornford to his fellow directors and he duly joined the board at the July AGM. That appointment would have a sting in the tail but, for now, the old guard was changing. Vacancies had been created by the resignation of director Henry Harrison and, more significantly, Pink. As well as the appointment of Cornford, it paved the way for the return of Blyth, who was brought in to provide the board with knowledge of professional football. Alderman Pink JP gave much to the town and, from 1926, city of Portsmouth. After leaving Fratton Park, he continued his patronage of sport by being president of both the Portsmouth FA and the Portsmouth Lads League, which were also supported by Lewin Oliver. Pink died at Eastern Parade in Southsea in March 1939 and the **Southern Daily Mail** paid tribute to a life well lived: "[He] was a Conservative, and in his younger days served for 14 years in the 3rd Hants. Volunteers, rising to the rank of Major. He was interested in sport. He was one of the founders of the Portsmouth Football Club, serving for many years as a director. He was a member of the Corinthian Yacht Club. Pink was consul for Belgium and the Netherlands, vice consul for Norway, Sweden, and Portugal, and Consular agent for France and Italy, and these countries recognise his service by conferring honours upon him. Only last year the honour of knighthood was conferred on him by the three countries."

   The old ways and faces were falling as fast as the club's bank balance. Pink's departure had quickly precipitated a change – whether by accident or design - of colours from salmon pink to white shirts, then in March 1910 Richard Bonney resigned as manager and he would go back to tailoring. On the face of it, he didn't make a great job of it. In court in October 1912, he was formally declared bankrupt, a huge stigma in those days, with debts of over £900. He admitted he had been a "speculator" in his army days. That means he probably gambled. His army pension was £31 a year and he had contacted his creditors to see if they would let him stay in business. There is no record of him doing so. However, during the Great War he re-enlisted, joining the 5th Battalion Dorset Regiment at age 49 as a Private, promoted to Sergeant a day later. He then moved regiments and ended up a Colour Sergeant. His enlistment papers show the family had probably split up, Richard and daughter Lily were living apart from wife Emily. He served in the Expeditionary Force in France in 1918, earning a mention in dispatches. Bonney had a sister called Lily, and he is recorded as living with her and her husband on a farm near Lancaster in the 1921 census as a "Poultry Farmer Labourer". The dates of birth of everyone all tie up. The manager who had guided Pompey to second in the Southern League ended up a labourer. The 1931 census was lost in a fire in 1942, but in 1939 records show him as a "retired serviceman" still living in the Lancaster area, where he died on June 22, 1942.

At the July 1910 AGM Alfred Bone resigned as a director, with little in the way of eulogy, although the whole meeting was a sombre affair. In December at the shareholders' half year meeting Brickwood announced his intention to retire due to business commitments. In May the following year the shareholders were getting worried, so Lewin Oliver truly stepped up to the plate, by stating publicly "the club will go on". At the AGM in July 1911 the mood hadn't improved. An athletics' festival at Fratton Park in July 1910 had failed to fill the financial hole and neither had moving the reserves to the Hampshire League. The team had finished bottom of the Southern League with just eight wins from 38 Southern League games. Allen *et al* (2023) paints the dismal balance sheet picture: "The club's overall debts were ... £4,215, yet the true state of the monies owing was far worse. Debts to others included £4,000 on the mortgage [to the Goldsmiths] and £6,000 to the bank." Relegation meant fewer matches, and thus income, plus the prospect of long and expensive journeys to clubs in the Welsh valleys. Some hard decisions were needed.

Robert Brown was brought in from Sheffield Wednesday as the new manager in June 1911 and the **Sporting Life** reported he "will start immediately to engage a team for next season", but it was at board level that the old guard were almost all gone, age and the strain of keeping the club solvent taking its toll. William Wigginton resigned at the AGM, this time receiving many plaudits for his time with the club. Wigginton died in December 1918, shortly after the end of World War One, and his contribution to Portsmouth Football Club, not to mention sport in general, in the town was rightly centre stage. His obituary in the **Hampshire Telegraph** possibly wasn't as fulsome as it might have been in more normal times, but it still captured the essence of his contribution:

> By his death local sport loses one is its oldest loyal and generous supporters. He was among the pioneers of amateur football in the town and founded the old Southsea Rovers football and cricket club in Hambrook Street many years ago, and he was a strong supporter of the Southsea Alliance Cricket club, at one time one of the strongest local teams. As a services cricketer and an old member of the Hampshire County Cricket Club he was a familiar figure at all their home and many away matches and as one of the original directors of the Portsmouth Football Club he took a big part in the development and progress of professional football. A keen lover of boxing and athletics, he seldom missed a local meeting, in fact there was little doing in the sporting line that he was not either directly or indirectly involved in e.g. the Waverley Bowling Club.

By contrast, just a year later, when the architect of Fratton Park Alfred Bone died aged 73 in December 1919 at home in Southsea, his obituary ignored that fact, or anything else concerned with the football club, choosing to focus on his military exploits and civic service. The **Southern Daily Mail** may have hinted at the football ground though: "Subsequently [Bone] was appointed permanent architect to the Portsmouth School Board, and he has held that office under the Education Committee. He also served as one of the overseers for the parish of Portsea in 1893 and 1894. Colonel Bone designed several important public and private buildings in this borough." On reflection, it probably didn't.

Bernard Murtough also retired as a director, but it seems like ill health was more at the heart of his decision. He retired as a councillor in 1914 and a **Hampshire Telegraph** article at the time made reference to him stepping back from several public positions, including at the football club, for this reason. The same paper went with a banner headline on his death: It simply read: "Mr. B. Murtough Dead". Readers were told that he had died the previous Sunday July 1, 1917, at his home in St George's Square after a "lingering illness at the age of 81". The paper called him "a very vigorous and effective platform speaker, aligned totally with Gladstone's policies of that time". He had been made a magistrate in 1906, was involved with the football club from the start and had chaired the council's planning committee back in the day, probably paving the way for Fratton Park to be built. John Brickwood was still involved with the club but his direct influence was fast waning. To be fair, he still presided over the annual meeting on August 4, 1911 and had already helped to launch a 'Save Our Club' appeal in May 1911, which eventually yielded £400 to help over the summer. But he faced criticism in some quarters for the way he had stewarded the club. Investment in the ground rather than team was a constant criticism but very unfair along with the usual thought that a rich person should 'wave a magic wand' financially. A Mr W Dart stating at one AGM that he felt that Brickwood was "badly stuck in the financial mud and needed to personally do something about it" and his decision to leave – it would be a long farewell – didn't come as a huge surprise.

On the field, Brown had the desired effect in season 1911/12 and Pompey were promoted, in second place behind Merthyr, back to the Southern League first division. The success came at yet more financial cost however and, at the end of the season, debts now totalled £10,600 with the bank agitating for the club to reduce its overdraft of £6,000. Lewin Oliver's solution was for a root and branch restructure. The old company would be wound up and, in the summer of 1912, shares in a new company would be issued. Existing investors faced the prospect of putting in significantly more money to retain their free season ticket privilege or take a 60% loss on their original investment with no perks going forward. Given the alternative was a complete loss, the new structure was agreed. The Portsmouth Football Company was incorporated on July 27, 1912, in time for the new season. The team would going forward play in blue shirts, with white trim, white knickers and black stockings and a gold town emblem of a star and crescent was stitched on the left breast of each shirt. Lewin Oliver became the chairman, leaving just him and Preston of our baker's dozen still standing.

Sort of. Whatever the misgivings of the press and supporters over Brickwood's stewardship of the club, he was awarded a medal for his 'services to the club' in 1912 and the new board welcomed him back into the fold at once. He became club president, attending the new club's AGM and dinner in November 1913 in that capacity. He remained in role until his death in 1932 at his then home in

Horndean. His ashes were scattered at sea. His obituary in the **Evening News** was the epitome of fulsomeness and with good reason. One line of it suffices here though: "The life of Sir John Brickwood has been a romantic one, and his name will live long in Portsmouth." No one can argue with that.

And at the 1912 AGM the club reconnected with its roots, appointing as director Sidney Leverett, an accomplished deep-sea diver with Camper & Nicholson by profession, who had helped fix some of the transfers back in the spring of 1899 and who, in 1907, had been described as the 'bravest man in the world' for his exploits diving in the English Channel on a sunken torpedo boat 150 feet below the surface. Leverett would remain a director until his death in June 1959. The new Lewin Oliver-led club was able to negotiate the Great War, effectively by shutting down the professional club completely between 1915 and 1919, emerging to win the Southern League title for a second time in 1920. In April of that month, with Pompey closing in on the title, a boardroom spat almost cost them. Brown, still the manager, and backed by Lewin Oliver, wanted money to sign additional players. The other directors disagreed and Brown resigned, with Lewin Oliver stepping down as chairman to be replaced by ... the Rev Cornford. Despite the upheaval, Pompey still won the league and, represented by Cornford at an FA meeting in Llandudno, the club agreed in July 1920 to join a newly sanctioned third division of The Football League, comprising most of the top Southern League clubs. By then photographer Stephen Cribb had also joined the board, in October 1919.

As a director Lewin Oliver remained at the club as it quickly rose through the leagues, in 1924 winning the southern section of the third division (a northern section had been formed in 1921) gaining promotion to Division Two. That year Blyth stepped up to become chairman and he would be the driving force behind the building of the South Stand in 1925 and then at the helm as the club reached the first division in 1927 and then Wembley twice in 1929 and 1934 as the club reached the FA Cup final, losing to Bolton Wanderers and Manchester City respectively. In December 1934, at his home at the Mile End School, the pillar of his professional life, Lewin Oliver, still on the board, died aged 81. Looking back, Lewin Oliver's contribution to the club was immense. Even the **Daily Mirror** reported his death, noting his "services to football". However, it was the **Evening News** which truly gave the clue as to his contribution. Times change, along with social mores, but compared to some of the scant or non-existent references to football on the obituaries of other founders, Lewin Oliver's puts his efforts for the club on a par with his work in education:

> "Skipper" Oliver as he was known to those inside football was a great sportsman and he was mainly responsible for the formation of the Portsmouth football club prior to the 1899-1900 season and he has fathered it ever since. The club has had its ups and downs and it is said that but for his generous financial backing in lean times particularly during the war period we might not be in a position to witness first division football at Fratton Park. It must've been a great joy to him in the last few years to know

that Pompey had progressed to financial solvency after being at one time so badly in debt. He was one of the original directors of the club and he was for many years chairman, a position from which he retired after the Southern League championship was won in the first post war years when he disagreed with his co-directors on a matter of policy but he retained his seat on the board keeping his interest in the club right to the end although he has not been seen on the ground since his serious accident. On the occasion of his 80th birthday he was presented by the directors with a silver cigar case which I know he prized very much. The players always had respect and esteem for the skipper and, travelling about as I do, I met some of these old timers that I know. Just one instance will do - last season I met Pompey's original centre half back Harry Stringfellow "how is 'Skipper' getting on?" he asked and "give him my respects and best wishes" and he proceeded to tell me about Christmas gifts the players and their wives and families always had in the early days. Mr Oliver did not confine his sporting interest to Pompey as for a considerable period until quite recently he was president of the Portsmouth Lads Football League which he helped very materially to finance and keep going. We shall all miss "The Skipper".

Shortly before Lewin Oliver's death, Blyth had retired from the board, stepping down as chairman. He would be at Wembley in April 1939 though to see the club win the FA Cup for the first time and would have died a happy man in February, 1941. Such was the esteem in which he was held, his coffin was laid out on the boardroom table prior to the hearse picking up and taking him to his last resting place in Milton Cemetery.

Of our founding 13, that left George Preston. When he retired as secretary in 1946 he had already joined the board in December 1945 and he served there until his death in November 1950 in Portsmouth. A **Football Mail** from December 1950 quoted the ever and omni-present *Sentinel*: "[George] was as straight as a gun barrel. He left a widow and two sons when he died. His dominant characteristics were his loyalty, unswerving fidelity and honesty". The reporter clearly had a lot of time for Preston, describing him as a man who "threw himself into the establishment of the club". His funeral was held at St Peter's Church Southsea, with then first-team captain Reg Flewin among the mourners. By that time, Portsmouth were Champions of England. The team were the best in the land, having won the title in 1949 then retained it in May 1950. A little over fifty years on from when it had all began, what better place to end the story of the making of modern Pompey, and the men who made it.

APPENDIX 1 - 1899/1900 IN NUMBERS Compiled by Paul Boynton

SOUTHERN LEAGUE DIVISION ONE

	Date		Opponent		F - A	Gate	Goalkeeper	Right back	Left Back	Right Half	Centre Half	Left Half
1	Sep 1	A	Chatham	W	1 - 0	4,000	Reilly	Turner H	Wilkie	Blyth	Stringfellow	Cleghorn
2	Sep 9	H	Reading	W	2 - 0	8,073	Reilly	Turner H	Wilkie	Blyth	Stringfellow	Cleghorn
3	Sep 16	A	Sheppey United	D	0 - 0	1,000	Reilly	Turner H	Wilkie	Blyth	Stringfellow	Cleghorn
4	Oct 7	H	Bristol Rovers	W	8 - 2	7,064	Reilly	Turner H	Wilkie	Blyth	Stringfellow	Cleghorn
5	Nov 4	A	New Brompton	L	0 - 1	1,500	Reilly	Turner E	Wilkie	Blyth	Stringfellow	Hunter
6	Nov 11	H	Gravesend	W	2 - 1	4,693	Reilly	Turner E	Wilkie	Blyth	Stringfellow	Hunter
7	Nov 25	H	Bristol City	W	2 - 0	5,923	Reilly	Turner E	Wilkie	Blyth	Stringfellow	Hunter
8	Dec 16	A	Millwall Athletic	L	1 - 2	4,000	Reilly	Turner E	Struthers	Blyth	Cleghorn	Hunter
9	Dec 23	H	Queens Park Rangers	W	5 - 1	3,783	Reilly	Turner E	Struthers	Blyth	Stringfellow	Cleghorn
10	Dec 25	A	Tottenham Hotspur	L	0 - 3	15,000	Reilly	Turner E	Struthers	Blyth	Stringfellow	Hunter
11	Dec 26	H	Bedminster	W	2 - 0	10,617	Reilly	Turner E	Struthers	Blyth	Stringfellow	Cleghorn
12	Dec 30	H	Chatham	W	2 - 0	2,962	Reilly	Turner E	Struthers	Blyth	Stringfellow	Cleghorn
13	Jan 6	A	Reading	L	0 - 2	3,000	Reilly	Turner E	Struthers	Blyth	Stringfellow	Cleghorn
14	Jan 13	H	Sheppey United	W	3 - 0	3,871	Reilly	Wilkie	Struthers	Blyth	Stringfellow	Cleghorn
15	Feb 3	A	Bedminster	L	0 - 2	500	Reilly	Wilkie	Struthers	Blyth	Stringfellow	Hunter
16	Feb 10	A	Bristol Rovers	L	0 - 4	3,000	Reilly	Turner E	Wilkie	Hunter	Stringfellow	Cleghorn
17	Feb 24	H	Thames Ironworks	W	2 - 0	3,216	Reilly	Turner H	Turner E	Blyth	Stringfellow	Cleghorn
18	Mar 3	H	Tottenham Hotspur	W	1 - 0	6,892	Reilly	Turner E	Wilkie	Blyth	Stringfellow	Cleghorn
19	Mar 10	H	New Brompton	W	5 - 1	5,639	Reilly	Turner E	Wilkie	Blyth	Stringfellow	Cleghorn
20	Mar 17	A	Gravesend	W	1 - 0	2,500	Harms	Turner E	Wilkie	Blyth	Stringfellow	Cleghorn
21	Mar 24	H	Swindon Town	W	1 - 0	4,653	Reilly	Turner E	Wilkie	Blyth	Stringfellow	Cleghorn
22	Mar 31	A	Bristol City	W	6 - 3	3,500	Reilly	Turner E	Wilkie	Blyth	Stringfellow	Cleghorn
23	Apr 5	A	Thames Ironworks	W	4 - 2	1,000	Reilly	Turner E	Wilkie	Blyth	Stringfellow	Cleghorn
24	Apr 7	A	Queens Park Rangers	W	4 - 0	3,000	Reilly	Struthers	Wilkie	Blyth	Stringfellow	Hunter
25	Apr 14	A	Southampton	W	2 - 0	4,000	Reilly	Turner E	Wilkie	Blyth	Stringfellow	Cleghorn
26	Apr 16	H	Southampton	W	2 - 0	13,003	Reilly	Turner E	Wilkie	Blyth	Stringfellow	Cleghorn
27	Apr 21	H	Millwall Athletic	W	2 - 0	5,220	Reilly	Turner E	Wilkie	Blyth	Stringfellow	Cleghorn
28	Apr 30	A	Swindon Town	L	1 - 3	1,500	Reilly	Turner E	Struthers	Hunter	Stringfellow	Cleghorn

SOUTHERN DISTRICT COMBINATION

	Date		Opponent		F - A	Gate	Goalkeeper	Right back	Left Back	Right Half	Centre Half	Left Half
1	Sep 18	A	Tottenham Hotspur	L	0 - 2	4,000	Reilly	Turner H	Wilkie	Blyth	Stringfellow	Cleghorn
2	Sep 27	H	Chatham	W	4 - 0	2,479	Reilly	Turner H	Wilkie	Blyth	Stringfellow	Cleghorn
3	Oct 18	H	Southampton	W	5 - 1	7,883	Reilly	Turner H	Wilkie	Blyth	Stringfellow	Turner E
4	Oct 23	A	Woolwich Arsenal	W	2 - 0	1,000	Reilly	Turner E	Wilkie	Hunter 1	Stringfellow	Blyth
5	Nov 1	H	Millwall Athletic	L	1 - 3	3,471	Reilly	Turner E	Wilkie	Hanna	Hunter	Digweed
6	Nov 8	A	Reading	L	0 - 2	2,000	Reilly	Turner E	Wilkie	Blyth	Stringfellow	Hunter
7	Nov 29	A	Bristol City	W	3 - 1	3,000	Reilly	Turner E	Wilkie	Blyth	Stringfellow	Hunter
8	Dec 13	H	Reading	W	4 - 1	1,235	Reilly	Turner E	Struthers	Blyth 1	Cleghorn	Hunter
9	Jan 17	H	Tottenham Hotspur	D	2 - 2	3,059	Reilly	Wilkie	Struthers	Blyth	Stringfellow	Cleghorn
10	Feb 7	H	Woolwich Arsenal	W	3 - 1	1,216	Reilly	Turner E	Wilkie	Hunter	Stringfellow	Cleghorn
11	Feb 21	A	Queens Park Rangers	W	2 - 0	1,200	Reilly	Turner H	Turner E	Blyth	Stringfellow	Cleghorn
12	Mar 14	H	Queens Park Rangers	W	1 - 0	1,549	Reilly	Turner E	Wilkie	Blyth	Stringfellow	Cleghorn
13	Mar 28	H	Bristol City	D	0 - 0	1,056	Reilly	Turner E	Wilkie	Blyth	Stringfellow	Cleghorn
14	Apr 2	A	Southampton	L	0 - 1	1,000	Reilly	Turner E	Wilkie	Blyth	Hunter	Cleghorn
15	Apr 19	A	Millwall Athletic	L	0 - 2	NK	Reilly	Turner H	Struthers	Hunter	Hill	Digweed
16	Apr 25	A	Chatham	L	1 - 2	500	Reilly	Turner E	Wilkie	Blyth	Stringfellow	Cleghorn

ENGLISH CUP

	Date		Opponent		F - A	Gate	Goalkeeper	Right back	Left Back	Right Half	Centre Half	Left Half
1Q	Sep 30	H	Ryde	W	10 - 0	3,841	Reilly	Turner H	Wilkie	Blyth	Stringfellow	Turner E
2Q	Oct 14	H	Cowes	W	3 - 2	6,062	Reilly	Turner H	Wilkie	Blyth	Stringfellow	Turner E
3Q	Oct 28	H	Swindon Town	W	2 - 1	9,630	Reilly	Turner E	Wilkie	Blyth	Stringfellow	Cleghorn
4Q	Nov 18	A	Bristol Rovers	D	1 - 1	4,000	Reilly	Wilkie	Struthers	Blyth	Stringfellow	Hunter
4QR	Nov 22	H	Bristol Rovers	W	4 - 0	4,467	Reilly	Turner E	Wilkie	Blyth	Stringfellow	Hunter
5Q	Dec 9	A	Bedminster	W	2 - 1	10,000	Reilly	Turner E	Wilkie	Blyth	Stringfellow	Hunter 1
R1	Jan 27	H	Blackburn Rovers	D	0 - 0	16,835	Reilly	Turner E	Wilkie	Blyth	Stringfellow	Cleghorn
R1R	Feb 1	A	Blackburn Rovers	D	1 - 1	5,000	Reilly	Struthers	Wilkie	Blyth	Cleghorn	Hunter
R1R2	Feb 7	N	Blackburn Rovers	L	0 - 5	6,000	Reilly	Wilkie	Struthers	Blyth	Stringfellow	Cleghorn

THE MAKING OF MODERN POMPEY

Right Wing	Inside Right	Centre Forward	Inside Left	Left Wing
Marshall	Cunliffe	Brown A	Smith	Clarke 1
Marshall	Cunliffe 1	Brown A	Brown J	Clarke 1
Marshall	Cunliffe	Brown A	Brown J	Clarke
Marshall 1	Cunliffe 4	Brown A 2	Smith	Clarke 1
Marshall	Cunliffe	Brown A	Smith	Clarke
Marshall	Cunliffe	Brown A 2	Smith	Clarke
Marshall	Cunliffe	Brown A 2	Smith	Clarke
Marshall	Cunliffe	Brown A 1	Smith	Clarke
Marshall 2	Cunliffe 1	Brown A 2	Smith	Clarke
Marshall	Cunliffe	Brown A	Smith	Clarke
Marshall	Cunliffe 1	Clarke	Smith 1	Barnes
Marshall	Cunliffe 1	Brown A 1	Clarke	Barnes
Marshall	Clarke	Brown A	Smith	Moore
Marshall	Cunliffe 1	Brown J	Smith 2	Clarke
Barnes	Cunliffe	Brown A	Smith	Clarke
Marshall	Cunliffe	Brown J	Smith	Moore
Marshall 1	Cunliffe 1	Clarke	Smith	Barnes
Marshall	Cunliffe 1	Brown A	Smith	Clarke
Marshall 1	Cunliffe 1	Brown A 2	Smith 1	Barnes
Marshall	Barnes	Brown A 1	Smith	Clarke
Marshall	Clarke 1	Brown A	Smith	Barnes
Marshall 1	Cunliffe 2	Brown A	Smith 1	Clarke 2
Marshall 1	Cunliffe	Clarke 2	Smith	Barnes 1
Marshall	Cunliffe 1	Brown A 2	Smith 1	Clarke
Marshall	Cunliffe 1	Brown A 1	Smith	Clarke
Marshall	Cunliffe	Brown A 1	Smith 1	Clarke
Marshall 1	Cunliffe 1	Brown A	Smith	Clarke
Marshall	Cunliffe	Brown A	Smith 1	Clarke
Marshall	Brown J	Brown A	Smith	Clarke
Marshall	Cunliffe	Brown J 2	Smith 1	Barnes 1
Marshall	Cunliffe 2	Brown A 1	Smith 2	Clarke
Marshall	Cunliffe 1	Brown A	Smith	Clarke
Marshall	Cunliffe 1	Brown J	McKenzie	Clarke
Marshall	Cunliffe	Brown A	Smith	Clarke
Marshall 1	Cunliffe 2	Brown A	Smith	Clarke
Marshall	Cunliffe	Brown A	Smith 1	Barnes 2
Marshall 1	Cunliffe 1	Brown J	Smith	Clarke
Marshall	Cunliffe 1	Brown J 2	Smith	Clarke
Marshall	Cunliffe	Clarke 2	Smith	Barnes
Marshall	Cunliffe 1	Brown A	Smith	Clarke
Marshall	Clarke	Brown A	Smith	Barnes
Marshall	Cunliffe	Brown J	Smith	Clarke
Cotton	Cooke	Brown J	Halliday	Barnes
Marshall	Cunliffe	Brown A 1	Smith	Clarke
Marshall 2	Cunliffe 1	Brown A 3	Smith 3	Clarke 1
Marshall	Cunliffe 1	Brown A	Smith 2	Clarke
Marshall	Cunliffe	Brown A	Smith 1	Clarke OG
Marshall	Cunliffe	Brown	Smith	Clarke
Marshall 2	Cunliffe	Brown A 1	Smith	Clarke 1
Marshall	Cunliffe	Brown A	Smith 1	Clarke
Marshall	Cunliffe	Brown A	Smith	Clarke
Marshall	Cunliffe 1	Brown A	Smith	Clarke
Marshall	Cunliffe	Hunter	Smith	Clarke

APPEARANCES & GOALS

		SL	SDC	FAC	Tot	SL1	SDC	FAC	Tot
1	Barnes	8	5		13	1	3		4
2	Blyth	26	13	9	48		1		1
3	Brown A	23	9	8	40	17	2	4	23
4	Brown J	4	7		11		4		4
5	Clarke	26	13	9	48	8	2	3	13
6	Cleghorn	22	10	4	36				
7	Cooke		1		1				
8	Cotton	1			1				
9	Cunliffe	25	13	9	47	17	9	3	29
10	Digweed		2		2				
11	Halliday		1		1				
12	Hanna		1		1				
13	Harms	1			1				
14	Hill		1		1				
15	Hunter	9	8	5	22		1	1	2
16	Marshall	27	15	9	51	8	2	4	14
17	McKenzie		1		1				
18	Moore	2			2				
19	Reilly	27	16	9	52				
20	Smith	25	14	9	48	8	4	7	19
21	Stringfellow	27	12	8	47				
22	Struthers	10	3	2	15				
23	Turner E	21	12	7	40				
24	Turner H	5	5	2	12				
25	Wilkie	20	13	9	42				
	Own Goals (OG)							1	1

SOUTHERN LEAGUE DIVISION ONE

		Pld	W	D	L	GF	GA	Pts
1	Tottenham Hotspur	28	20	4	4	67	26	44
2	Portsmouth	28	20	1	7	59	29	41
3	Southampton	28	17	1	10	70	33	35
4	Reading	28	15	2	11	41	28	32
5	Swindon Town	28	15	2	11	50	42	32
6	Bedminster	28	13	2	13	44	45	28
7	Millwall Athletic	28	12	3	13	36	37	27
8	Queens Park Rangers	28	12	2	14	50	58	26
9	Bristol City	28	9	7	12	44	47	25
10	Bristol Rovers	28	11	3	14	46	55	25
11	New Brompton	28	9	6	13	39	49	24
12	Gravesend United	28	10	4	14	38	58	24
13	Chatham Town	28	10	3	15	38	58	23
14	Thames Ironworks	28	8	5	15	30	45	21
15	Sheppey United	28	3	7	18	24	66	13
16	Brighton United*	0	0	0	0	0	0	0
17	Cowes*	0	0	0	0	0	0	0

*Resigned in season

SOUTHERN DISTRICT COMBINATION

		Pld	W	D	L	GF	GA	Pts
1	Millwall Ath	16	12	2	2	30	10	26
2	*Tottenham H	15	10	3	2	40	16	23
3	Portsmouth	16	8	2	6	28	18	18
4	*Woolwich Arsenal	15	7	1	7	26	21	15
5	Southampton	16	6	2	8	24	29	14
6	Bristol City	16	5	3	8	25	32	13
7	Reading	16	4	4	8	16	28	12
8	Chatham	16	5	2	9	12	37	12
9	QPR	16	4	1	11	19	29	9

*Tottenham v Woolwich Arsenal not played

APPENDIX 2 - SHAREHOLDERS INVESTING £25 OR MORE

This list shows all those who purchased 25 or more £1 shares from the first offer in May 1898 until December 1899. With initial sales sluggish, the club very soon offered fans a free season ticket if they bought a minimum of 25 for as long as they kept the shares.

Name	Surname	Occupation	No	Name	Surname	Occupation	No
Horace	Abingdon	Park Surveyor	25	James	Gardiner	Pensioner	25
William	Archer	Licensed Victualler	25	John	George	Dual Instructor	25
James	Bailey	Farmer	25	William	Gill	Gentleman	25
Lewis	Barnes	Wine Merchant	25	James	Godfrey	Manager	25
Robert	Barnes	Gentleman	25	James	Golding	Licensed Victualler	25
Joseph	Barnes	Surgeon	25	James	Goldring	Oyster Merchant	25
Charles	Barnett	Gentleman	25	William	Grant	Baker	25
Percy	Barrow	Gentleman	25	Albert	Guy	Architect	25
Alice	Barry	No occupation	100	Ernest	Hall	Surveyor	25
Allen	Barry	Publican	100	Thomas	Handy	Gentleman	25
Ellen	Bedford	Writer	100	Gratton	Hardy	Licensed Victualler	25
William	Berry	Schoolmaster	25	Joseph	Hatchard	Carter	25
Charles	Bevis	Architect	25	Arthur	Heath	Joiner	25
Alfred	Bone	Architect	200	Robert	Hewett	Greengrocer	25
John	Bone	Builder	25	Alfred	Hicks	Baker	25
Richard	Briant	Hotel keeper	25	William	Hill	Police Constable	25
Harry	Brickwood	Student	100	Albert	Hipkin	Gentleman	25
John	Brickwood	Brewer	200	Arthur	Hockmouth	Clerk	25
George	Brisley	Tobacconist	25	Thomas	Holding	Band Sergeant	25
Herbert	Briant	Licensed Victualler	25	Albert	Hooper	Fish Salesman	25
Frederick	Burghard	Licensed Victualler	25	Harry	Hooper	Licensed Victualler	25
William	Chalcraft	No occupation	25	George	Hooper	Fishmonger	25
Robert	Chandler	Beer Retailer	25	James	Hooper	Fishmonger	25
George	Churcher	Solicitor	50	William	Hooper	Fish Merchant	25
William	Clarke	Coal Merchant	25	Charles	House	Farmer	25
Hamilton	Coad	Chief Engineer	25	William	Hunt	Accountant	25
Charles	Cockerell	Builder	25	Alfred	Hunt	Wine Merchant	25
John	Coffin	Solicitor	25	William	Hunt	Wine Merchant	25
George	Coffin	Solicitor	25	Harry	Hurle	Gentleman	25
Harry	Collins	Licensed Victualler	25	Alfred	Hutchins	Gentleman	25
Lawrence	Cook	Fishmonger	25	Edgar	Hutchins	Licensed Victualler	25
Arthur	Cooke	Gentleman	25	William	Hutchins	Gentleman	25
Edwin	Cooper	Stockbroker	25	Henry	Jago	Hairdresser	25
James	Cowan	Outfitter	25	Charles	James	Shipwright	25
Eliza	Cowling	No occupation	25	Stephen	James	Master Mariner	25
Thomas	Cripps	Poulterer	25	William	Jeffery	Licensed Victualler	100
James	Crockerell	Builder	25	Alfred	Jelks	Managing Clerk	25
Albert	Crumplin	Licensed Victualler	25	Henry	Jones	Builder	25
Wiilaim	Dart	Bootmaker	25	Arthur	Jurd	Architect	25
Joseph	Davis	Writer	25	Leonard	Kellett	Surgeon RN	25
Henry	Dexter	Baker	25	Thomas	Kendall	Licensed Victualler	25
Alfred	Dunn	Company Secretary	25	James	Kennett	General Dealer	50
John	Edney	Builder	25	Walter	Killpatrick	Gentleman	25
George	Elliott	No occupation	25	Frank	Kinch	Licensed Victualler	25
Richard	Ellis	Licensed Victualler	100	Frederick	King	Photographer	50
Alfred	Embling	Master Mariner	25	George	King	Solicitor	25
John	Farlow	Beer Retailer	25	John	Kingswell	Foreman	25
Jonathan	Farrow	Pensioner	25	Charles	Kingswell	Gentleman	25
Harry	Fellgate	Gentleman	25	Charles	Kingswell	Schoolboy	25
Ernest	Fry	Licensed Victualler	25	Annie	Kingswell	No occupation	25

THE MAKING OF MODERN POMPEY

Name	Surname	Occupation	No	Name	Surname	Occupation	No
Thomas	Larkcom	Outfitter	25	John	Roffey	Electrician	25
William	Lavis	Carpenter	25	Charles	Rufus	Gentleman	25
Alfred	Lewis	Architect	25	George	Salter	Builder	25
Arthur	Lockmouth	Clerk	25	Samuel	Salter	Builder	50
William	Loxton	Messman RN	25	Sarah	Salter	No occupation	25
Robert	Luing	Butcher	25	Arthur	Saxby	Organist	25
Joseph	Malling	Schoolboy	25	Harold	Seward	Brewer	25
James	Malpas	Surgeon	25	Arthur	Short	Gentleman	25
Charles	March	Gentleman	25	George	Skeers	Gentleman	100
Herbert	Martins	Lady's Tailor	25	Walter	Slade	Timber Merchant	25
Thomas	Mason	Gentleman	25	George	Smith	Architect	25
Frederick	May	Estate Agent	25	Harry	Smith	Builders Manager	25
Theophilus	Mead	Surgeon	25	Emma	Smith	No occupation	25
William	Meadus	Engineer RN	50	George	Sprigings	Builder	25
Malcolm	Melrose	Gentleman	25	William	Stainer	Staff Commander RN	25
Thomas	Mindego	Licensed Victualler	25	James	Stapleton	Builder	25
Beda	Mindego	No occupation	50	John	Stevenson	Engineer (Retd.)	25
Harry	Moody	No occupation	25	William	Stilges	Licensed Victualler	25
Elizabeth	Moore	No occupation	25	Charles	Stokes	Dockyard Writer	100
Alfred	Moth	Printer	25	John	Tayler	Engineer	25
Alfred	Mountifield	Master Mariner	25	Albon	Taylor	Gentleman	25
Lewis	Moutrie	Contractor	25	Francis	Taylor	Gentleman	25
Charles	Mumby	Gentleman	25	Percy	Teir	Licensed Victualler	25
Bonner	Mumby	Asylum Doctor	25	Tom	Thomas	Fish & Game Dealer	25
Bernard	Murtough	Mineral Water Manufacturer	50	Charles	Tipper	Cellerman	25
George	Nelder	Steward RN	25	John	Titheridge	Beer & Wine Retailer	25
Elizabeth	Oliver	No occupation	25	Matthew	Totterdell	Corset Manufacturer	25
Herbert	Oliver	No occupation	25	William	Uniacke	Licensed Victualler	25
Margarite	Oliver	No occupation	25	Thomas	Vevren	Beer Retailer	25
George	Oliver	Schoolmaster	125	Anne	Way	No occupation	25
Thomas	Page	Baker	25	Thomas	Webb	No occupation	25
Ernest	Page	Licensed Victualler	25	Keith	Welsh	Surgeon RN	25
Ellen	Pannell	Hotel Keeper	125	William	White	Fish Merchant	25
John	Parker	Refreshment Contractor	25	Alfred	White	Solicitor	25
Richard	Payne	Cork Cutter	25	Harry	Whybro	Hotel keeper	25
Matthew	Pearce	Painter	25	Maurice	Whyham	Gentleman	25
John	Peters	Wine Merchant	200	Robert	Wigginton	No occupation	26
John	Phillips	Yacht Captain	25	Frank	Wigginton	No occupation	26
Frank	Pinhorn	Shipwright	25	Sidney	Wigginton	No occupation	26
John	Pink	Solicitor	100	Percy	Wigginton	No occupation	26
James	Poole	Rate Collector	25	William	Wigginton	Builder	26
Arthur	Purdue	Fishmonger	25	Emma	Wigginton	Provision Merchant	25
Joseph	Radford	Teacher Music	25	William	Wigginton	Contractor	50
John	Rake	Architect	25	Frederick	Windrum	Army	50
Mabel	Rake	No occupation	25	John	Woodhouse	Clothier	25
John	Riddell	Officer Merchant Service	50	James	Young	Grocer	25
William	Robbins	Builder	25				
James	Roffey	No occupation	25				

Name *Walter Finch Andrews*
Address *Portsmouth Cemetery, Eastney.*
Occupation *Superintendent.*

Appendices

BIBLIOGRAPHY

BOOKS & JOURNALS

Allen, Neil, Bone, Steve, Comben, Mick & Spraggs, Gerry
Farmery, Colin (Ed) — **The Official History of Portsmouth FC** / Bishops Printers / 2023

Arnold, AJ — **A Game That Would Pay** / Gerald Duckworth & Co / 1988

Arthur, Owen — **The World's First Football Superstar** / Pen & Sword Books / 2022

Bolsmann, Chris — **The 1899 Orange Free State Football Team Tour of Europe: 'Race' Imperial Loyalty & Sporting Contest** / The International Journal of the History of Sport / 2011

Brown, Paul — **The Victorian Football Miscellany** / Goal-Post / 2013

Brown, Paul — **The Portsmouth Dockyard Story** / The History Press / 2018

Carder, Tim & Harris Roger — **Seagulls! Story of Brighton & Hove Albion FC** / Goldstone Books / 1993

Coates, Richard — **Pompey as a Nickname For Portsmouth** / Journal of the Society For Name Studies In Britain & Ireland / 2009

Corbett, James — **Everton: School of Science** / Macmillan / 2005

Cousins, Richard — **The Hayling Bridge & Wadeway** / Havant Borough History Booklet No 25 / 2016

Durman, William — **Portsmouth Education** / 1942

Edwards, Leigh (Ed) — **The Official Centenary History of the Southern League** / Paper Plane Publishing / 1994

Eley, Phillip — **Portsmouth Breweries Since 1847** / Portsmouth Paper / 1994

Farmery, Colin — **Seventeen Miles From Paradise** / Desert Island Books / 2004

Gannaway, Norman — **William Pickford: A Biography** / Hampshire FA / 2009

Gibson, Alfred & Pickford, William — **Association Football & the Men Who Made It** / Caxton / 1906

Goodwin, Bob — **Spurs - A Complete Record 1892-1988** / Breedon Books / 1988

Green, Geoffrey & Fabian, AH (Eds) — **Association Football** / Caxton / 1960

Inglis, Simon — **The Football Grounds of England & Wales** / Willow Books / 1983

Johnston, Frank (Ed) — **The Football Encyclopedia** / Associated Sporting Press / 1937

Juson, Dave & Bull, David — **Full Time at The Dell** / Hagiology Publishing / 2001

Juson, Dave with Aldworth, Clay, Bendel, Barry, Bull, David & Chalk, Gary — **Saints v Pompey: A History of Unrelenting Rivalry** / Hagiology Publishing / 2004

Keoghan Jim — **The Rise of Fan Ownership** / Pitch Publishing / 2014

Korr, Charles — **West Ham United: The Making of a Football Club** / University of Illinois Press / 1986

Lapp, John A — **British Companies Act** / American Political Science Review / 1908

McArdle, David — **One Hundred Years of Servitude: Contractual Conflict in English Professional Football before Bosman,** / Cavendish / 2000

Mason, Tony — **Association Football & English Society 1863-1915** / Harvester / 1980

Mason, Tony & Riedi, Eliza — **Sport & the Military** / Cambridge University Press / 2010

BOOKS & JOURNALS CONT.

Nash, Andy — **AE Cogswell – Architect within a Victorian City** / Portsmouth Polytechnic / 1976

Neasom, Mike, Robinson Doug & Cooper, Mick — **Pompey, The History of Portsmouth Football Club** / Milestone Publications / 1984

Palmer, Francis — **The Companies Act: 1900 - A Legal Milestone** / Leopold Classic Library / 1900

Rogers, George J — **Memories of Milton** / Unknown / 1985

Pickford, William — **A Few Recollections Of Sport** / Bournemouth Guardian / 1939

Pulsifer, Christian — **Beyond the Queen's Shilling: Reflections on the pay of other ranks in the Victorian army** / British, Journal of the Society for Army Historical Research / 2002

Russell, David — **Football & the English, a Social History of Association Football in England** / Carnegie Publishing / 1997

Sherman, Alfred — **Athletics & Football** / Longmans / 1887

Smith, Kevin — **Glory Gunners** / KS Publications / 1999

Sherlock Holmes Was A Pompey Keeper / Halsgrove / 2004

The Secret History of Fratton Park / e-book / 2012

Stavert Geoffrey — **A Study of Southsea** / Milestone Publications / 1987

Sutcliffe, Charles E, Brierley, JA & Howarth, F — **The Story Of The Football League** / The Football League / 1938

Vignes, Spencer — **Lost in France** / Tempus Publishing, 2007

Whicher, Alex — **Soccer - The Ace of Games** / Southern Publishing / 1940

Wilson, Jonathan — **Inverting The Pyramid** / Orion Publishing / 2014

ONLINE SOURCES

Jackson, Lee — **victorianlondon.org** / last accessed 2022

Kelly, Andy — **thearsenalhistory.com** / last accessed 2023

Moors, David — **historicalkits.com** / last accessed 2023

Pomeroy, Stephen — **pomeroyofportsmouth.co.uk** / last accessed 2023

Sawyer, Rob — **efcheritagesociety.com** / last accessed 2023

Walters, David — **greensonscreen.co.uk** / last accessed 2023

Marshallsay, John — *Memories of Bygone Portsmouth* **facebook.com/groups** / last accessed 2024

WEBSITES

ancestry.co.uk / last accessed 2024

brickwoods.co.uk / last accessed 2022

britishnewspaperarchive.co.uk / last accessed 2024

bsa.org.uk / last accessed

claptonfc.com / last accessed 2022

devonfa.com / last accessed

economicshelp.org / last accessed 2022

findmypast.co.uk / last accessed 2024

nationalarchives.com / last accessed 2022

thefa.com / last accessed 2022

visitportsmouth.co.uk / last accessed 2022

MEDIA SOURCES

Haywood, Maria — **BBC News Channel** / first broadcast 2004

ACKNOWLEDGEMENTS

This book could not have been written without the newspapers of the day in particular the **Evening News**. Mark Waldron, the editor-in-chief, and the staff at its present incarnation **The News**, allowed me access their archives and gave permission to use material. Thanks go also to the various other newspapers that we have used for giving their permission to use extracts from them. I have endeavoured to check the copyright status of all text and images used and acknowledge accordingly. If anyone feels their copyright has been infringed, please contact the Pompey History Society charity to discuss.

Specific thanks go to my wife Diane Comben for some of the proofreading and putting up with me during the last four years researching this book and also to my son William Comben and Roger Loader for some first draft thoughts. In addition, I am grateful to Michael Saunders, who helped write the chapter on building the ground. No one has a better knowledge of Fratton Park than him. Stephen Pomeroy who owns the most comprehensive database of all things Portsmouth was a huge help and Kevin Smith provided content, constructive suggestions and proofread the first draft. My society colleagues, Paul Boynton and Richard Wilson provided statistics and financial information and Mick Mulford, whose family did some of the research on the Pink family, generously shared it. Mark Parnell helped finalise the structure of the book. Thanks guys.

The staff at the Portsmouth Central Library - Gareth, Dianne, Helen, Michael, Ellie, Gail, Anna and everyone else - put up with me day after day as I trawled through all the old local newspapers and asked question after question. Without the means to access old copies at the library, as well as the British Library and the fantastic online British Newspaper Archive, writing this book would have taken far longer, if not been impossible. I would like thank Keith Allen for his wise counsel about the Southern League and also the football history community, particularly Dave Juson, at Southampton who, along with Gary Chalk, provided much of the Saints input. In addition I am grateful for the time and advice of David Downs at Reading, Tim Carder and Roger Harris at Brighton, Roger Walters and Steve Dean at Plymouth, John Fennelly at Tottenham, Rob Sawyer at Everton and James Woodrow at Norwich. I also made contact with various relatives of the founders and learnt so much from them, so to the Blyth family, the Brickwood and the Oliver families, particularly Jane and Richard, thank you. Finally, thanks go to editor, Colin Farmery, for his help, although the words "Can we cut that bit out..." and "I've had a thought..." have started to give me nightmares! He helped tell the story of the birth of this great club in a way that flowed better than I ever imagined.